Dear Andy and Ro.

Hope you enjoy Dis. I'm sure
Andy can use some in her next
quiz!

    Happy Christmas 2006
love The van Weiders.

A Concise Dictionary of English Idioms

Other dictionaries edited by B. A. Phythian

A Concise Dictionary of Correct English

A Concise Dictionary of English Slang

A Concise Dictionary of Foreign Expressions

A Concise Dictionary of Confusables

A Concise Dictionary of English Idioms

B A Phythian

Headway · Hodder & Stoughton

British Library Cataloguing in Publication Data

Phythian, B. A.
  A Concise dictionary of English idioms.–
  4th ed.
  1. English language – Idioms –
  Dictionaries
  I. Title   II. Freeman, William. Concise
  dictionary of English idioms
  423'.1   PE1460

  ISBN 0 340 39271 1 (Pbk)
  ISBN 0 340 40597 X (Bds)

First published 1951
Fourth edition copyright © 1986 B. A. Phythian
Fifth impression 1990

Printed in Great Britain for
Hodder and Stoughton Educational
a division of Hodder and Stoughton Ltd,
Mill Road, Dunton Green, Sevenoaks, Kent
by Richard Clay Ltd, Bungay, Suffolk

Preface

This dictionary has two objects. The first is to furnish the reader with a simple and practical guide to the most frequently used idiomatic expressions in English—those countless expressions which everyone uses, which usually evade the normal rules of grammar, and which often have implications quite unconnected with the normal meanings of the words themselves. The second is to give the origin and history of some of these. Wherever it is felt helpful to show the idiom 'in action', the explanations of idiomatic expressions are accompanied by illustrations.

The reader should be aware that it is frequently difficult to decide under what word an idiom should be entered. Should 'See how the land lies' be entered under 'See', 'Land' or 'Lie'? Cross-references have frequently been used, but complete cross-referring would have increased the size of this volume several times; accordingly, if an expression does not appear in the place expected, the reader is asked to look it up under another key word in the expression. Similar difficulties have occurred in deciding on the correct alphabetical order of idioms within any one entry; idioms usually consist of several words, and have more than one key word, with the result that exact alphabetizing is impossible. Again the reader is requested to bear with the editor, and to be prepared to look in more than one place under an entry.

There are a number of deliberate omissions from the Dictionary: foreign words or phrases, commercial and technical idioms, dialect words, and, for the most part, single words—the idiomatic variations of which can be discovered in any ordinary dictionary. Only a few slang expressions are included; for a more comprehensive coverage of slang, the reader should consult the companion volume, *A Concise Dictionary of Slang*.

B A Phythian

Abbreviations

LIT Literal meaning

MET Metaphorical meaning

Old f. Old fashioned

Or. Origin

A

A B C The first rudiments; the beginning; the alphabet.

Abeyance **Be in** *or* **fall into abeyance** Be in a state of waiting or suspense (until some decision is made).
The whole matter is in abeyance until after Christmas.

Abide **Abide by** Remain faithful to (an agreement or decision).

About **Out and about** Outdoors and moving around.
Up and about Out of bed and moving around.

Above **Above all** That which is of the greatest importance.
Above all, be careful.
Above-board Honest and unconcealed.
His conduct has been entirely above-board.

Abuse **Terms of abuse,** *or* **abusive terms** Bad, uncomplimentary, or violent language.

Accident **Chapter of accidents** Succession of mistakes.

Accommodate
Accommodate oneself Adjust oneself to the circumstances; accept the conditions.
Accommodate with Supply with; allow the use of.

Accord **Of one's own accord** Voluntarily; without being compelled.
With one accord Unanimously; all together.
According to 1. As agreed or arranged. In a manner consistent with
2. As reported by. On the authority of.
According to the newspaper, it will rain later today.

Account **Account for** Explain (the cause of).
Did they account for the delay?
An account to settle [LIT] A debt to pay. [MET] A grudge or a grievance to avenge.
By all accounts In everyone's opinion.
Call to account Summon, in order that statement of justification be made.
A good account of A satisfactory story about or impression of.
Give a good account of oneself Behave in a way which brings credit to oneself.
The whole team gave a very good account of themselves.
Keep an account of Keep a record of.
Of no account Of no value or importance.
On account As partial payment.
He owed £50, and sent me £10 on account.

On account of Owing to; because of.

On no account In no circumstances.

On no account walk home by yourself.

On that account For that reason.

Open an account Deposit a sum of money (e.g. in a bank) for the first time.

Settle an account Pay a bill.

Square accounts Take some action which will cancel out a wrong or disadvantage, and make one equal.

Take account of Estimate. Include in one's calculations.

Take into account Make allowance for. Consider.

Taking into account all the circumstances, he felt it wise to say nothing further.

Turn to (good) account Make useful.

She turned her illness to good account by writing letters all day.

Accountable

Be accountable for Be responsible for something or to a person.

Ace **Play one's ace** Use one's strongest resource.

Within an ace of Within a very little distance of; very near indeed to.

The boy was (came) within an ace of being drowned.

Achilles **Achilles' heel** The weak or vulnerable spot in a person's character or circumstances. [Or. According to the legend, Achilles, with the exception of one heel, was protected against every weapon his enemies might use.]

Acquaint **Acquaint one with** Make one aware of.

Be acquainted with Know (person, subject etc.)

Acquire **An acquired taste** A liking for something unusual; a taste developed gradually.

I don't know whether you'll like this drink; it's rather an acquired taste.

Acquit **Acquit oneself** Conduct or exhibit oneself; behave; perform a part or function.

Act **Act a part** Conceal one's real emotions, etc., as an actor does.

Act on *or* **upon** Take definite action as a result of (what one knows).

The police immediately acted on the information they received.

Act up Misbehave.

In the act In the process (of doing something) (i.e. while doing it).

He was caught in the act of stealing the car.

Put on an act Pretend. Behave ostentatiously to gain attention.

Action **Go into action** Start work.

Out of action Not working.

Adam **Not known from Adam** Completely unknown and unfamiliar.

Addition **In addition to** Furthermore; as well as.

Address **Address oneself to** Direct one's attention or energy to.

Advantage **Have the advantage of** Be in a superior position to.

Take advantage of 1. Gain through another person's ignorance or innocence.
The dealer took advantage of the student's ignorance.
2. Act at a propitious or fortunate moment.
I took advantage of the fine weather to play tennis.

To advantage In a way that displays merit.

Turn to advantage Benefit from.

Affirmative **In the affirmative** Yes. Opposite: **in the negative**.

After **After all** In spite of everything that has been said or done.

Be after 1. Intend. Want.
What are you after?
2. Pursue.
He knew the police would be after him.

Again **Again and again; time and again** Repeatedly.

Half as much again One and a half times as much.

Now and again Occasionally.

Age **At an advanced age** Very old.

Age before beauty Those who are old must take precedence.

Come of age Attain the age of legal responsibility.

For ages (and ages) For a very long time.

From age to age From one long historical period to another.

Ripe *or* **green old age** Very old (but often with the implication of being healthy as well).

Under age Less than the age specified by law.

Agog **All agog** In a state of excitement.

Agree **Agree to differ** Agree that there must be a difference of opinion.

Aid **In aid of** To help; with the object of assisting.

Air **Air a grievance** Bring forward for discussion some hardship, grievance or other matter which should be made public.

By air In an aircraft.

In the air 1. In a state of uncertainty; unsettled.
We go to Lancaster on Monday, but after that all our plans are in the air.
2. Spreading about.
Rumours of rebellion are in the air.
See **Castle**.
Into thin air Into nothingness. (To 'vanish into thin air' is to disappear entirely.)
Take the air Go out of doors.

Airs **Give oneself airs** Try to show one's (sometimes imaginary) superiority, usually to impress. Similar to **put on airs, put on side, show off.**

Alarm **Give the alarm** Give warning, usually when some danger or disaster is discovered. Also **raise the alarm**.
False alarm Untrue report of disaster.

Alert **On the alert** In a state of awareness; ready for anything that may happen.

Alive **Alive and kicking** Vigorous and active.
I'm glad to see that Ann is still alive and kicking.
Alive with Crowded with.
The streets were alive with people.

All **All along** All the time; from the beginning.
I suspected all along that she was unhappy.
All at once; all of a sudden Suddenly; unexpectedly.
All at once there was a tremendous crash.
All for the best All for the ultimate good. (Commonly used to console someone for bad news.)
All the best A common form of farewell, an abbreviation for May all the best things happen to you.
All but Very nearly.
The proposals are all but meaningless.
All ends up In every way.
All for In favour of.
All in 1. Exhausted.
They're all in after their swim.
2. With everything included.
The holiday will cost £40 all in.
All in a day's work Part of one's responsibilities.
All in all In summary.
All one Of no importance; immaterial. Just the same.
It's all one to me whether you stay here or go home.
All out Using full power.
The builders are going all out to finish the job before the winter.
All over 1. Entirely covering.

There was ice all over the pavement.
2. Finished.
The funeral was all over by the time I arrived.
All over the place 1. Scattered untidily.
Collect your papers; they are all over the place.
2. In many directions.
Her work takes her all over the place.
All right 1. Certainly.
2. I agree.
3. Satisfactory.
All-round Complete. Many-sided. Hence **all-rounder**:
a person with many skills, talents, etc.
All the same 1. Alike, in a general sense.
It's all the same to me if we go today or tomorrow.
2. Nevertheless.
All the same, I'm not going.
All the time Continuously.
All set Fully prepared.
All set? Then let's go.
All and sundry Everyone, individually and collectively.
All-time Record.
Unemployment is at an all-time low.
All very well Possibly true (usually followed by
expression of dissent).
At all In any way.
Did he promise anything at all?
For all that Nevertheless; in spite of that.
In all In total number.
There are seventeen buses in all.
Get away from it all Remove onself from one's
everyday life and anxieties.
On all fours On one's hands and knees.
One and all Everybody.
When all's said and done The conclusion, stated
briefly. When all the facts are considered.

Allow **Allow for** Take into consideration. Excuse. Leave
a margin of time or space for.
Allow half-an-hour for the journey.

Allowance **Make allowance for** Similar to **allow for**.
We must make some allowance(s) for his inexperience.

Alone **Go it alone** Act independently.

Along **All along** see *All*.
Along with In company with. In conjunction with.
We need to buy chairs along with the table.

Go along with Agree, co-operate, with.

Ambition **The height of ambition** Strongest, most powerful desire.
To be an airline-pilot was the height of her ambition.

Amends **Make amends** Compensate (e.g. for some injustice or wrong).
This will make amends for his disappointment.

Analysis **In the final** *or* **last analysis** After all consideration.

Anchor **Anchor-man** Person playing vital part, especially compère in radio or tv programme.
Come to anchor Lower anchor, and cease to move.
Ride at anchor Be anchored. (Sometimes, move gently with the tide while anchored.)
Weigh anchor Pull up the anchor prior to sailing away.

Angel **On the side of the angels** Supporting what is right.

Answer **Answer back** Retort; reply impudently.
Answer *or* **be answerable for** Accept responsibility.
Answer to Have. Use. Correspond to.
A man answering to that description lives next door.
Answer to the name of Be called.
Know all the answers Be alert and well-informed.

Anybody **Anybody's guess** Unpredictable.

Anything **Anything but** Far from.

Apart **Joking apart** Seriously.
Tell apart Distinguish between.

Appear **Appear for** Represent legally or officially.
Keep up appearances Maintain an outward show.
Make (put in) an appearance Show oneself.
To all appearances To the eye; outwardly.

Apple **Apple of one's eye** See under *Eye.*
Apple-pie order Perfectly tidy and neat.
Upset the apple-cart Spoil plans.

Apron **Tied to one's (mother's) apron-strings** [MET] In the position of a small child who is compelled to rely on its mother for everything; humiliatingly dependent.

Argue **Argue something away** Argue that something does not exist. Attempt to destroy by argument.
Argue the toss Be disputatious.

Arm **At arm's length** [LIT] The length of one's extended arm.
She held the picture at arm's length.
[MET] In a state of formality and unfriendliness.
He prefers to keep his neighbours at arm's length.
A baby in arms [LIT]A child too young to walk. [MET] An inexperienced or immature person.

Up in arms Angrily roused to protest or action.
With open arms With warmth and pleasure.

Around **To have been around** To have acquired worldly
experience.

As **As it were** In other words; speaking metaphorically.
*He was intoxicated, as it were, by the soft air and sunshine
of spring.*
Similar to **so to speak** and **in a manner of speaking**.
As yet Up to this or that time.

Ascendant **In the ascendant** Rising in power or popularity.
Increasing in influence or ability. Hence:
One's star is in the ascendant One is growing in
influence, etc.

Ask **Ask for it** Behave in a way which invites trouble.
Also **ask for trouble**.
Asking price Price set by the seller.
For the asking Available. To be easily acquired.
If you ask me In my opinion.

Ass **Make an ass of** Make (person) look foolish.

Astray **Go astray** Stray. [LIT] Wander from the right path.
[MET] Depart from what is correct. Become lost.

At **At it** At work.

Attach **Strings attached** Conditions. Restrictions.
We can have the use of the premises with no strings attached.

Attention **Call (draw) attention to** Ask for consideration to be
given to.
Pay attention to Attend to; listen to.
Rivet one's attention Concentrate; fix one's mind
upon.

Attitude **Attitude of mind** Settled way of thinking.
Strike an attitude Stand or sit in a dramatic, self-
conscious position.

Avail **Of** *or* **to little** *or* **no avail** Almost (or quite)
without any result.

Avenue **Leave no avenue unexplored** *or* **explore every
avenue** Employ every possible source of information;
make every possible enquiry.

Aversion **Pet aversion** Special object of dislike.

Away **Do away with** Abolish.
Get away with Do with impunity.

Axe **Axe to grind** A private and personal object to achieve
(or favour to obtain). A grievance.

B

Baby **Holding the baby** Bearing an (unwanted) responsibility.
Throw away the baby with the bathwater Dispense with something essential while disposing of something unwanted.

Back **At the back of one's mind** In one's thoughts, but not uppermost in them.
Back and forth From one place to another, then back again.
Backbone [MET] Chief support. Main strength.
Back down Abandon a claim.
Back out of Withdraw from an agreement.
Back stairs Indirect and unofficial. [Or. The inferior staircase used by servants in a large house. Hence **backstairs gossip**: gossip by subordinates.] Also **by the back stairs**: indirectly, unofficially.
Back up Give support to.
Behind one's back When one is absent. Deceitfully.
Break one's back Overburden one. Hence **backbreaking**: very burdensome.
Break the back of Complete the most difficult or the chief part of.
We shall break the back of the work by tonight.
Go back *(a)* **on a person;** *(b)* **on one's word** *(a)* Betray; desert; *(b)* contradict or withdraw (a statement, etc.).
Hang back Linger; fail to advance.
Have on one's back Be harassed by.
Have one's back to the wall Be in difficulties.
Like the back of one's hand Intimately.
On one's back 1. Ill in bed.
2. Harassing one.
Put one's back into Use all one's efforts.
Put one's back up Annoy; make hostile. [Or. From the way a cat arches its back when angered.
Take a back seat Occupy an inconspicuous position.
Turn one's back on Abandon. Ignore.
When one's back is turned When one is absent, or occupied over some other matter.

Background **Keep** *or* **remain in the background** Remain inconspicuous and unnoticed.
I'm going to keep in the background during the discussion.

Backwards **Know backwards** Know very well.

Bacon **Save one's bacon** Enable one to escape or succeed.
He would have failed the examination, but his history paper saved his bacon.

Bad **Bad blood** Ill feeling.
There has been bad blood between the two countries for centuries.

A bad egg; a bad hat; a bad lot A person with a bad character.

Bad debts Debts which are 'written off' as complete losses. See *write off.*

Bad form Not accepted as socially correct; ill-mannered.

Go from bad to worse Deteriorate still more.

Go bad Become stale or rotten.

Not (so) bad Fairly good.

With bad grace Reluctantly.

Bag **Bag and baggage** Luggage; with all one's portable possessions.

Bag of bones Very thin person or animal.

It's in the bag It is concluded successfully. [Or. The bag, behind the Speaker's Chair in the House of Commons, into which petitions are placed.]

Bail **Bail out** [LIT] Pay money as security so that a prisoner may be released pending trial. [MET] Come to the rescue in any way. See *Bale.*

Balance **In the balance** Uncertain.

Keep one's balance Not fall.

Lose one's balance Fall from precarious position.

Strike a balance Balance or weigh certain objects or facts against one another, in order to discover their comparative value or importance.

On balance Taking everything into consideration. Having regard to all aspects of a matter.

Bald **Bald as a coot** Absolutely hairless. [Or. A coot is a water-bird, one species of which has a flat covering on its forehead, which gives it an appearance of baldness.]

Bale **Bale** *or* **bail out** 1. Remove water or other fluid from a vessel by means of a ladle, pail, etc.
2. Escape from an aeroplane by parachute.

Ball **Ball of fire** Very energetic person.

Have the ball at one's feet Have every quality and opportunity of being successful. [Or. Football.]

Have the ball in one's court Be responsible for the next move. [Or. Tennis.]

Keep one's eye(s) on the ball Remain alert.
Keep the ball rolling Continue (the conversation, proceedings, etc.) successfully.
On the ball Alert. Efficient.
Play ball Cooperate.
Start the ball rolling Make a beginning.

Balloon **The balloon went up** Trouble began. Uproar broke out.

Bare **Bare-faced** Impudent.
With one's (own) bare hands By hand. Unaided.

Bargain **Bargain for** Anticipate; prepare for.
We didn't bargain for so many people coming to tea.
Drive a hard bargain Conclude a bargain the terms of which are harsh.
Into the bargain In addition; moreover.
He bought the house, and the furniture into the bargain.
Make the best of a bad bargain Accept difficulty, misfortune, etc., cheerfully.
Strike a bargain Reach a final compromise.
We argued for a long time over what I should pay, but finally struck a bargain.

Bark **One's bark is worse than one's bite** What one threatens to do is worse than what one actually does. One's manner of speaking is deceptively severe.

Barrel **Over a barrel** Helpless.
Scrape the (bottom of the) barrel Use the (unsatisfactory) remains of one's resources.

Bat **Have bats in the belfry** Be crazy.
Not to bat an eyelid Show no sign of emotion.
Off one's own bat On one's own initiative. Unaided. [Or. Cricket.]

Battle **Battle royal** A general fight.
Half the battle A great help.
Pitched battle One in which both sides are fully engaged.

Bay **At bay** In a situation so desperate that one is compelled to turn and face one's enemies.
Keep at bay Keep at a distance.

Be **Be-all and end-all** Whole (of a matter).
Be that as it may Even so.
Let it be Do not disturb it.

Beam **On one's beam-ends** In a desperate and almost hopeless condition. [Or. Nautical. The term is applied to a ship when it is tilted so far over that it is resting on the ends of its cross-beams, or supports, and is consequently in great danger of sinking.]

Tom's already spent all his pocket-money, and is on his beam-ends.

Bean **Full of beans** In high spirits. Having plenty of energy.

Bear **Bear a charmed life** Be almost incredibly fortunate in escaping disasters and accidents.

Bear down upon To approach with determination or with an obvious purpose.

Bear enquiry, investigation, *etc.* Produce a satisfactory answer to enquiries. (Frequently used in the negative.)

The business he has been connected with won't bear enquiry.

Bear fruit Have results.

Bear-garden Scene of uproar and confusion.

Bear malice *or* **a grudge** Retain bitter or angry feelings, usually as the result of a dispute or quarrel.

Bear a meaning Convey a meaning.

That sentence doesn't bear the meaning you seem to think it does.

Bear in mind Retain in one's memory. Take note.

Bear in mind that the train leaves at midnight.

Bear the name of Possess the name of. Have the same name as.

Their son bore the name of his grandfather, and was christened Joseph.

Bear oneself Behave

Bear out 1. [LIT] Carry away.

They bore out the body.

2. Confirm; support.

Her statement bears out what the police told me.

Bear up Sustain one's strength and spirits.

Her father's death was a terrible shock, but she is bearing up well.

Bear with Endure as sympathetically as possible.

Bear witness Act as a witness. Give evidence.

Bring to bear Apply. Aim.

The outcry in the local newspapers brought a good deal of pressure to bear on the Council.

Grin and bear it Endure.

Like a bear with a sore head In a bad temper.

Lose one's bearings Lose one's way or sense of direction.

No bearing on No connection with; irrelevant.

Bear a date, signature, *etc*. Have written upon it.

His latest letter bears the date April 1st.

Beard **Beard the lion in his den** Confront boldly one's opponent (or superior) on his own ground (e.g. in his own home or office) to discuss a matter in dispute.

Beat **Beat about the bush** Avoid or delay a straightforward discussion; approach a subject in a roundabout way. [Or. Hunters beating bushes and similar hiding-places cautiously, to discover if game is hiding there.]

Beat down 1. Crush opposition.

The rebellion was beaten down.

2. Compel a person to reduce his price.

He wanted five pounds, but I beat him down.

Beat hollow Be entirely superior to.

Beat off Repel.

The garrison beat off all the enemy attacks.

Beat up Strike repeatedly and severely.

Dead beat Utterly exhausted.

After walking all day in the rain, we were dead beat.

Off the beaten track Away from main roads.

Beauty **Beauty is only skin deep** One must not judge by appearances.

The beauty of it is The especially satisfying thing is.

Beaver **Eager beaver** (Over-) zealous person.

Beck **At one's beck and call** In a position of being under one's domination.

Bed **Bed and board** Accommodation and meals.

Bed of roses A state of ease and luxury. (Frequently used with a negative.)

Between you, me and the bedpost In confidence.

Die in one's bed Die of natural causes, or peacefully.

Get out of bed on the wrong side Behave in a disagreeable fashion.

Have made one's bed and must lie in it Must endure consequences of one's own actions.

Bee **Bee in one's bonnet** Obsession; some particular idea or conviction, usually slightly crazy.

Make *or* **follow a bee line** Proceed in a straight line (as a bee does on its way home).

Beer **Beer and skittles** Amusement.

Think no small beer of How high opinion of.

Beg **Beg the question** Assume that something which is a matter for dispute is in fact true. (Often loosely used to mean 'avoid the issue being discussed'.)

Beg to differ Disagree.

Beggar **Beggars can't be choosers** People in need must take what is offered them. [Or. Proverbial.]

Beggar description Be so extraordinary that one cannot find words in which to describe it.

Behaviour **Be on one's good** or **best behaviour** Conduct oneself as correctly and properly as possible.

Behind **Behind the scenes** In private. Secretly and unofficially. [Or. Theatrical.]
Plans for the next election are going on behind the scenes.

Behind the times Late; unfashionable. Antiquated.
You are behind the times with your information.
Similar to **out of date**.

Come from behind Succeed from unpromising position.

Fall behind Lag.

Belief **Beyond belief** Unbelievable; astounding.

To the best of my belief In my genuine opinion.

Believe **Believe one's ears** or **eyes** Accept the truth of what one hears or sees.

Bell **Clear** or **sound as a bell** Very clear or sound. [Not confined to what one hears.]

Below **Below one's breath** Almost inaudible (but intended to be heard). In a mutter, so as to be heard privately, not publicly.

Belt **Hit below the belt** Attack unfairly. [Or. Boxing. A boxer may not strike his opponent below the belt worn round the waist.]

Under one's belt As part of one's experience.

Bend **Catch one bending** Have one at a disadvantage.

Beneath **Beneath contempt** So despicable as not to deserve even the effort of expressing one's dislike of it.

Beneath one's breath See *Below*.

Benefit **Give one the benefit of the doubt** Assume that one is right, or innocent, when it is not certain.

Bent **Bent upon** Determined to take a certain action.
Jane was bent upon walking the entire distance that same night.

Berth **Give a wide berth to** Avoid; keep as far from as possible. [Or. Nautical. A berth is any place in which a ship can anchor.]

Beside **Beside the mark** or **point** Irrelevant; unconnected with the matter being discussed.

Beside oneself In such a state of emotion that one is incapable of knowing what one is doing.

Best **At best** Even in the best possible circumstances.
At the best of times In the most favourable conditions.
Best man The bridegroom's chief friend and assistant at a wedding.
Best part Most.
For the best; all for the best The best that can happen; for the ultimate good.
Have the best of Win (an argument, contest, etc.).
Make the best of (a bad bargain *or* **job)** Be contented with (something unsatisfactory).
Put best foot forward Walk as quickly as possible. Exert effort.
To the best of one's ability As well as one can.
With the best As well as anyone.

Better **Better half** Wife (a gently ironic complimentary phrase).
Better oneself Improve one's worldly position.
Get the better of Triumph over; prove stronger than.
His anger got the better of him, though he was sorry later.
Know better (than) Not to be so foolish (as).
He should have known better than to take the risk.
No better than The same as.
Think (all) the better of Have more favourable opinion of.
Think better of Reconsider, and decide to alter one's plan (usually from prudence or fear).
He was going to protest, but thought better of it.

Between **Between ourselves; between you and me; between these four walls; between you, me and the bed-** *or* **gate-post** Speaking privately and confidentially.
Betwixt and between In the middle.
Read between the lines Find information which is not stated but implied.

Beyond **The back of beyond** The most remote part of the world.
Beyond (one's) expectation Beyond anything (one) expected.
The beauties of Florence were far beyond his expectation.
Beyond measure Exceedingly. Very much indeed.
Beyond the pale Unacceptable. [Old f.: beyond the

limits of decent society, good manners and moral limitations.] [Or. In Ireland, the property of the English kings used to be separated from that owned by the inhabitants, which was thus beyond 'the pale' = heraldic term = sovereignty. 'Pale' also = fence, boundary—a more likely origin of the phrase.]

Bib **Best bib and tucker** Best clothes.

Bid **Bid fair to** Appear likely to.

Bid welcome, farewell To express a welcome, or a farewell greeting.

Make a bid for Make an attempt to secure.

Bill **Bill and coo** Speak lovingly and intimately. [Or. An allusion to the sound—billing and cooing—made by doves and pigeons.]

Clean bill of health Assurance that one is in sound health.

The doctor gave her a clean bill of health.

Bird **A bird in the hand** Immediate possession is worth much more than a mere promise. [Or. The proverb, 'A bird in the hand is worth two in the bush.']

An early bird An early arrival. [Or. The proverb, 'The early bird catches the worm.']

The entertainment did not begin till eight, but we were early birds and got to the hall at seven-thirty.

Bird-brained Foolish.

Bird has flown Person has escaped or left.

Birds of a feather Similar people (e.g. having similar views, etc.).

[Or. The proverb, 'Birds of a feather flock together.']

Bird of ill omen [LIT] A bird—e.g. the raven, the owl or the crow—whose appearance is supposed to indicate the coming of bad luck. [MET] Any person who has a reputation for bringing bad news. [Old f.]

Bird of passage [LIT] A bird like the swallow, starling, etc., which migrates from one country to another according to the season. [MET] A person who is constantly travelling from place to place and has no permanent home; one who remains only temporarily.

Kill two birds with one stone Produce two results with a single action.

Like a bird Without difficulty.

A little bird told me I don't want (I refuse) to say who told me.

Birthday **In** *or* **wearing one's birthday clothes** *or* **suit**

Wearing no clothes at all; naked (as one is born).

Bit **A bit of** Rather. Some.
It's a bit of a nuisance.
Do one's bit Make one's contribution.
Every bit as Just as.
Not a bit (of it) Not at all.
Take *or* **have the bit between one's teeth** Become (or be) uncontrollably eager (to do something, etc.).

Bite **Bite** *or* **lick the dust** Be killed in battle. Be finished.
At the next election, I expect the Tories will bite the dust.
Bite off more than one can chew Undertake more than one can cope with.
Bite one's head off Speak angrily and sharply to a person.
Bite (on) the bullet Show endurance.
Bite the hand that feeds one Injure one's benefactor.
Two bites at a cherry Two separate attempts to achieve a result.
What's biting him? What is worrying or annoying you?

Bitten **Once bitten, twice shy** Once having been hurt (damaged, disappointed, swindled, etc.), one is understandably careful.

Bitter **The bitter end** The very end (however painful). See under *Pill*.

Black **Black art** Art or craft derived from the Devil; vile or supernatural practices.
(As) black as thunder *or* **a thundercloud** Very angry.
Black and blue Discoloured with bruises.
In one's black books In disfavour; with a bad reputation.
Black looks Angry (sometimes evilly threatening) appearance.
Black out 1. Obliterate; obscure.
2. Become unconscious.
In black and white In writing or print.
In the black Solvent.
Not so black as one is painted Not as unpleasant as people say.

Blank **Draw a blank** Fail (usually to gain a response).

Blanket **Wet blanket** A person who by his manner or conversation extinguishes the cheerfulness and

enthusiasm of others (as, literarlly, a wet blanket
extinguishes fire).

Bleed **My heart bleeds (for)** I am very sorry (for).

Blind **Blind alley** Unprofitable line of enquiry or course of
action.

Blind impulse An illogical, sudden or thoughtless
impulse.

Acting on blind impulse, she turned the car to the left.

Blind side The aspect of a man's character in which
he is tenderhearted or weak. Also, in sport, the
unguarded part of the field.

Blind spot Area where one's understanding is lacking.

None so blind No one is so difficult to persuade as a
man who is determined not to listen to arguments or
persuasion. [Or. Proverb, 'There's none so blind as those
who won't see.']

Turn a blind eye to Pretend not to notice or know
about.

Block **A chip off the old block** One exhibiting the
characteristics of his parents or ancestors.

Blood **Bad blood** Ill-feeling; antagonism.

There's been bad blood between them for ages.

One's blood being up Being excited and angry.

His blood was up, and a quarrel was inevitable.

Blood-and-thunder Highly sensational; melodramatic.
Hence, a story, book, film, etc., having such
characteristics.

See *penny dreadful.*

Blood is thicker than water Relations are more
closely connected than mere friends or acquaintances,
and should receive better treatment.

Blood-letting 1. Bloodshed.
2. Quarrel etc. having victim(s).

Blood sports Sports that involve the shedding of
blood, usually of animals (e.g. fox-hunting, bull-
fighting, etc.).

Blue-blooded Aristocratic. [Or. The now discredited
idea that the blood of aristocrats was bluer than that of
other people.]

First blood First success (in a contest, debate, trial of
strength, etc.).

Fresh *or* **new blood** New members (of an organisation,
club etc.).

Get blood out of a stone Find evidence of human

feeling in someone who lacks it. (More generally) Attempt the impossible.

Hot blood Quick temper. Anger.

In cold blood Deliberately; coolly.

In the blood Part of one's nature; born with one. Hence **runs in the blood** Is a family trait.

Make one's blood boil Make one furiously angry.

One's blood runs cold One experiences fear, acute apprehension or disappointment.

His ruthlessness makes my blood run cold.

Out for blood Determined to win.

Taste blood Be stimulated by success.

Young blood New young members (of an organisation, etc.).

Blot **Blot one's copy book** Spoil one's previously good reputation.

Blot out Efface; obliterate; forget.

It will be many years before memories of the accident will be blotted out.

Blow **Blow-by-blow description, account etc.** Detailed description etc.

Blow hot and cold Be inconsistent and unreliable. [Or. Æsop's fable of the countryman who blew on his fingers to warm them, and then on his porridge to cool it.]

Blow *or* **hang it!** *or* **the expense,** etc. Disregard it.

Blow (let) off steam Get rid of surplus energy.

Blow one's own trumpet Boast.

Blow out 1. (Verb) Extinguish.

Blow out the candles.

2. (Noun) A large and luxurious meal.

We had a tremendous blow out at the hotel.

Blow over Subside. [LIT] Applied to a storm of wind, etc.

The storm will soon blow over.

[MET]Applied to quarrels, disagreements, etc.

We have frequent quarrels, but they soon blow over.

Blow up 1. Explode.

The mine blew up soon after the soldiers passed.

2. Inflate.

The tyre needs blowing up.

Hence: [MET] Exaggerate.

Its importance has been blown up out of all proportion.

Come to blows Fight.

Strike a blow for *or* **against** Act in support *or* opposition.

Blue **Blue-eyed boy** Favourite.

Blue murder An angry scene. (Also used in a number of phrases as emphasis, e.g. **shout blue murder** (= loudly), **like blue murder** (= very quickly).
There'll be blue murder when she hears of this.

Blue riband *or* **ribbon** Highest attainable honour or prize. [Or. The blue ribbon worn with the Order of the Garter.]

See also under *Bolt.*

Bluff **Call a man's bluff** Challenge a statement or action which one believes has nothing to support it. [Or. The card game of poker.]
If you think he's asking too much for the house, call his bluff by pretending you're not interested in buying.

Blush **At (the) first blush** At first sight.
At first blush the proposals seeem generous.

Spare one's blushes Not embarrass one by praise.

Board **Above board** Honest and unconcealed. Straightforward. In order.

Across the board For everyone. In all respects.

Go by the board Be lost, forgotten or eliminated.

Sweep the board Take all the available rewards or prizes.

Boat **In the same boat** Similarly situated.
It's no use grumbling—we're all in the same boat.

Bob **Bob up** 1.[LIT] Rise suddenly.
2. [MET] Arrive suddenly.

Body **In a body** Collectively; all together.

Keep body and soul together Remain alive. (Usually jocular.)
I'm managing to keep body and soul together.

Boil **Boil down to** Amount to.

Boil over 1.[LIT] Boil so that the fluid rises above the edge of the saucepan or kettle.
2. [MET] Become so angry that self-control is lost.

Make one's blood boil Make one extremely angry.

Bold **Make bold to; make so bold as to** Presume to. Dare to. (Used ironically, usually.)

Bolster **Bolster up** Add to (e.g. one's confidence, a statement, etc.) in order to strengthen.
The Government bolstered up its position by imprisoning all its outspoken opponents.

Bolt **A bolt from the blue** A complete surprise. A sudden and entirely unexpected disaster. [Or. 'Bolt' = thunderbolt; 'blue' = a cloudless sky from which no storm is to be expected.]

Bolt upright Absolutely straight and perpendicular. [Or. 'Bolt' = short arrow of crossbow, therefore straight.]

Shoot one's bolt Do everything one can.

Bone **A bone to pick** A matter for reproof or blame.

Bone of contention The subject of argument or dispute.

Bone-dry Quite dry.

Bone idle Utterly idle.

Feel in one's bones Be quite sure.
The train will be full; I can feel it in my bones.

Make no bones about Not attempt to disguise.
I'm disappointed, I'll make no bones about it.

See also under **Finger**.

Book **Bring to book** Bring to justice; punish.

Closed book Something one does not understand.

Go by the book Adhere strictly to rules.

In my book As I see matters.

In one's good *or* **bad** *or* **black books** Liked and appreciated (or the reverse).

Read someone like a book Understand person's character, motives, etc., fully.

Suit one's book Agree with one's plans.
That arrangement will suit my book very well indeed.

Take a leaf out of a person's book Follow his example. Imitate him.
I think I'll take a leaf out of his book and go to bed early.

Throw the book at Make all possible accusations against.

Boot **Put the boot in** Take decisive, usually harsh, action.

The boot's on the other foot (*or* **leg**) The advantage (power, responsibility, truth, etc.) now lies on the opposite side to where it formerly did.

Born **Born before one's time** Possessing ideas and theories that belong to a later period in history.

In all one's born days In all one's life. (Used to emphasis.)
I've never been so surprised in all my born days.

Not born yesterday Not without experience.

Borne **Borne in upon one** Impressed upon one's mind.
It was borne in upon her that they would never meet again.

Borrow **Borrowed plumes** Anything worn or assumed to which one is not entitled. [Or. Æsop's fable of the jay who made herself ridiculous by adding peacock's feathers (or plumes) to her own.]

Borrowed time Unexpected prolongation of time, especially of life.

Bosom **Bosom friend** Intimate friend.

Both **Having something both ways** Choose two contradicting or alternative lines of action, etc., for one's own benefit, when only one is available.
If you don't give up smoking, you won't be able to afford a holiday: you can't have it both ways.

Bother **Cannot be bothered** Will not take trouble.

Bottle **Bottle-neck** A passage which becomes suddenly narrow, like the neck of a bottle, through which objects are compelled to move slowly; hence [MET] anything which causes a delay.

Bottle up Suppress.
He bottled up his anger and said nothing.

Bottom **At the bottom of** Really responsible for.

Bet one's bottom dollar Stake everything one possesses.

Bottom falls out Collapse takes place.

Bottomless pit Hell.

From the bottom of one's heart Genuinely. Most sincerely.

Get to the bottom of Find the truth, cause, meaning of.

Knock the bottom out of Show to be of no value.

Touch bottom [LIT] Reach the bottom of the sea.
The boat's keel touched bottom.
[MET] Reach the lowest depths (e.g. of misery, etc.).
See **rock-bottom**.

Bound **Beyond the bounds of** Outside the limits of.

I'll be bound I am certain.
He'll be late again tomorrow, I'll be bound.

Out of bounds Beyond the official boundary or limit.
All the hotels in the town have been placed out of bounds to the troops.

Within bounds 1. Within the official boundary or limit.
2. Within reasonable limitations and restraint.
She could never keep her temper within bounds.

Within reasonable bounds Within restraint.

Within the bounds of possibility Just possible.

It is, of course, within the bounds of possibility that the shipwrecked crew may have reached some desert island.

Bow **Bow to the inevitable** Accept what is unavoidable.
Shot across the bows Warning.
Two strings *or* **another string to one's bow**
More resources than one. An alternative, a second plan in case the first should fail.

Bowl **Bowl along** Go fast and smoothly.
Bowled over 1. [LIT] Overturned; knocked down.
The nun was bowled over in the rush to the train.
2. [MET] Overcome (usually with surprise, joy).
When I heard the news I was completely bowled over.

Box **Box on the ears** Blow on the side of the head.

Boy **Boys will be boys** Immature behaviour must be tolerated.
Jobs for the boys Favours for one's friends.

Brain **Brain wave** Sudden good idea, plan; inspiration.
Brains trust A group of experts, meeting publicly to discuss and answer questions, problems, etc.
Cudgel *or* **rack one's brains** See *Cudgel*.
Have something on the brain Be totally preoccupied with something.
Make one's brain reel Stagger one mentally. Applied to an almost incredible statement or fact.
Pick a person's brains Question a person (sometimes informally or tactfully) to extract information, advice, etc., from him.
See under *Crack, Hare, Scatter*.

Brake **Put the brake(s) on** [LIT and MET.] Cause to slow down.

Branch **Branch out** Develop (into or away from) (as branches grow from trees). Become independent.
The chip-shop is branching out into a café as well.
He's left the firm, to branch out on his own.

Brand **Brand-new** Absolutely new. [Or. Anglo-Saxon *brandoz* = burning stick. Thus applied to metal goods taken straight from the fire in which they were made.]

Brass **Bold as brass** Extremely or excessively self-assured.

Brazen **Brazen out** Defiantly defend, or deny.

Breach **Breach of the peace** (*strictly speaking,* **the Queen's peace**) Any action which breaches or breaks the law and may lead to violence and disturbance.
Heal the breach Bring a serious or prolonged quarrel to an end.

Step into the breach Deputize.
The organist fell ill, but his assistant stepped into the breach at the last moment.

Bread **Bread and butter** Routine daily work.
Bread-winner The person whose earnings support the family.
Know which side his bread is buttered on Know where his interest, advantage, etc., lies.
Want one's bread buttered on both sides Want undue benefits.

Break **Break away** Free, or detach oneself, by a definite effort.
I broke away from the association ten years ago.
Break the back of Complete the most difficult or main part of.
I should break the back of this piece of work before the end of the week.
Break the bank Exhaust the bank's resources.
Break a blow *or* **fall** Mitigate its effect.
Break down 1. Smash by force.
We shall have to break down the door to get in.
2. Cause to diminish and finally disappear.
It took a long time to break down his shyness.
3. Collapse under great pain or emotion.
When she heard he was dead, she broke down completely.
Break even Show neither profit nor loss.
Break from *or* **forth** Escape from. Sound from.
Cheers broke from the crowd when the teams appeared.
Break a habit Cease to be subject to a habit.
Break new ground Begin something new or different.
Break of day Dawn.
Break one's heart Cause profound distress.
It will break his heart to retire.
Break the ice Break an uncomfortable silence; put an end to formality or stiffness.
Break in 1. Enter a building by force.
2. Interrupt.
I could tell this story better if so many people didn't break in.
3. Train someone, usually an animal, in obedience.
I've spent nearly six months breaking in my pony.
Break in on Interrupt.
Break a journey Interrupt it by stopping at some point on the way, and resuming the journey later.
We are breaking our journey at Chester for one night.

Break loose Escape.
The dog broke loose from its chain.
Similar to **break away.**
Breakneck speed (Dangerously) fast pace.
Break one's neck Be in a considerable hurry.
I broke my neck to arrive in time.
Break the news Pass on information. (Usually, startling or bad news, as tactfully and gently as possible.)
Break off End (suddenly, or temporarily).
We were discussing our plans, but had to break off when the telephone rang.
Break out 1. [LIT] Force one's way out.
He broke out of prison, but was caught again later.
2. [MET] Begin.
A roar of cheering broke out.
Break ranks Leave one's position (usually in disorder).
Break the record Surpass all previous performances.
Break the thread Interrupt a story, a line of thought, etc.
Break through (Verb) Penetrate (the surroundings or impediment, etc.).
The sun broke through the clouds.
The crowd broke through the lines of police.
Break-through (Noun) Successful development.
Break up [LIT] Break into small pieces. [MET] End, dismiss, destroy, depart.
Break with Have no further connection with.
Break one's word, *or* **promise** Fail to do what one has undertaken to do.
Make the break Similar to **break away (from).**
The weather breaks The weather changes. Hence **a break in the weather**: a change.
Breast **Make a clean breast (of)** Confess all.
Breath **A breath of (fresh) air** [LIT]
Let's go into the garden for a breath of air.
[MET] Someone or something invigorating, refreshing, delightful.
The new typist is a real breath of fresh air.
The breath of one's nostrils Vital; absolutely necessary.
Hold one's breath Stop breathing (out of fear etc.).
In the same breath At the same time; simultaneously.

(Usually in connection with two contradictory statements.)

Keep one's breath to cool one's porridge Not speak.

Out (short) of breath Unable to breathe (because of exertion, illness, etc.).

Take away one's breath Leave one breathless through intense astonishment, delight, etc. Thus **breathtaking** Astonishing.

Your offer is so generous that it takes my breath away.

Under *or* **below one's breath** Very softly; almost in a whisper.

With one's last breath To the end of one's life; to the last. (Used metaphorically to add emphasis to a statement.)

See under *Save, Waste.*

Breathe   **Breathe again** Recover (from fear, inconvenience, etc.).

The floods subsided, and the villagers breathed again.

Breathe down one's neck Supervise closely.

Breathe one's last Die.

Breathe (e.g. **revenge, curses, blessings,** *etc.*) Murmur; utter in low intense tones, or passionately.

Breathing-space Pause (for recovery or relaxation from effort).

Not to breathe a syllable *or* **word** Remain absolutely silent; keep secret.

See **fire and brimstone.**

Bred   **Born and bred** Born and brought up.

Brick   **Brick up** Fill up an opening in a building, etc., with bricks.

There was once a window there, but it has been bricked up for centuries.

Make bricks without straw Make something without having the necessary materials. [Or. Biblical. The Israelites were commanded to make bricks without straw.]

Bridge   **Cross a bridge when one comes to it** Deal with a difficulty when it occurs, not anticipate it.

Brief   **In brief** In short. Concisely.

Hold no brief for Refrain from arguing in favour of.

Bright   **Bright and early** Very early.

Bright idea Clever idea.

Bright lights Places of entertainment. Town where these may be found.

Bright spark Quick-witted person.

Brim **To the brim** [LIT] To the edge of any vessel made to contain fluid. [MET] To completion. Also **brim-full.**
She was filled to the brim with happiness.

Bring **Bring about; bring to pass** Cause to happen.

Bring-and-buy sale Sale, usually for charity, at which people donate items for sale.

Bring to bear Apply (influence, etc.). Concentrate one's efforts with some special object.

Bring to book Detect someone in a mistake; bring a wrongdoer to punishment.

Bring *or* **call into being** Cause to exist.

Bring into play Cause to operate.

Bring into the world Give birth to.

Bring to a close End; conclude.

Bring down 1. Cause a penalty to fall on.
He'll bring trouble down on himself.
2. Lower.
Prices are being brought down.
3. Cause to end.
This controversy could bring down the Government.

Bring forth Produce; display.

Bring forward Introduce; initiate.

Bring home to one Cause one to realize, to feel, to understand. Convince one.

Bring the house down Cause uproarious laughter or applause. [Or. Theatre: house = theatre building.]

Bring in Introduce. Produce (as income or profit). Deliver (verdict).

Bring off Succeed.

Bring to mind Recall.

Bring into play Cause to operate.

Bring up the rear Follow at the end. [Or. Military.]
Policemen on horseback brought up the rear.

Bring on 1. Cause.
The heat brings on my headaches.
2. Cause to appear.
Bring on the dancing girls!
3. Advance progress of.
Pruning will bring on the roses.

Bring oneself to Persuade oneself to.
He couldn't bring himself to apologize.

Bring out 1. Exhibit clearly.
Hardship sometimes brings out the best in people.
2. Publish.
*The new edition of the dictionary will be brought out
next year.*
Bring round 1. Bring from a short distance.
2. Restore to consciousness. Also **bring to.**
We threw water over the woman to bring her round.
3. Persuade (to a point of view).
*The strikers are taking a long time to be brought round to
accepting the management's offer.*
Bring up 1. Refer to some matter requiring discussion
(also **bring forward**).
Please bring up the matter at our next meeting.
2. Care for and educate.
He was very well brought up.
Bring word Convey information.

Bristle **Bristle with** Be (unpleasantly) full of.
The whole plan bristles with difficulties.

Bristol **(All) shipshape and Bristol fashion** In good order.
[Or. High repute of ships from port of Bristol.]

Broad **It's as broad as it's long** Either alternative will lead
to the same result.
Broadly speaking Speaking generally; stated in simple
terms.
Broad-minded Tolerant.

Broken **Broken accents** Imperfect or hesitating speech.
Broken English Inaccurate and imperfect English.
Broken reed An ally or support who has proved
useless or unworthy. [Or. A reed is a tall kind of grass
which, although stiff, snaps very easily.]
See under *Break.*

Broom **New broom** Newly appointed person eager to improve
matters.

Brow **Lowbrow** Having to do with popular, undemanding
forms of art, literature, music, etc.
Highbrow Having to do with highly developed,
intellectual tastes in the arts.
Knit one's brows Frown (usually in thought).

Brown **In a brown study** In a reverie. Apparently thinking
deeply; sometimes hardly thinking at all. [Or. A faulty
translation of the French *sombre pensée. Sombre,* like *brun*
(brown) = gloomy, melancholy. (?)]

Brush **A brush** A light, not serious, encounter.

He's out of sorts because he's just had a brush with a traffic-warden.

Brush up Renew one's memory of. Revise.
You can brush up your French by watching the TV programme.

Brute **Brute force** Physical force or strength.
The police had to use brute force to take her to the station.

Buckle **Buckle (down) to** Get to work vigorously. Set about.
We shall have to buckle to if we are to catch that train.

Bud **Nip in the bud** Prevent at an early stage.

Build **Build up** (Verb) 1. Gradually build or increase.
2. Praise.
Build-up (Noun) Advance publicity creating anticipation.
Build upon [MET] Rely upon.

Bull **Bull-at-a-gate** Forceful.
Bull in a china shop Clumsy wrecker.
Take the bull by the horns Tackle problem boldly.

Buoy **Buoy up** Support; encourage. [Or. Nautical.]

Burn **Burn one's bridges** *or* **boats** Make a change of
plan impossible; make certain that the decision is final.
[Or. If a general or sea captain wished to make his own
retreat impossible, he burned the bridges he had crossed
or the ships he had sailed in before the battle began.]
Burn the candle at both ends Fail to conserve one's
energy. Work hard or for long hours, or live very
energetically, usually with consequent exhaustion.
Burn one's fingers Suffer because of rashness,
meddling or financial speculation.
Money burns a hole in one's pocket One is very
eager to spend money.
Money to burn Plenty of money to spend.
One's ears are burning One is being talked about
while not present.

Burst **Burst into laughter** *or* **tears** *or* **out laughing**
Suddenly erupt into laughter or tears.

Bury **Bury the hatchet** Forget past quarrels, and become
friends. [Or. The custom of the American Indians of
ceremoniously burying their war-hatchets after making
peace with an enemy.]
See **pipe of peace** and **bygones be
bygones.**
Bury one's head in the sand Obstinately refuse to
accept or face facts. [Or. The legendary (and false) idea
that ostriches bury their heads in the sand when in
danger, believing that since they are unable to see their
enemies, their enemies cannot see them.]

Business **Get down to business** Begin seriously.
Go out of business Cease to trade; discontinue one's usual work.
Have no business Have no right.
Like nobody's business In a remarkable way.
Make it one's business to Assume personal responsibility for. Undertake to.
I'll make it my business to call on him.
Mean business Intend to take definite (and sometimes unpleasant) action.
There's a bull in the field, and I'm afraid he means business.
Mind one's own business Refrain from interfering.

Butt **Butt in** Interrupt. Intervene. Interfere.

Butter **Look as if butter wouldn't melt in one's mouth** Appear demure, innocent.
Fine words butter no parsnips The truth can not be hidden or changed by mere words.

Buttonhole Intercept and speak privately to. Detain a reluctant listener.

Buy **Buy off** Pay to be rid of (usually person).
Buy out Pay person(s) to give up business, prosperity, etc.
Buy up Purchase large quantities or whole of.
A good buy A bargain.

By **By and by** Soon; in the near future.
By and large In general terms; comparing the advantages and disadvantages. On the whole.
By and large, the bus service is getting worse.
By himself, herself 1. Unaided.
The baby can now walk by himself.
2. Alone.
I spent all the afternoon by myself.
By the by Incidentally.
By the way See under ***Way.***

Bygones **Let bygones be bygones** Let past quarrels or disagreements be ignored or forgotten. See **bury the hatchet** and **pipe of peace** (under ***Peace***).

Byword **Become** *or* **be a byword** Become (be) notorious, proverbial.

C

Cake **Cakes and ale** A very enjoyable experience. Merry-making.

Have one's cake and eat it Obtain two contradictory advantages from the same thing or by the same means. Similar to **have it both ways.**

Like hot cakes Very quickly.

Slice of the cake Share of the benefit.

Calculate **Calculated to** Likely to; tending to.

His conduct is calculated to offend people.

Calculate upon Expect; estimate.

We calculate upon a hundred people attending.

Call **Call away** Summon.

Call to the bar Admit as a barrister. [Or. Legal. Qualified law students are 'called' from the body of the hall to take part in legal proceedings. To be called *within* the Bar is to be made a Queen's (or King's) Counsel.]

Call down Invoke.

Call for 1. Demand.

The present emergency calls for special measures to be taken.

2. Arrive to take away or accompany.

We will call for you on our way to the concert.

Call a halt End. Order to end.

The referee called a halt to the bout in the fourth round.

Call in Recall something that has been issued, e.g. coins or stamps.

Call in question Express doubt about. Dispute.

Call to mind Recall; remember.

I can't call to mind where I've met you.

Call names Abuse.

She called him every name she could think of.

Call off 1.Order to cease. Cancel.

The search was called off at nightfall.

2. Change one's mind, and abandon plans previously made.

We were going to give a party, but had to call it off.

Call on 1. Visit.

2. Request.

Call one's bluff Challenge one's attempt to deceive.

Call out 1. Raise one's voice; shout.

Call out the name of the winner.

2. Summon to keep public law and order.

Rioting began, and troops were called out.

Call over Read through a list of names aloud, in order to ascertain who are present. Also **call the roll.**

Call a spade See *Spade.*

Call a thing one's own Have normal benefits of possession.

Call to account. See *Account.*

Call the tune Give the orders. Be in a position of superiority.

Call up Summon.

No call to No need to.

There's no call to be alarmed.

On call Ready when wanted.

Pay a call Make a visit.

Camel **Break the camel's back** Go too far. See **last straw** under *Straw.*

Camp **Camp-follower** Hanger-on.

Can **Can of worms** Very complicated matter.

Candle **Burn the candle at both ends** See *Burn.*

Not fit to hold a candle to Not fit even to assist; not good enough even to be compared with.

Not worth the candle Not justifying the trouble, cost etc.

Cap **Put on one's thinking-cap** Give a problem some thought. [Or. A legendary magic cap worn by Eric XIV of Sweden which gave him special powers.]

A feather in one's cap See *Feather.*

Cap and bells Part of the equipment of a professional jester or fool of the Middle Ages.

Cap in hand Humbly. Hence **go cap in hand**: solicit meekly; ask a favour.

If the cap fits (wear it) If something (e.g. remark, statement) is appropriate or true (take note of it).

Set one's cap at Attempt. Also applied to a woman who is making a determined effort to persuade a man to marry her. [Or. The idea that she put on her most attractive cap to catch his attention].

Take (send, pass) the cap round Make a collection of money by circulating some container among people.

To cap To go one better (e.g. **to cap a joke**: to tell a better one). Outdo.

Capital **Make capital out of** Turn to good account.

Captain **Captain of industry** Industrial magnate.

Cards **Get one's cards** Be dismissed from one's employment.

Have card(s) up one's sleeve Have plan in reserve.

House of cards Unstable plan or operation.

On the cards Possible; likely to happen.

It's on the cards that I may go to Australia.

Play one's cards (right *or* **well,** etc.) Act or plan, negotiate, etc. (sensibly).

Put one's cards on the table Be absolutely candid, and conceal nothing.

Care **Have a care!** Be careful.

Take care Be careful.

Take care to Be sure to.

Take care of Protect.

Career **Chequered career** One including many changes; successes and failures. [Or. A 'chequered' pattern is one resembling a chessboard, with alternate squares of light and dark colours.]

Carpet **Sweep under the carpet** Conceal. Ignore.

Carry **Carry all before one** Be overwhelmingly successful.

Carry (along) with Persuade.

Carry away 1. Transport.

2. Deprive of self-control.

Carry coals to Newcastle Do something superfluous. [Or. Newcastle has plenty of coal.]

Carry conviction Be very persuasive.

His arguments don't carry much conviction.

Carry the day Reach final success; win.

Their greater skill eventually carried the day.

Carry off 1. Take away by force.

The invaders carried off many hostages.

2. Conduct oneself successfully (in a difficult situation).

He carried off the interview very well.

Carry on 1. Continue (e.g. one's work or recreation.)

2. Grieve.

3. Behave irregularly and badly.

Carry one's point Succeed in convincing one's opponent . [Or. Archery.]

Carry out Put into practice.

Carry over Postpone.

Carry through Complete. Bring safely out of difficulties.

Carry weight Exert influence.

Cart **Put the cart before the horse** Make two statements in reverse order of their importance; put the second and less important thing first; place the effect before the cause.

Case **As the case may be** Whichever of several things may happen.

Suppose your son becomes an artist, or a poet, as the case may be?

A case in point See under *Point.*
In any case Whatever may occur.
In case Lest. In the event that.
Close the window in case it rains while we're away.
In case of In the event of. Also **just in case.**
In that case If that is true or should happen. That being so.
In the case of As regards. In the matter of.
Is *or* **is not the case** Is true *or* false.
Make out a case for Argue in favour of.

Cash **Cash down** Immediate payment.
Hard cash Currency (not cheques etc.).
Cash in on Benefit from.
Cash on the nail Money (not cheques or any other substitute).

Cast **Cast about** Seek for.
I've been casting about for some village in which I can spend a quiet holiday.
Cast adrift Abandoned.
Cast aside Reject as worthless.
Cast aspersions on Comment unfavourably upon; decry. See **run down.**
Cast away Wrecked.
Cast a clout Discard one's winter clothing. [Or. Proverb: 'Cast not a clout till May be out.'
Clout – piece of clothing.]
Cast down Depressed; unhappy.
Cast an eye over Look at, usually quite casually.
Similar to **cast a glance at.**
Cast *or* **throw light upon** Reveal; exhibit.
Pepys' diary casts a light on life in England in the seventeenth century.
Cast *or* **throw in one's lot** Decide to share the life, the good and bad fortunes, of another person or society.
Cast the net Search widely.
Cast off (Verb) 1. Unfasten the mooring ropes, chains, etc., preparatory to sailing.
2. Repudiate. Throw away.
Cast-off (Noun) Unwanted. Used up.
Cast out Expel.
Cast pearls See under *Pearl.*
Cast a shadow over Have a dispiriting influence on.
Cast a spell over Bewitch; control by magic.
Casting vote A vote given by the chairman of a meeting when the number of votes for and against any

proposal is equal. It is the casting vote that then decides the matter.

Castle **Castle in the air** A dream building; a mere vision of happiness which has no basis in fact.

Castle in Spain The French version *(Château d'Espagne)* of the above.

An Englishman's home is his castle One's home is private, and may not be entered by force.

Cat **A cat may look at a king!** Whatever may be our (social) positions, one person is as good as another.

Cat-call Expression of disapproval (usually whistling) at theatre, etc.

Cat-and-dog life A life of continual quarrelling and fighting. Also **fight like cat and dog.**

Cat-and-mouse game Cautious manœuvring, bargaining, negotiation, etc.

Cat-nap Brief sleep.

Curiosity killed the cat Do not be inquisitive.

Enough to make a cat laugh Very funny.

Let the cat out of the bag Allow a secret to escape unintentionally.

Like a cat on hot bricks Restless. Fidgety. Uneasy.

Like something the cat brought in Bedraggled.

Not room to swing a cat Confined space.

Put the cat among the pigeons Create a sensation, uproar, contention, by doing something, e.g. by taking some initiative in a given situation.

Rain cats and dogs Rain very heavily.

Which way the cat jumps What events indicate as a probability.

Similar to **which way the wind blows** (under *Wind.*)

Cat's paw On who is used merely for the convenience of a cleverer or stronger person. [Or. Æsop's fable of the monkey who, wanting to eat some chestnuts that were on a hot stove, but not wishing to burn himself getting them, seized a cat and holding its paw in his own, used it to knock the chestnuts to the ground.)

Catch **Catch-all** Designed to include every contingency.

Catch cold Become ill with a common cold.

Catch fire (catch light; catch alight) Ignite; burn. *The spilt oil caught fire, and the house was burnt down.*

Catch a glimpse of See momentarily.

Catch hold of Take a hold on. Take hold of.

Catch someone napping [LIT] Discover someone asleep. [MET] Obtain an advantage through discovering someone being careless or ignorant.

Catch out Find out; expose. Discover someone making a mistake.

Catch penny Cheap, or superficially attractive, because purely commercial.

Catch-phrase Phrase in common use.

Catch a person's eye See under *Eye.*

Catch sight of See for a moment.

Catch up 1. Snatch up; seize suddenly.
He caught up his briefcase and dashed out.
2. Become level with.
He ran so fast that he soon caught up with me (or *caught me up*).

Catchword Slogan.

Caught **Be caught bending** *or* **napping** *or* **out** Be put at a disadvantage by someone else's greater alertness.

Cause **Good cause** Organisation, event, etc. deserving support (e.g. charity).

Lost cause Undertaking that has no hope of success.

Caution **Throw caution to the winds** Behave rashly.

Caviare **Caviare to the general** Something good which is beyond the appreciation or understanding of the general public. [Or. *Hamlet.* Caviare is an expensive preparation made from sturgeon's roe; it is highly popular in Russia.]

Centre **Centre of attraction** Person or thing attracting principal attention.

Ceremony **Stand on ceremony** Insist on formal behaviour.

With no further (without) ceremony Promptly. Informally.

Chain **Chain reaction** A result which, in turn, produces an effect which, in turn, produces a similar result, and so on.

Chain store One of a number of precisely similar stores, controlled by the same company, and selling goods of the same type and price.

Chair **Take the chair** Occupy the chair, i.e. the seat of the chairman. Preside over a meeting as chairman.

Chalk **By a long chalk; by long chalks** By a great deal; thoroughly. [Or. An ancient custom of recording merit by chalk marks.] Thus **chalk up**: score.
The boy will win the race by a long chalk.

As different as chalk from cheese Totally different.
The music of Strauss is as different from Bach's as chalk from cheese.

Chance **An eye to the main chance** See under *Eye*.
Game of chance Game depending on luck, not skill.
On the off chance In the hope.
Sporting chance A chance, though not a great one.
There's still a sporting chance that the horse will win.
Stand a good *or* **fair chance of** Be very (quite) likely to.
We stand a good chance of being late.
Take a chance *or* **take chances** Run a risk.
Taking no chances Taking no risks.
He has two bolts on every door, and an extra one on the window; he's taking no chance of burglars getting in.
The chances are The probability is.
The chances are that there will be a strike.
The chances are against it *or* **even** It is unlikely *or* reasonably likely.

Change **Change hands** Change owners.
That shop has changed hands only once in a hundred years.
Change of air Different climate.
Get no change out of Fail to receive satisfaction from.
I complained to the manufacturers, but I didn't get any change out of them.
Ring the changes Do something in a variety of ways. [Or. Bell-ringing.]
Small change Coins of small value.
I had to give the conductor a pound note; I had no small change.

Chapter **Chapter of accidents** A series of accidents or misfortunes.
Chapter and verse Exact authority for a statement; details by which the truth of a statement can be checked. [Or. The divisions of the Bible.]

Character **In character** In harmony with a person's known habits or temperament. Opposite: **out of character.**

Charge **Charge with** 1. Formally accuse of some crime.
2. Entrust with.
Charged with 1. Filled, loaded with.
2. Entrusted with.

In charge of Responsible for.

Charity **Charity begins at home** Kindness is due first to one's kith and kin. One should look after one's own interests, and those of one's relatives and friends, before showing kindness to strangers.

Cold as charity Very cold. Unsympathetic.

Charm **Work like a charm** Work very well.

Bear a charmed life Appear to have magical powers enabling one to succeed, escape, etc.

Cheap **Cheap as dirt; dirt cheap** Extremely cheap; a bargain.

On the cheap Cheaply.

Check **Check out** [U.S.A.] Pay one's bill and leave.

Keep in check Restrain.

Cheek **Cheek by jowl** Close together, very near.

Have a cheek Be impertinent.

Have the cheek to Have the impertinence, effrontery, to.

Turn the other cheek Fail to retaliate.

Cheer **Cheer up** Recover your cheerfulness!

Cherry **Two bites at the cherry** A second attempt or opportunity.

Chest **Get something off one's chest** Say something (usually something one has been intending to say for some time).

Play something *or* **one's cards close to one's chest** Act secretively.

Chestnut **Old chestnut** Very familiar device, anecdote, rumour, etc.

Chicken **Chicken-hearted** Cowardly; easily terrified. [Or. Chickens run to their mother for shelter at the slightest danger.]

Count one's chickens before they are hatched Make definite plans about profits or advantages before it is certain that you will obtain them.

Child **Child's play** Very simple task.

Chill **Cast a chill over** Have a depressing influence on.
If he comes, he'll only cast a chill over the proceedings.

Catch a chill Develop a cold.

Take the chill off Warm slightly.

Chime **Chime in** Add in support of something already said. [Or. The chiming of bells.]

Chime in with Harmonize with.
Those blue curtains will chime in with the carpet.

Chin **Keep one's chin up** Stay cheerful.
Take on the chin Receive blow courageously.
Chip **Chip off the old block** See under **Block.**
Have a chip on one's shoulder Be touchy or bitter.
When the chips are down When it comes to the point.
Choice **Hobson's choice** No choice at all; the acceptance of
what one is offered. [Or. The custom of a Cambridge
stable-keeper named Hobson, who insisted on every
customer who wanted to hire a horse taking the one
nearest the stable door.]
Spoiled for choice Presented with many choices.
Take one's choice Decide between several
possibilities.
Chop **Chop and change** Frequently alter one's decisions or
methods. Be inconsistent, vacillating, variable.
Chord **Strike a chord** Bring back to one's memory.
Touch a chord *or* **the right chord** Appeal to emotions.
Chorus **Chorus of approval** *or* **applause** etc. General
approval.
Chuck **Chuck away** Waste. Lose. Throw away carelessly.
Chuck out Expel. Throw out.
Chuck up Stop; abandon (in disgust).
Church **Broad church** A term applied to those who think the
Church's religious belief should be broad-minded
enough to include all variations of ritual.
High church comprises those who follow more
elaborate ritual; those who give a 'high place' to the
importance of the priests and bishops and have much in
common with the Roman Catholic procedures and
beliefs.
Low church is the term applied to those who follow
simpler and less-formalized ritual. Protestant.
Evangelical.
Circle **Come full circle** End at starting-point.
Go round in circles Make no progress.
Run round in (small) circles Be very busy.
Vicious circle Actions and consequences which make
each other worse and worse.
Circumstance
Extenuating circumstances Excuses; causes which
make forgiveness possible.
In (under) the circumstances In the present
condition or state of affairs; after consideration of what
has happened.

Circumstantial

Circumstantial evidence Evidence which gives no direct proof. Known facts which are hard to explain unless one accepts that they *appear* to constitute proof.

Claim **Stake a claim** Claim.

Clamp **Clamp down on** Be stricter about.

Clap **Clap eyes on** Catch sight of. See. (Usually used in negative.)
I haven't clapped eyes on him for some weeks.
Clap-trap Worthless, valueless talk, generally used in an attempt to become popular or appear learned.

Clapham **The man on the Clapham omnibus** Ordinary people.

Class **In a class of its own** Unequalled.

Clean **Clean bill of health** [LIT] An official document certifying that a ship has left port with no case of infectious illness on board. [MET] Indication that there is no risk of infection, or, alternatively, that no illness, infectious or otherwise, exists.
Clean down Rub until clean.
Clean out Empty.
Clean sheet No record of wrong-doing.
Clean slate Freedom from commitments. Freedom from blame.
Clean up Make (person or thing) clean.
Make a clean breast of See *Breast.*
Make a clean sweep of See under *Sweep, Heel.*
One's hands are clean One is innocent.

Clear **Clear away** 1. Remove.
I'll clear away all this rubbish.
2. (*With* **get**) Escape completely.
The burglars got clear away.
Clear conscience Feeling that one is innocent.
Clear as crystal Obvious; absolutely plain. Also **crystal clear.**
Clear-cut Clearly defined.
Clear the decks for action Prepare. Get ready. [Or. Nautical. Before a sea battle or 'action' begins, the deck of each ship was cleared of all unnecessary or impeding objects.]
Clear of Free from.
The river is clear of weeds, and delightful to swim in.
Clear off Go away; depart.
Clear out 1. Make clean; remove impurities, etc.
2. Similar to **clear off.**

Clear the air Remove misunderstandings, quarrels, ambiguities, etc., which are impeding progress towards the successful outcome of a particualr matter.

Clear up 1. Make plain and clear.
I am trying to clear up any misunderstanding.
2. Make tidy by removing or rearranging.
You'll have to clear up the things on the table before we have tea.
3. Become fine.
The weather has cleared up.

Clear the way Remove obstructions [LIT or MET].
This new law will clear the way for many educational improvements.

Clearing-house Office for the exchange of information.

Steer clear of Avoid.

The coast is clear No one is about to see or interfere.

Cleft **In a cleft stick** In a state of uncertainty. In a dilemma.

Cliff **Cliff-hanger** Event, story, etc. with thrillingly uncertain outcome. Also **cliff-hanging.**

Climb **Climb down** Withdraw from decision, position, etc., previously taken.

Clinch **Clinch (an argument, a dispute, the matter,** *etc.***)** Settle finally and completely; conclude.

Clip **Clip the wings of** [LIT] Cut the wing-feathers of a bird so that it is unable to fly at any height. [MET] Limit the powers or authority of a person.

Clipped speech Words uttered in short, staccato tones, with the final consonants sharply stressed.

Cloak **Cloak-and-dagger** Surreptitious.

Clock **Against the clock** Under pressure of time.

Beat the clock Finish before a stated time.

Like clockwork Without a hitch.

Put the clock back Return to previous (outmoded) ways.

Round the clock All day long.

Watch the clock Be anxious to finish working-day on time. Hence **clock-watcher** Person who does this.

Close **At close quarters** Near to.

Behind closed doors Privately; secretly.

A closed book Something unknown.

Close down Shut permanently.

Close in upon Approach and surround.

Close on Almost.

Close with Grapple with; grasp violently.

Close season Period of time during which sporting events, etc., do not take place.

Close up 1. Move closer together.
2. Fill. Block.
3. Same as **Close down.**

Closed shop See under *Shop.*

Cloud **Cloud-cuckoo-land** An ideal realm.

Every cloud has a silver lining Every misfortune has its consolations. [Or. Proverb.]

In the clouds Day-dreaming, with one's thoughts elsewhere.

Under a cloud Regarded with disfavour and distrust; with an injured reputation.

With one's head in the clouds Unrealistic.

Clover **In clover** In a condition of luxury; very well off.

Club **Club together** Join, combine together (usually to share payment).

Clutch **Clutch at a straw** *or* **straws** Eagerly seize any help, support, solution, etc., however flimsy it may be.

Coach **Drive a coach and four** *or* **horses through** Easily evade or make ineffective.

Coals **Carry coals to Newcastle** Do something superfluous. [Or. Proverbial. Newcastle = important coal port.]

Haul over the coals Find fault; blame for some error. [Or. In the Middle Ages money was extorted by the King by hauling or pulling people over a slow-burning fire until they agreed to pay the amount demanded.]

Coast **The coast is clear** There is no enemy in view; no probability of interference.

Coat **Cut one's coat according to one's cloth** Limit oneself (or one's expenses) to the resources (or money) available.

Trail one's coat Seek to pick a quarrel.

Cobweb **Blow away the cobwebs** Revive oneself, usually by going into the open air.

Cock **Cock-a-hoop** Triumphant. Exultant. Boastful. [Or. The almost obsolete sport of cock-fighting. A winning bird erected his *houpe*, the feathered crest on his head.]

A cock-and-bull story A fantastic and unbelievable story.

Cock-eyed Having a squint. Crooked, not straight or level. Irregular.

Cock a snook at Express contempt for. Make a contemptuous gesture at. (Strictly speaking, placing thumb to nose with fingers outspread.)

Cock sure Aggressively sure and certain. Very self-confident. Also **cocky.**

Cock of the walk The chief; the dominant person. [Or. Walk = the name of the feeding-place of poultry, among whom there is always a cock who is master.]

Go off at half cock Succeed only partially, disappointingly. Proceed half-heartedly, with sense of anti-climax.

Knock into a cocked hat Make to appear insignificant.

Live like fighting cocks Live on the best and richest food. [Or. Sporting. Fighting cocks were so fed in order to make them fiercer and stronger.]

Cockles **Warm the cockles of one's heart** Make one's body glow, as with wine. Be deeply moving, delightful. Be emotionally affecting.

Coffin **A nail in one's coffin** A mistake contributing to one's downfall.

Coin **Coin money** Produce riches very rapidly.

Pay back in his own coin Retaliate or retort by the same method as the one he used. Similar to **give tit for tat.**

Other side of the coin Opposite aspect of a matter.

To coin a phrase Invent new expression. [Usually ironic apology for using cliché or stating the obvious.]

Cold **Cold comfort** Very slight satisfaction (the phrase is generally used ironically).

Give the cold shoulder to Avoid. Shun. Adopt an aloof manner towards.

In cold blood Deliberately. With premeditation.

Leave one cold Fail to impress one.

Left out in the cold Ignored.

Pour *or* **throw cold water on** Discourage. Behave very unenthusiastically towards (an idea, proposal, etc.).

Collar **Hot under the collar** Angry. Embarrassed.

Colour **Colour-blind** Unable to distinguish colours correctly, though otherwise possessing normal sight.

Give *or* **lend colour to** Support; help to prove.

In one's true colours As one really is (as distinct from what is pretended, or supposed).

Nail one's colours to the mast Adopt a position from which one does not intend to budge. [Or. Nautical.

Colours = flags. If nailed, they cannot be changed, or lowered to express surrender.]

Off-colour Slightly ill.

See the colour of one's money See proof that one has money.

Under false colours Falsely; pretending to be what one is not.

With flying colours Triumphantly.

Column **Dodge the column** Avoid duty.

Come **Come about** Occur; happen.

Come across 1. [LIT] Cross.

He came across the road to speak to me.

2. [MET] Find casually, discover.

Yesterday, when tidying my desk, I came across some old letters of yours.

3. Project.

On television he comes across very unsympathetically.

Come along Make haste.

Come to an arrangement Agree; mutually arrange.

Come away Leave. Become detached.

Come back (Verb) Return. Recur to memory.

Come-back (Noun) A return from obscurity to the prominence and success of the past.

He's far too old to stage a come-back to professional football.

Come to blows Proceed to fight.

Come by Acquire.

Come down Reduce. Fall. Decide. Lose status.

Come down on Rebuke. Punish. Also **come down (on one) like a ton of bricks.** See under *Ton.*

Come into Inherit.

Come into one's own Be seen to one's best advantage.

Come into existence Exist; be born; function.

The regulations came into existence on June 1st.

Come forward Present oneself.

Come to grief Suffer disaster.

Come in for Receive; inherit. Encounter.

He came in for a good deal of praise for his action.

Come-hither Flirtations.

Come into force Begin to operate.

Come of Become; result from.

I don't know what will come of all these developments.

Come off [LIT] Be removable.

I can't make the lid come off the saucepan.

[MET] Reach a successful result.

The comedian did his best to amuse us, but it didn't quite come off.

Come off well, badly, *etc.* End with credit, discredit, etc.
For over an hour he was examined in court by the lawyer, and came off well.
Come on 1. Hasten! Move more quickly! Also **come along.**
2. Begin.
It came on to rain soon after midnight.
Come out with Utter.
Come over 1. Affect, overpower, master, with emotion or illness.
I don't know what came over me.
2. Sound. Project. Make an impression. Perform.
His speech on the radio came over very well.
3. Similar to **come round** (2).
Come right Prove itself to be correct.
I can't make this sum come right.
Come round 1. Recover (from a faint).
We splashed water on her face, and she soon came round.
2. Visit someone not far away.
Come round and see us when you've time.
3. Modify one's own account or accept another person's view.
I discussed the subject for an hour before he came round to my opinion.
Come to (oneself) Identical with **come round** (1).
Come to grief Encounter disaster.
Come to light Be revealed.
No further information has come to light.
Come to pass Happen.
Come to terms Reach a formal agreement.
We expect to come to terms about the house very soon.
Come true Actually happen.
Come under 1. Be classed among.
2. Be subordinate to.
Come upon Encounter. Similar to **come across** (2).
Come up to Reach the level of [LIT and MET].
The water came up to the top of the bath.
This picture does not come up to the one you showed me yesterday.
Come up to scratch See under *Scratch.*
Come up with 1. Draw level with.
We came up with the travellers at the top of the hill.
2. Produce. Devise. Suggest.
Can you come up with a better way of doing it?
Come what may Whatever may happen in the future.
Coming man Person of growing importance.

Easy come, easy go What is gained without difficulty may be lost without pain.

Have it coming to one Deserve it.

How come? How did that happen?

If it comes to that In that case.

It comes *or* **amounts to this** Summarizing the situation; stated briefly.

Comfort **Creature comforts** Things which give physical comfort (e.g. food, clothes).

Command **At one's command** At one's service; available; capable of being used.

Commission **Out of commission** Not working.

Common **By common consent** By general agreement.

Common ground Basis for agreement.

Common knowledge Something generally known.

Common or garden Ordinary.

Common origin An origin in common. The same beginning.

Common parlance Plain, ordinary speech.

In common Shared; possessed by each (or all).

In common with Together with.

Short commons Not much food.

Company **Be good company** Be a pleasant companion. Hence **in good company.**

In bad company With people of poor reputation.

In company with Together with.

In good company With (counted among) people of merit.

Keep person company Be companion to person.

Part company Separate; part.

Compare **Compare notes** Discuss impressions and opinions.
Comparison

Comparisons are odious Any comparison between two persons or things is almost certain to lead to dissatisfaction and trouble.

In comparison with When compared to.

Compliment

Complimentary tickets Free tickets, given as a compliment to the receiver's position and importance.

Compliments of the season Traditional Christmas and New Year greetings.

Fish for compliments Speak deprecatingly of oneself in the hope of being contradicted.

Give *or* **pay a compliment** Express praise politely.

Give *or* **send one's compliments** Transmit an expression of formal greetings.

Return the compliment Repay a pleasant speech or a kindly action by another.

Concern **As far as I am concerned** In my opinion.

Concert **In concert** Unitedly; all together.

Conclusion **Arrive at** *or* **come to the conclusion** 1. Perceive; realize after considering all the facts.

I think you'll arrive at the conclusion that it is suitable for the job.

2. End.

The debate came to a conclusion soon after midnight.

Foregone conclusion An end so obvious that one is justified in assuming it.

Jump to a conclusion Assume rashly and without justification.

Try conclusions Test by opposing; fight against.

Condition **On condition that** If. Provided that.

Out of condition In a poor state (e.g. of health, fitness, etc.).

Conduct **Line of conduct** Behaviour.

Confidence **Confidence trick** Swindle based on persuading someone to entrust money, etc., to one as a sign of confidence in his honesty.

In strict confidence Absolutely privately.

Confusion **Confusion worse confounded** Disorder and confusion made even worse than before. [Or. Milton's *Paradise Lost.*]

Conjecture **Hazard a conjecture** Guess.

Conjunction **In conjunction with** Added to; together with.

What you've told me, in conjunction with what I already know, fills me with confidence.

Conjure **To conjure with** Of great importance.

Connection **In connection with** Relating to. Referring to. Regarding. About.

In that connection As far as that matter is concerned.

Miss the connection Miss a train, boat (etc.) which one's present mode of transport is intended to arrive in time for.

My train arrived late at Crewe, and I missed the connection to Manchester.

Conscience **Conscience money** Money paid to settle one's conscience.

Have on one's conscience Feel guilty about. Also
have a conscience about.
In all conscience In any imaginable set of
circumstances.

Consequence

Of no consequence Totally unimportant.
Don't apologize for breaking the cup—it's of no consequence.
Take the consequences Accept the results (usually of
one's own behaviour, actions, etc.).

Consideration

In consideration of In return for.
Take into consideration Make allowance for.
Under consideration Being considered.

Construction

Put a false construction on Misinterpret; assume
wrongly.

Contact **Come in contact with** Meet; encounter.

Contempt **Bring into contempt** Cause to be despised.
Fall into contempt Become despised.
Hold in contempt Regard with contempt or scorn.

Contradiction

Contradiction in terms A statement which
contradicts itself.

Contrary **On the contrary** The reverse; the opposite.
I haven't finished. On the contrary, I've only just started.
Contrary to expectation The reverse of what was
expected.
Contrary to expectation, he was not present.
To the contrary To contradict. The opposite.
*Unless I hear to the contrary, I'll expect you to arrive on
Sunday.*

Convenience

At your convenience When, where, etc. it suits you.
At your earliest convenience As soon as you can.
Make a convenience of Use for one's own purpose,
irrespective of feelings of others.

Convert **Convert into** Change into.

Conviction **Carry conviction** Convince; compel belief in.
His excuse doesn't carry much conviction.

Cook **Cook the books** Falsify statements (usually financial
ones).
Cook one's goose Create problems for one.
Cook up Prepare. Concoct.

Too many cooks spoil the broth One organizer is enough.

What's cooking? What's happening?

Cool **Cool as a cucumber** Completely calm and unexcited.

Cool customer (card, hand) A calmly audacious person.

Cool down [LIT] Become less heated. [MET] Become calmer.

Cool one's heels Wait. Be kept waiting (often as punishment, etc.).

Copy **Copy-cat** Imitator.

Core **To the core** Throughout.

Corner **Cut corners** Do something in straightforward way.

In a (tight) corner In a difficult position, awkward situation.

Just around the corner Very close.

Turn the corner Be improving.

Correct **Speak under correction** May be wrong.

Stand corrected Accept correction.

Cost **At all costs** Whatever may be involved; whatever efforts or sacrifice may be needed.

Count the cost Consider the risks before acting.

Counsel **Keep one's own counsel** Remain discreetly silent; say nothing of one's own plans.

Count **Count on** Rely on: be sure of.

Count one's chickens See under *Chicken.*

Does not count Is immaterial; does not make any difference.

Personal friendship does not seem to count in politics.

Countenance

Keep one's countenance Refrain from laughing. Maintain one's composure. Similar to **keep a straight face** (under *Face*).

Counter **Go** *or* **run counter to** Be opposite to. Also **act counter to**: behave contrary to.

It is a philosophy which runs entirely counter to everything I beleive in.

Courage **Dutch courage** Temporary courage created by drinking. [Or. In the seventeenth-century wars with Holland, Dutch sea-captains had barrels of brandy placed on deck from which the sailors helped themselves before beginning a fight.]

Have the courage of one's convictions Be brave enough to speak and act as one really believes.

Take one's courage in both hands Nerve oneself (to do something difficult).

Summon *or* **pluck up courage** Succeed in showing bravery in spite of fears.

Course **Adopt a course** Take a certain definite and considered action.

Change course Change direction.

In due course Eventually; ultimately; at the appropriate time.

In the course of During.

Embark on *or* **continue a course** Begin a connected series of actions or words. [Or. Nautical. The 'course' is the direction in which a ship travels.]

A matter of course The normal or expected procedure.

Run *or* **take its course** Complete its natural development.

Court **Ball is in one's court** It is one's turn to act.

Hold court Preside (usually over hangers-on, admirers etc.).

Coventry **Send to Coventry** Disregard completely; refuse to associate with. [Or. The dislike the inhabitants of Coventry had at one time for soldiers. Any woman seen speaking to one was thereafter treated as an outcast and ignored.]

Cover **Cover-up** Improper concealment of error (or crime).

From cover to cover From beginning to end (of a book, document, etc.).

Take cover Shelter.

Under cover 1. [LIT] (*a*) Sheltered.
We were under cover when the rain fell.
(*b*) Covered by a wrapping or envelope.
I am sending you a parcel under separate cover.
2. [MET] Concealed by a pretence.
Under cover of friendship, he betrayed their trust.

Cow **Till the cows come home** For an indefinite period; for ever.
If we wait for him, we shall wait till the cows come home.

Crack **Crack-brained** Crazy. Similar to **hare-brained, scatter-brained.**

Crack of doom The Day of Judgement, the last day. Commonly used to indicate an infinitely future period.
This shed is built to last till the crack of doom.

Crackpot Eccentric (person).

C

Crack the whip Show one's authority. Demand more effort (as of man driving a horse).

Wisecrack Joke.

Creature **Creature comforts** The material things which make life comfortable—good food, warm clothing, etc.

Credit **A credit to** A source of honour to or for.

Get the credit for Receive due praise for.

Give credit to Give praise where it should be given. Believe. Also **credit where credit is due.**

Redound to one's credit; reflect credit upon Be worthy of praise or honour.

Creeps **Give one the creeps** Cause one to shudder with nervous fear. (Generally used less literally to express dislike.)

Make one's flesh creep Make one feel as if things were crawling over one's skin (as result of repugnance, fear, etc.).

Crest **Crestfallen** Dejected.

On the crest of a wave Enjoying success.

Crocodile **Crocodile tears** Hypocritical show of regret. [Or. Belief that crocodile sighs to attract victim and weeps while eating prey.]

Crop **Crop up** Appear unexpectedly (above the surface) [LIT] and [MET].

Weeds always crop up in our flower-bed.

I never expected that this problem would crop up again.

Cross **Cross one's mind** Occur to one.

Talk at cross purposes Discuss from incompatible points of view, owing to a misunderstanding.

Cross *or* **pass the Rubicon** Take any irrevocable step. [Or. The Rubicon was a small river dividing ancient Italy from Caesar's territory, and when he and his army crossed it, he automatically invaded Italy.]

Cross as two sticks In an extremely bad temper. [Or. The cross formed when two sticks are placed one across the other. Thus pun on two meanings of the word 'cross'.]

Cross swords *See Sword.*

Got *or* **have one's wires crossed** Misunderstand.

Keep one's fingers crossed *or* **cross one's fingers** Hope for good luck.

Paths do not cross Ways of life do not cause people to meet each other.

Crow **Crow's foot** The small wrinkles which age, ill-health or trouble cause to form at the corners of one's eyes.

As the crow flies In a straight line, regardless of obstructions. [Or. A crow flies in a straight line from point to point.]

The villages are ten miles apart as the crow flies, but nearly fifteen miles by road.

Crow over Boast about one's triumph over.

Crown **To crown it all** As a final misfortune.

Cruise **Cruising speed** An economic travelling speed, less than full speed.

Crumb **Crumb of comfort** A tiny amount of comfort.

Cry **Cry for the moon** Ask for the impossible.

Cry off Refuse, or cease, to share in or co-operate.

Cry one's eyes *or* **heart out** Weep bitterly.

Cry out for Stand in obvious need of.

Cry over spilt milk Express regrets too late, or when nothing is to be gained by expressing them.

Cry stinking fish Speak unfavourably about one's own profession, trade, family, endeavours, etc.

Cry wolf Cause excitement or anxiety by spreading false news. [Or. From Æsop's fable of the shepherd boy who shouted 'Wolf' and brought his neighbours from their work so many times that when a wolf really did attack his sheep no one paid attention to his cries.]

A far cry A long way. Very different.

Farm eggs are a far cry from the ones we get in the local shops.

In full cry Noisily pursuing.

Cuckoo **Cuckoo in the nest** Unwanted intruder.

Cud **Chew the cud** Reflect.

Cudgel **Cudgel** *or* **rack one's brains** [LIT] Beat one's brains (a 'cudgel' is a stick) to compel them to work. [MET] Try to compel one's brain to function, and to understand or remember. Think hard.

I've cudgelled my brains, but I can't recollect where I put it.

Take up the cudgels Vigorously defend or support a cause.

Cue **Take one's cue from** Follow example or advice of.

Cuff **Off the cuff** Without prior thought, planning, preparation, etc.

I won't prepare a speech: I'll talk off the cuff.

Cup **One's cup (of happiness) is filled** One's happiness is absolutely complete.

With his family around him and no fears for the future, his cup was filled.

Cup that cheers Tea. [Or. William Cowper's *Task*: 'The cups that cheer but not inebriate.']

In one's cups In the process of getting drunk. Intoxicated.

Not one's cup of tea Not something that interests or suits one.

Cupboard **Cupboard love** Affection shown only in the hope of obtaining something in return.

Curl **Curl up** Experience embarrassment.

Enough to make one's hair curl. Frightening.

Currency **Acquire** *or* **obtain** *or* **gain currency** Circulate; become publicly discussed.

Curry **Curry favour** Attempt by flattery, bribery, etc., to become popular.

Customer **Ugly (awkward, tough,** *etc.***) customer** A difficult or dangerous person to deal with.

Cut **Cut across** Transcend.

Cut back Reduce. Also **cut-back.** Reduction.
Production at the factory has been cut back because of the strike.

Cuts both ways Has a second and compensating effect. Has an effect on both sides (of an argument, etc.).
Her refusal to live with him cuts both ways—he won't be responsible for maintaining her.

Cut a dash, a figure Exhibit oneself as a smart or fashionable person.

Cut down 1. [LIT]
Her cut down a tree.
2. [MET] Reduce.
He has to cut down his expenses since he changed his job.

Cut and dried Already arranged or prepared.
His plans for leaving were all cut and dried.

Cut fine Allow little margin for accident, etc.
You may catch the train, but you are cutting it rather fine.

Cut in 1. Interrupt.
Simon cut in with an interesting suggestion.
2. Admit.
Shall we cut them in on the plans?
3. (Of a car, pedestrian, etc.) Obstruct, or neatly obstruct, by placing oneself in front of another after overtaking.
The taxi cut in very sharply, and I had to brake.

Cut the (Gordian) knot Take a quick and drastic method of ending a difficulty. [Or. The knot tied by Gordius, a peasant who, on being chosen King of Phrygia, dedicated his wagon to Jupiter and tied the yoke to the beam with a knot that no one could untie. Alexander, on being told that whoever untied it would rule the whole of the East, solved the problem by cutting the knot with his sword.]

Cut of one's jib The face and general appearance. [Or. Nautical. The shape, or cut, of a ship's jib indicates to a sailor what type she is.]

Cut one's coat See *Coat.*

Cut one's losses Abandon any further attempts to continue a business or enterprise which has not been profitable, and limit one's losses to those already incurred.

Cut off 1. Sever; cut.
She is going to have all her hair cut off.
2. Separate. Also (of telephone) disconnect.
That remote village will entirely cut her off from her friends.

Cut off one's nose to spite one's face Behave spitefully, damaging oneself.

Cut off with a shilling Bequeath nothing, or practically nothing, to a person. [Or. The custom of leaving an unpopular member of the family only a shilling in one's will — the shilling merely being to make it impossible for the recipient to plead that his or her name had been omitted by accident.]

Cut one's teeth on Gain early experience from.

Cut out 1. [LIT] Cut round, as with a pair of scissors.
2. [MET] Supplant.
3. Designed for, suitable for.
I don't think you're cut out to be a soldier.

Cut *or* **wounded to the quick** Hurt intensely. [Or. Old meaning of 'quick' = 'living'; hence the part of one's nails which is below the skin, which still has feeling, is called the 'quick'.]

Cut and thrust Rapid exchange. [Or. Swordfighting.]
A barrister needs to be quick-witted to survive the cut-and-thrust of the court-room.

Cut short End abruptly.
The preacher cut short his sermon when the church caught fire.

Cut throat Ruthless.

Cut up 1. [LIT] Cut into small pieces.
2. [MET] Distressed, unhappy.
She was terribly cut up when she heard the news.
Short cut See *Short*.

D

Daggers **At daggers drawn** In a state of open and bitter
hostility.
Look daggers Look at fiercely and angrily.
Damn **Damn with faint praise** Praise in so formal and
limited a manner that it is an obvious cloak to adverse
criticism or dislike. [Or. Quotation from Alexander
Pope.]
(I'll be) damned if I know I don't know (emphatic).
Damp **A damp squib** A squib is a small firework which sends
out showers of sparks and finally explodes. If, however,
it is not dry, it will do neither. Hence, anything which
has failed is said to have 'gone off like a damp squib'.
Damp down Suppress.
Put the damper on Prevent by repression.
Dance **Dance attendance** Attend obsequiously to every whim
or requirement of a person.
Lead person a dance Cause person inconvenience
over a time.
Darby **Darby and Joan** An aged and devoted husband and
wife. [Or. From an eighteenth-century ballad called
'The Happy Old Couple'.]
Dare **Dare-devil** A daring and reckless person.
I dare say It is probable.
Dark **A dark horse** A person whose qualities are not well
known.
In the dark In ignorance.
Keep it dark Keep it secret.
Leap *or* **shot in the dark** Rash action, taken without
being able to see the consequences.
Dash **Dash off** 1. Hurry Away.
He dashed off for help.
2. Write in great haste.
He dashed off a note to his wife.
Dash one's hopes Abruptly destroy one's hopes.
Date **Out of date** Obsolete; belonging to an earlier period.

Up to date Recent. Fashionable. Current.

Davy Jones **Davy Jones' locker** The sea-bed. A 'locker' or box is one used by seamen and others for their personal possessions. 'Davy Jones' (a corruption of 'Jonah', who was thrown into the sea) is a legendary character who lives at the bottom of the ocean. 'To go to Davy Jones' locker' is therefore to drown.

Dawn **Dawn on** Become perceptible to.

Day **All day** *or* **night long** Continuously; throughout the day (or night).

All in a day's work Part of one's usual routine.

Any day At any time or in any circumstances.

At the end of the day In the final reckoning.

Broad daylight Full and complete daylight.
The house was robbed in broad daylight.

Call it a day Consider work on any particular job ended for the day or for the present time.

Carry the day See *Carry.*

Dark days Days of trouble and distress.

Daydream A reverie or flight of the imagination. Also used as a verb.

Day in, day out All day and every day.

Days *or* **hours are numbered** The end (e.g. death) is inevitable, and is approaching.
The revolution became less vigorous; it was plain that its days were numbered.

Days of old *or* **of yore** A long time ago; the remote past.
In days of yore people believed in dragons.

Day off Day spent away from work.

Days to come The future.

Every dog has his day Every person has some good fortune at some time or other.

Fallen on evil days In misfortune.

The livelong day All day; the whole of the time. [Old t.]

Make one's day Make one happy.

Name the day Literally, the day which a girl nominates as her wedding-day. (But frequently used in the sense of 'consent to marry', no exact date being specified.)

Not one's day An unsuccessful time.

The good old days The past, when things were better.

The old *or* **olden days** The past.

One of these (fine) days Soon.

A rainy day An emergency, a period of misfortune for which money, etc., has been reserved.

See better days Be happier and more prosperous (almost always used in the past tense).

Dead This word is commonly used in the sense of 'absolute' and 'absolutely', e.g. **dead centre, dead level, dead straight, dead certain, dead sure.**

Dead as a doornail (Emphatically) dead. Also **dead as mutton.**

Dead as the dodo Obsolete.

Dead beat Utterly exhausted.

Dead end Having no way out.

Dead hand Stultifying influence.

Dead heat Event in which two competitors finish at exactly the same time.

Dead letter A law or regulation which exists but is never enforced.

(Waiting for a) dead man's shoes (Waiting for) an advantage that may be obtained when someone dies, or retires, or is promoted, etc.

(In) dead(ly) earnest Extremely seriously.
He spoke quickly, in low tones, and in deadly earnest.

Dead of night The darkest, most silent time of night.

Dead to the world Utterly exhausted; sleeping deeply; or unconscious for any other cause.

Dead wood Useless thing or person.

Over my dead body Exaggerated expression meaning 'over-ruling my strongest wishes'.
If that dog comes into the house again, it will be over my dead body.

Wouldn't be seen dead in Would under no circumstances wear.

Deaf **Deaf as a post** Unable to hear.

Fall on deaf ears Be ignored.

Turn a deaf ear Ignore.

Deal **A raw deal** Unfair or unduly harsh treatment.

A square deal An honest bargain.

It's a deal I agree.

Death **At death's door** On the verge of dying; desperately, almost hopelessly, ill.

Be the death of Cause death to.

Do to death Overdo.

In at the death Arriving in time to see the climax. [Or. Hunting].

Jaws of death Extreme danger; risk of death.
The firemen rescued the child from the jaws of death.
Like grim death With all one's strength.
Pale as death As pale as though already dead.
Sick *or* **tickled to death** Extremely disgruntled or
amused.
(The phrase **to death** is added to many other verbs to
intensify them).
A death-warrant [LIT] A legal warrant authorizing
execution. [MET] State of being in serious difficulties, on
the verge of extinction.
*The defeat at Culloden was the death-warrant of the hopes of
the Jacobites.*
To the death Till one combatant is killed.

Deep **Go off the deep end** Become very angry. [Or. The
deep end of a swimming pool—the most dangerous end,
suitable for rash behaviour.]
In deep water(s) Into complex matters.
Still waters run deep What appears quiet (e.g. a
person) may have hidden emotions, etc.

Default **By default** As a result of failure to act or appear.

Degree **To a degree** To a certain extent.

Deliver **Deliver the goods** Keep one's promise to do
something.

Delusion **Delusions of grandeur** Belief that one is important,
or capable of becoming more powerful.

Demean **Demean oneself** Lower one's dignity.
I would not demean myself by apologizing.

Demon **A demon for** Very committed to.

Depend **Depend upon** Rely upon; have faith in.
You may depend upon our goods; they are of the best quality.
Depend upon it Be certain; have no doubt.
That depends That can only happen in certain
conditions.

Depth **Out of** *or* **beyond one's depth** Literally, one's
'depth' is the depth of water beyond which one's feet no
longer touch the bottom, so that one must either swim
or drown. Used as an idiom, 'out of one's depth'
indicates a subject beyond one's knowledge or
understanding.

Deserve **Richly deserve** 'Richly' here means thoroughly,
completely.

Design **By design** Deliberately.
Have designs on Have (usually harmful or
unpopular) plans for.

Despair **Yield** *or* **give away to despair** Give up hope.

Devil **Between the Devil and the deep (blue) sea** Between two equally dangerous or unpleasant alternatives.

Devil-may-care A reckless person.

Devil's advocate One who makes unpopular suggestions without seriously believing them, i.e. simply to ensure that all sides of a case have been considered.

Devil take the hindmost The outcome does not matter.

Give the Devil his due Admit good, even in someone of whom one disapproves.

Hold a candle to the Devil (From fear or caution) assist someone of whom one disapproves. [Or. From the story of the old woman who lit one candle to St Michael and another to the Devil he was trampling underfoot, so that whether she went to Heaven or Hell she would have a friend.]

Needs must when the Devil drives If something must be done, then it must be done.

Play the very devil with Create disorder in.
Too much garlic plays the very devil with my digestion.

Talk of the Devil Applied (usually jocularly) to someone who has been a topic of conversation and who then unexpectedly arrives.

Diamond **Rough diamond** Worthy person with roughness of manner, speech, dress, etc.

Die **Be dying for** Long for.

Be dying of Be vexed by.

Die away Become more and more faint, until the sound cannot be heard at all.

Die down Subside; become calm after violence.

Die hard Be slow to diminish.

Die in harness Die while still at one's work.

Die laughing Laugh so much that one is completely exhausted.

Never say die Do not surrender.

The die is cast An irrevocable decision has been taken.

Difference **Make all the difference** Be very significant.

Split the difference Halve the amount in dispute.
You ask twelve pounds; I offer eight. Will you split the difference and accept ten?

Dig **Dig one's heels** *or* **toes, feet in** Be stubborn.

Dignity **Stand on one's dignity** Require that one is treated with respect.

Dilemma **On the horns of a dilemma** In a position where a choice has to be made between alternatives that are unpleasant in either case; in a difficult position. (Or. 'Lemma', from the Greek, means taken for granted, and dilemma is a double acceptance—*two* things accepted, a bull with horns that will toss you whichever you grasp.]

Dim **Take a dim view of** Feel dissatisfaction for.

Dint **By dint of** By means of.

Dip **Dip into (one's pocket** *etc.*) Spend from.

Discount **At a discount** Not required, or not fully appreciated. (Also [LIT] At a reduced price.)
Books about the war are at a discount just now.

Discretion See **Valour.**

Discussion **Open a discussion** Begin a discussion.

Distance **Keep one's distance** Refrain from becoming familiar or intimate.

Ditch **Dull as ditch-water** Extremely dull.

Divine **Divine right** A right supposedly received direct from God, applied chiefly to the right of sovereigns to occupy their thrones regardless of their suitability, or of their subjects' wishes, but also applied to other situations.
He behaves as if has a divine right to be unpleasant.

Do 1. Be sufficient or suitable.
A small loaf will do for the family's breakfast.
2 Exert oneself.
I'll do all I can.
3. Visit a theatre, etc., as part of a plan.
We did two concerts and the Royal Academy last week.
Do *or* **make away with** Dispose of, usually by destroying. Abolish.
Do or die Not be deterred.
Do to death Kill; murder. Also [MET] Repeat so frequently that all interest is 'killed'.
The whole subject has been done to death in the newspapers.
Do up Repair.
Do with need.
Doing Happening.
Done Completely cooked.
The pudding is done.

Have done with Cease to have any connection with.
Have to do with Have dealings, relationship with.
I refuse to have anything to do with that matter.
It isn't done It is socially forbidden; taboo.
Nothing doing No chance of success.

Dog **A dog's chance** No chance at all.
A dog's life A very unpleasant existence.
Dog-days (Traditionally July 3rd to August 4th.) The hottest weeks of the summer. So called because Sirius, or the dog-star, rising with the sun, combines to add his heat to it.
Dog doesn't eat dog See **honour among thieves.**
Dog-eared Applied to pages which, by constant handling, have become bent or curled at the corners.
Dog in the manger A person so selfish that he will not allow people to enjoy something he himself cannot enjoy. Also adjective: *A dog-in-the-manger attitude.* [Or. Æsop's fable of the malicious dog who barked and snarled in the manger containing the cow's hay, and refused to let them eat it, though he did not want it himself.]
Dog-tired Very tired.
Every dog has his day No one is always unlucky.
Give a dog a bad name When one has acquired a bad reputation, it is difficult to lose.
Hair of the dog that bit you A drink taken to cure the effects of too much drinking.
Help a lame dog over a stile Help someone who is in need of assistance, usually financial.
Let sleeping dogs lie Avoid any action leading to unnecessary friction or trouble; allow matters to remain as they are. [Or. Proverbial.]
Like a dog with two tails Very happy.
Not a dog's chance No chance at all.
Rain cats and dogs Rain very heavily.
Throw to the dogs Throw away, sacrifice, carelessly.
Under-dog One who is in a helpless or inferior position, who has no power to assert his wishes or authority.

Doldrums **In the doldrums** Depressed and miserable. [Or. Part of the ocean, near the equator, known as the doldrums, in which the wind is so slight that sailing vessels are frequently unable to proceed.]

Donkey **Talk the hind-legs off a donkey** Talk incessantly.

Door **Close the door to** Exclude.
Foot in the door Chance of success.
Leave the door open to Leave available the possibility of.
Show a person the door [LIT] Escort him to the door. [MET] Order him to leave.

Dot **Dot the i's and cross the t's** Put the final details to a piece of work.
On the dot Exactly. Precisely. Promptly.
The year dot Very long ago.

Double **Double-crossing** Tricking or betraying people who believed they were dealing with trustworthy friends.
Double-dealing Trickery and deceit.
Double-edged Possessing a double significance. Sarcastic. Ironical. [Or. A sword sharpened at both edges.]
Double-quick Extremely quickly. At the double.
I dashed to the door, double-quick, but was too late to catch him.
Double-talk Ambiguous statement, deliberately intended to be evasive.
Double time Twice the normal amount of wages.
We earn time and a half on Saturday afternoons, and double time on Sundays.

Doubt **Beyond a doubt; without doubt** With absolute certainty.
In doubt Uncertain; hesitant.
When in doubt, do what your conscience advises.
Shadow of doubt Very slight uncertainty. (Frequently in the negative to indicate complete certainty.)
The judge said he had no shadow of doubt of the prisoner's guilt.

Down **Be down on** Disapprove of.
Do down Vilify.
Down-hearted Dejected.
Down on one's luck Temporarily unfortunate.
Down in the mouth Depressed-looking; miserable. Similar to **in the doldrums** and **in the dumps**.
Down and out In a state of complete destitution. [Or. Boxing. A boxer is said to be down and out when he has been knocked down and is unable to rise before he is 'counted out'.]
Down-to-earth Straightforward.
Have a down on Disapprove of.

Dozen **Baker's dozen** Thirteen. [Or. A baker may be fined if his loaves are under the official weight. To ensure that this should not happen, he used to include an extra loaf in each dozen.]

Dozens of Lots of

Talk nineteen to the dozen Talk incessantly.

Drag **Drag one's feet** Display reluctance.

Drag in Introduce, usually unnecessarily.

Drag on Continue in tedious way.

Drag out Lengthen.

Drag up *or* **in** Talk about some subject which it is not tactful or necessary to discuss.

Draw **Draw a blank** Have no success.

The police searched all day, but drew a complete blank.

Draw aside 1. [LIT] Draw, as one draws a curtain.

2. [MET] Separate a person from others.

After the meeting, he drew me aside to discuss the situation.

Draw away Withdraw from; shrink from. Leave.

Draw back Withdraw from an undertaking.

Draw to an end Reach the end; finish.

Draw (person's) fire Weaken person's attack by deflecting it.

Draw in 1. Shrink; become shorter. (Applied especially to the period between summer and winter, when the hours of daylight decrease.)

After September the days seem to draw in very quickly.

2. Move to the side of the road, or stop entirely.

See **draw up** (3).

Draw near Approach; come near.

Draw off 1. [LIT] Cause to flow away.

We must draw off the water from the tank.

2. [MET] Cause to depart, to lead away. [Old f.]

Draw out 1. Remove money from a bank or company.

I drew out a hundred pounds last week.

2. Encourage to talk.

The boy was very shy, but we succeeded in drawing him out about his hobbies.

Draw rein Pull at a horse's rein to compel it to stop.

Draw up 1. Arrange in correct order (applicable both to people and to legal documents).

He drew up an agreement.

The troops will be drawn up on the parade ground.

2. Raise; pull up.

The people used to draw up water from the well.

3. Stop; halt.

The taxi drew up at the station entrance.

Drawn game *or* **draw** Term applied to any match or competition which ends in both sides being absolutely equal. Similar to **dead heat.**

Go back to the drawing-board Begin again (usually to make plans).

Dream **Like a dream** Exactly as one would wish.

Drink **Drink like a fish** Drink (alcohol) heavily.

Drive **Drive away, off** 1. Depart, in a vehicle.
I must drive away in five minutes.
2. Compel someone or something to leave quickly.
These flies are a nuisance; please drive them away.
Drive a bargain Arrive at an agreement, usually after forceful negotiation.
Drive home 1. [LIT] Hammer a nail, etc., as far as it can go.
2. [MET] Emphasize.
The message was driven home by frequent repetition in the course of his speech.
Driving *or* **getting at** implying; hinting.
In the driver's seat In charge.

Drop **At the drop of a hat** Very readily.
Drop 1. Cease to be friends with (a person).
2. Abandon, cease to discuss (a subject).
I don't wish to discuss the matter further, so let's drop it.
Drop behind Be overtaken.
Drop in Call casually and informally.
Drop in for tea whenever you're passing.
Drop a hint See under *Hint.*
Drop a line Send a short letter.
Drop in the ocean *or* **bucket** A small and inadequate matter compared with the whole subject.
Drop off Fall asleep.
Drop on 1. Select for questioning, etc.
2. Blame.
Drop out Absent oneself; cease to compete.
A drop too much An intoxicating amount of drink.
Fit to drop Very tired.

Duck **Like water off a duck's back** Having no effect.
Make a duck *or* **duck's egg** *(cricket only)* Be dismissed without scoring.
Make ducks and drakes 1. Send small flat stones skimming horizontally over the surface of the sea, a pond, etc.
2. Scatter one's fortune in extravagant living.
Take to something like a duck to water Become used to something very readily.

Due **Give person** *or* **the Devil his due** Be fair to person, how little he or she may deserve it.

Dull **Dull the edge of** Make less enjoyable, interesting, significant, etc.

Dumb **Our dumb friends** Animals.

Dumps **In the dumps** Thoroughly depressed. Similar to **in the doldrums; down in the mouth.**

Duration **For the duration** For a very long time.

Duress **Under duress** Compelled by moral or physical force. *He confessed, under duress, to several crimes.*

Dust **Throw dust in the eyes** Hoodwink; mislead and confuse.

Shake the dust from one's feet Leave.

Dutch **Double dutch** Gibberish.

Dutch courage Courage induced by drinking.

Talk to one like a Dutch uncle Advise in a firm but friendly manner.

Duty **In duty bound** Compelled by a sense of duty.

Dye **Of the deepest dye** Of the most extreme type, usually unpleasant. [Old f.]

Dyed in the wool Permanently ingrained.

E

Ear **All ears** Listening attentively.
When they came in, they were all ears.
Box a person's ears Administer a sharp slap on the side of the head.
If you don't go to bed at once I'll box your ears.
(Play) by ear 1. Without any technical knowledge, merely by a natural appreciation of the sounds.
She plays the piano entirely by ear.
2. Without preparation.
I haven't decided what to say when he comes; I'll play it by ear.
Come to *or* **reach one's ears** Be heard or known.
An ear for A natural appreciation for.
Earshot Hearing distance.
Ear-splitting Deafening; distressingly loud and shrill.
Ears burning A sign that one is being talked about. (Used jocularly.)
A flea in the ear Truths, usually unpleasant.
A salesman came to the door, but I sent him away with a flea in his ear.
Give ear Listen to, and attend carefully. [Old f.]

Give one's ears Make almost any sacrifice to obtain.
I'd give my ears to visit Venice this spring.
Have one's ear to the ground Be aware of what is likely to happen.
Have the ear of Be in a position to advise someone.
If you want to get anything done about it, you'll have to find someone who has the ear of the manager.
Head over ears Completely.
In at one ear and out at the other Without being appreciated or remembered.
Everything we try to teach the boy goes in at one ear and out at the other.
Prick up one's ears Listen with sudden attention to something heard unexpectedly. (Animals 'prick up' or raise their ears at an unfamiliar sound.)
Set by the ears Make quarrel.
Throw out on one's ear Eject forcibly.
Turn a deaf ear Refuse to listen.
Up to the ears Deeply immersed.
Wet behind the ears Inexperienced.
Word in your ear Word in confidence or in private.

Early **Early bird** Person who arrives or gets out of bed early.
Early days Too early.
Keep early hours Go to bed early.

Earth **Come down to earth** Return to reality.

Earnest **In earnest; in dead** *or* **good earnest** Serious; the reverse of joking.
Go to earth Disappear from the places in which one is usually seen. [Or. Hunting. A fox 'goes to earth' when it vanishes into its 'earth' or burrow.]
On earth Emphatic addition to many expressions.
Run to earth Find after search.

Ease **Put** *or* **set at ease** Make unembarrassed and socially happy by friendliness.
He has a knack of putting visitors at their ease.
Ill at ease Uncomfortable. Anxious.

Easy **Easy on the eye** (Person) enjoyable to look at.
I'm easy I don't mind.
In easy circumstances Financially comfortable; rich enough to be able to live without worrying.
In Easy Street Enjoying wealth or comfort.
Easy money 1. One from whom money is easily obtained.
2. Money which is easily earned.

Take it easy Relax.

Eat **Eat away** Penetrate and use up.
The sea had eaten away much of the shore.
Eat one's cake See under **Cake.**
Eat humble pie Behave meekly, apologetically. [Or.
'Umbles', the inferior parts of a deer, which was served
as a pie to the servants of a medieval household, while
the host and guests received the better portions.]
Eat into Similar to **eat away.**
Eat one's hat Be very surprised.
Eat one's head off Eat very large quantities.
Eat one's heart out Pine. Grieve continuously.
Eat out of house and home Eat so much that one
would have to sell one's house to pay for food. (Often
used jokingly of hungry children.)
Eat out of one's hand Do as one asks.
Eat one's words Completely and ignominiously
withdraw a statement.

Edge **Edge away** Move gradually away (as a boat moves
very slowly from the edge of the shore).
Have an edge on one's appetite Be hungry.
On edge In a state of nervous tension.
We were all on edge to know the news.
Rough edge of one's tongue A reprimand.
Set one's teeth on edge Cause feelings of revulsion
and general discomfort, usually at unpleasant sound, but
also because of embarassing speech or action.
Take the edge off Reduce the effect of.

Educate **Educated guess** Guess based on knowledge,
experience, information etc.

Effect **Bring (carry) into Effect** Put into operation.
For effect In order to create a particular impression.
Give effect to Make operative.
In effect Stated briefly and in other words.
Take effect Operate; function.
To that effect With that meaning, result, etc.
With effect from Beginning at.

Egg **As sure as eggs is eggs** Stated with absolute
certainty.
As sure as eggs is eggs it will rain tomorrow.
A duck's egg *(cricket)* See under **Duck.**
Don't teach your grandmother to suck eggs
Don't offer advice to people who are more experienced
than you are.
Put all one's eggs in one basket Invest all one's

resources, financial or otherwise, in a single enterprise.

Elbow   **Elbow one's way** Push forward by thrusting with one's elbows. Frequently used metaphorically:
They're trying to elbow their way into the tennis club committee.
Elbow-room Space in which to move.
We're moving to an office in which we shall have more elbow-room.
Out at elbows (Of garment) Worn out.
Up to the elbows Very busy.

Element   **In one's element** In a congenial atmosphere and surroundings.
Out of one's element In an uncongenial atmosphere or surroundings. Similar to **a fish out of water.**

Elephant   **White elephant** Troublesome, unwanted and unused thing.

Eleven   **The eleventh hour** The latest possible time before it is too late.

Embargo   **Lay** *or* **place an embargo on** An embargo is a legal prohibition. The phrase is also loosely applied to any definite impediment.

Embark   **Embark on** Begin.

Empty   **Empty-handed** Bringing or taking nothing.
Emtpy-headed Stupid.
On an empty stomach Not having eaten for some time.

End   **At a loose end** Unoccupied.
Give me a ring if you're at a loose end tonight.
At an end Finished.
At one's wits' end Mentally desperate, and unable to find a solution. Also used jocularly (as an exaggeration) to mean simply 'in a state of confusion', or 'unable to think clearly'.
End of the road Point beyond which no progress is possible.
End on With the end of one thing next to the end of another.
End up Finish by.
To the bitter end To the extreme end, whatever may happen.
I intend to see this matter through to the bitter end.
Ends of the earth [LIT] The most distant parts of the world. [MET] A considerable distance.
The end of one's tether The limit of one's endurance or patience. [Or. Tether = the rope or chain by which a horse or other animal is secured.]
We had been walking all day, and were at the end of our tether.

E

The end of the road Conclusion of a matter.
In the end Finally.
Make (both) ends meet Make one's income enough for one's expenses. (More frequently used in the negative.)
I cannot make ends meet on my salary.
On end Continuously.
The rain has been falling for days on end.
Put an end to Finish; terminate. (Applied to something which has already existed for some time.)
The King decided to put an end to the barons' quarrels.
Tie up the loose ends Arrange the final details.
To no end *or* **purpose** Without effect or result.
The priest tried to put the fire out, but to no end.

Enemy **Be one's own worst enemy** Bring about one's own misfortunes.

English **Murder the Queen's English** 'Queen's English', or 'standard English', is the English language as spoken by educated people. To 'murder' the Queen's English is to use it incorrectly or to speak it with a very bad accent.

Enough **Enough and to spare** Ample; more than is needed.
Ten metres of carpet will be enough and to spare.
Enough to wake the dead Very loud, noisy.
The racket at the party was enough to wake the dead.
Oddly enough Unexpectedly; surprisingly. ('Enough' here is equivalent to 'in the circumstances', 'considering the conditions', etc.) Similarly, **curiously, strangely, remarkably enough,** etc.
We met by chance in Egypt, and a year later, oddly enough, in New York.
Sure enough As was to be expected.

Enquiry **In the course of enquiry** While enquiries were being made; during an investigation.
In the course of an enquiry, it was discovered that he had never been in the Army.
Searching enquiry Close, thorough and detailed enquiry.
The Government promise a searching enquiry into the whole matter.

Enter **Enter into** 1. Comprehend; understand.
We can enter into your feelings of relief.
2. Occupy oneself with.
We cannot enter into details at present.
The two old men entered into (or upon) a long discussion.

Enter into an agreement Agree; undertake.
The firm will enter into an agreement to supply five thousand pairs of shoes.
Enter a protest Complain. Register a protest.
Enter up Make an entry.
Please enter up these figures in the account book.
Enter upon Begin.
We are entering upon a new epoch in the history of civilization.

Entry **Make an entry** 1. Record in a book.
2. Enter formally or ceremoniously.

Err **Err on the right side** Risk possible error by attempting to avoid more serious one.

Error **Clerical error** Slip of the pen.

Escutcheon **Blot on one's escutcheon** Damage to one's reputation.

Esteem **Hold in (high) esteem, honour,** *etc*. Regard as deserving.

Estimate **Form an estimate** Judge in a general way.
Rough estimate A rough calculation; an approximation.

Eternity **For an eternity** For a very long time.

Even **Even so** In spite of, even after the circumstances have been considered.
Be *or* **get even with** Be revenged upon; pay back an injury.
He beat me, but I'll be even with him next time we play.
On an even keel 1. [LIT] Well balanced.
2. [MET] Smooth.
Their relationship has been stormy, but it now seems to be on an even keel.
There is an even chance It is as likely as not.

Event **At all events** Nevertheless; yet.
Similar to **at any rate.**
Coming events Events which are expected or planned.
Course of events A succession of events; a number of events that followed.
The course of events made it necessary for him to go to America.
In any event Whatever may happen.
I hope to go tomorrow; in any event I shall go before Saturday.
Similar to **in any case; in any circumstances; happen what may.**
In the event As things turned out.
In the event of If a specified event should take place.
In the event of fire, ring the alarm-bell.
Prophesy after the event State that something was certain to have happened after it has already happened.

Be wise after the event State what should have been done to avert a disaster when it has already occurred.

Ever Widely used as a form of emphasis.

Did you ever hear such nonsense. Come as quick as ever you can. Whatever will he do next?

Ever such a A very.

For ever and a day [LIT] Always; eternally. [MET] For a long time.

We won't reach agreement if we sit here for ever and a day.

For ever and ever Similar to **for ever and a day.**

Every **Every now and again. Every now and then.**

Every so often. From time to time.

Every other Every alternate. 1. [LIT]

2. [MET] (Applied only to the singular.)

1. Every other man carried a lighted torch.

2. She asks questions every other minute.

Everyday Commonplace.

Example **For example** To quote as an example.

Some English poems are extremely long—'The Faerie Queene', for example.

Make an example of Inflict punishment on an individual who has done wrong as a warning to others who might behave in the same way.

Exception **Take exception to** Object. Feel offended by.

I take exception to your statement that I am bad tempered.

The exception that proves the rule An action which draws one's attention to the fact that most people (as a rule) behave very differently, and that the action in question is an exception to the rule.

Excess **In excess of** More than.

Exchange **Exchange is no robbery** Unfair exchange is better than robbery. (Jocular excuse for unfair exchange.)

Excuse **Excuse oneself** Apologise for leaving (or not attending).

Execution **Put into execution** Do something already planned or arranged. Similar to **carry out.**

They wanted to go abroad, but realized that it would be some months before they could put their plan into execution.

Exercise **Exercise power** Exert power or influence.

The Queen cannot exercise political power, though she frequently offers advice.

Object of the exercise Purpose of what is happening or planned.

Exhibition **Make an exhibition of oneself** Act so as to appear foolish.

Expect **Expect me when you see me** I cannot say when I shall be back.

Expense **At one's expense** 1. [LIT] Causing financial expense to one.
2. [MET] Causing inconvenience, embarrassment, discredit, etc., to one.
At the expense of In a way that causes damage to.
Go to the expense of Spend money on.
Put one to expense Make one spend money.

Explain **Explain away** Remove uncertainty by persuasive and reasonable explanations.
I didn't believe her at first, but she managed to explain away my doubts.

Extent **To a certain** *or* **considerable** *or* **large extent** To a limited (considerable, large) degree; partially.

Extreme **Go to extremes** Take an extreme course of action.
Go to the other extreme Do the exact opposite.

Eye **Apple of one's eye** Loved and prized intensely.
Her son was the apple of her eye.
A black eye The result of being struck so violently in the fact that the flesh surrounding the eye is bruised and blackened.
Cast an eye over Glance at.
Catch someone's eye Meet the gaze of a person for a brief time.
The schoolboy caught the teacher's eye, and stopped talking.
An eye for Ability to appreciate (visual).
He has always had an eye for a bargain.
See also **an ear for; a taste for.**
An eye for an eye Revenge. Retaliation.
To eye To glance at, usually with suspicion.
Have a good eye for Be clever at assessing or choosing.
Have an eye to the main chance Be alert for opportunities of personal profit.
Have one's eyes about one Be observant and alert.
Have *or* **keep one's eyes skinned** As above.
In the eyes of Regarded by.
In the eyes of our grandparents, Picasso's paintings would have seemed absurd.
Keep an eye on Watch; devote some attention to.

Eye of the law See under *Law.*
Keep one's eyes skinned Watch intently.
Make eyes at Ogle. Look amorously, provocatively or seductively.
In one's mind's eye Mentally; as a mental vision.
In my mind's eye I can still see my old home.
Run an *or* **the eye over** Glance over; survey quickly.
Do you mind running your eye over these accounts.
See eye to eye Regard in the same way; agree.
I hope we shall see eye to eye in this matter.
See with half an eye Realize easily, and at once.
Up to the eyes *or* **eyebrows, in** Immersed; completely occupied with.
With an eye to With a definite object in one's mind.
I bought the barn with an eye to coverting it into a cottage.
With one's eyes open Fully aware of the circumstances.
With one's eyes shut 1. Carelessly.
He must have gone into the business with his eyes shut.
2. Very easily.
I could do it with my eyes shut.
Eye-witness One who actually sees an incident, etc.
According to an eye-witness, it was the car-driver's fault.

F

Face **Face; face up to** Accept and meet a situation without flinching.
Face about Turn in the opposite direction.
Face down Overcome (person) by boldness.
Face to face Directly opposite; confronting one another.
The brothers came face to face in a crowd.
Face the music Accept the unfortunate consequences.
We were in the wrong, so we'll have to face the music.
Face it out Meet a situation. Show effrontery.
He knew he was in the wrong, but was determined to face it out.
Face value Nominal or superficial value.
The face value of the stamp was a penny, but it was worth fifty pounds.

Fly in the face of Commit an act which is obviously rash, foolish or provocative.

Have the face *or* **the nerve to** Have the effrontery or impertinence to.
I'm surprised that you have the face to ask again.

Keep a straight face Remain serious.
Similar to **keep one's countenance.**

Look one in the face (Dare to) meet one without shame.

Lose face Be humiliated. Lose some of one's credit or reputation, etc.

Make faces Twist and contort one's features, usually in contempt or dislike, or to make someone laugh.

On the face of it As it appears; judging from what has been stated.
On the face of it, you have been very badly treated.

Pull a (long) face Look miserable and depressed.
We've lost a good deal of money, but it's no use pulling a face about it.

Put a good *or* **brave** *or* **bold face upon it** Behave cheerfully, and as though there was nothing wrong.

Put a new face on Alter.
Moon-landings have put a new face on our scientific knowledge.

Save face Avoid shame.

Set one's face against Oppose.

Show one's face Appear.

To one's face Openly, when one is present.

Fact **Fact of life** Reality that cannot be ignored.

Facts and figures All the relevant details.

In fact Stated exactly or briefly.
He will not come; in fact, I think he never intended to.

Fag **Fag-end** The latter, the final remaining part. [LIT] The rough end of a piece of cloth.
We spent the fag-end of our holiday on the river.

Fail **Words fail me** I cannot express what I feel.

Failing **Failing that** If that does not happen.

Fair **All's fair in love and war** In any competition, the competitors must fend for themselves (*or* have equal conditions).

Fair copy A neat copy, unspoilt by corrections.

Fair deal A transaction which is fair and just to both sides.

Fair enough I agree.

Fair game A suitable object of amusement and ridicule.

(By) fair means or foul (In) any way possible.

Fair play Correct and courteous treatment between opponents; justice according to accepted rule.

Fair's fair We must act fairly.

Fair and square Just; openly honest.

The terms of the contract are absolutely fair and square.

Fair-to-middling Moderately well.

In a fair way to Likely to; behaving so that a certain event is probable.

Fair-weather friend One who is a friend only during prosperity, and who ceases to be one when trouble comes.

Fair words butter no parsnips Polite and friendly speeches are of no practical value unless accompanied by kind actions. [Or. Proverb.]

Faith **Bad faith** Treachery; dishonesty.

It was an act of bad faith to betray his friend.

Breach of faith A dishonourable action; a broken promise, given or implied.

It was a breach of faith to reveal the information I gave you.

In (all) good faith Honestly believing. With honest intention.

Even though he was wrong, he acted in good faith.

Pin one's faith on Place one's entire faith in; believe in.

Put one's faith in Trust. Believe.

Shake one's faith Make one doubtful of one's previous beliefs.

What you tell me shakes my faith in human nature.

Shatter one's faith Destroy one's belief completely.

Fall **Fall about** Be helpless (with laughter).

Fall apart, asunder Break up in separate pieces.

Fall into arrears Fail to pay a sum due at regular intervals.

Fall astern Go more slowly, till instead of being level one is behind. [Or. Nautical.]

Fall away 1. Diminish; dwindle.

Trade always falls away during the summer.

2. Separate from; desert.

Fall back 1. Retire; retreat.

The crowd fell back to let the ambulances through.

2. Make use of in an emergency.

One can always fall back upon condensed milk.

Fall *or* **drop behind** 1. Be passed by; be overtaken.
2. Similar to **fall into arrears.**
Fall between two stools Attempt to combine two plans, and succeed with neither.
Fall flat 1. [LIT] Be prostrate.
The man staggered, and fell flat on the floor.
2. [MET] Fail to amuse or interest; end in an anti-climax. ('Flat' here is used as the reverse of 'sparkling', a term applied to effervescent drink which has been spoilt by exposure to the air.)
What was meant to be a funny story fell completely flat.
Fall foul of [LIT] Collide with; crash into. [MET] Quarrel with. Be in a state of dispute with.
He has a knack of falling foul of everyone he meets.
Fall into a habit Form or acquire a habit.
Fall in place [LIT and MET] Take up the proper and logical place or position.
When he told me his story, all the facts I had known before fell into place.
Fall in with Encounter. Meet and accompany. Agree with. Coincide with.
It would be very convenient if you could fall in with my plans.
Fall on evil days Be in misfortune.
Fall on one's feet Be successful as the result of good fortune or luck.
Fall off Deteriorate.
Fall out Disagree; quarrel.
If we talk politics we are bound to fall out.
Fall over Cease to be upright.
Fall short Be less than, or below.
My income falls short of my expenditure by five hundred pounds.
Fall through Collapse; fail to happen.
Fall to one's lot Happen to one.
It will probably fall to my lot to die a bachelor.
Fall to pieces Break up completely.
Fall under Be classed among.
Fall upon Attack.
The wolf fell upon the lamb and devoured it.
Fall upon a person's neck Embrace [Or. Biblical, now used only facetiously].
Fall within Be included in.

False **False step** Mistake.
Strike a false note Cause awkwardness.
Fan **Fan the flame** Increase excitement, tension, pressure etc.
Fancy **Catch the fancy of** Please. Attract.

It caught my fancy and I bought it without thinking.
Fancy free Not in love. Hence, carefree. [Or. Shakespeare, *A Midsummer Night's Dream*.]
Fancy price High cost.
Flight of fancy *or* **imagination** Something visualized which is entirely imaginary; unconnected with actual events.
Take a fancy to Be attracted by.
On second thoughts, I've rather taken a fancy to the idea.
Take one's fancy Please.
Tickle one's fancy Amuse; divert. Attract.
Do you see anything in the shop which tickles your fancy?

Far **As far as in one lies** As much as one is capable.
Far and away; by far To a much greater extent or degree.
I was far and away happier before I changed jobs.
Far and near Everywhere.
Far and wide; far and near Many places, both near and distant.
People came from far and wide to hear him.
A far cry A remote connection only; distant or slightly connected.
Far be it from me An apologetic phrase for interfering or criticizing.
Far-fetched Exaggerated and over-elaborate.
Far-flung Widely extended.
Far from Almost the opposite of.
The answer is far from easy.
Far gone In a dangerously critical condition.
I'm afraid he is so far gone that there is no hope.
In so far To the extent or degree.
I am able to help you, in so far that I can arrange an appointment.
Go far Succeed.
Go too far Go beyond what is acceptable.
So far as one can As much as one can.
So far so good Progress has been satisfactory.

Farm **Farm out** Delegate. Sub-contract.

Fashion **After a fashion** In an amateurish and ineffective way.
He cooked the dinner after a fashion.

Fast **Fast dye** 'Fast' here is equivalent to 'fixed'; immovable. Dye which will not wash out.
Play fast and loose Act irresponsibly, and without regard to one's duties.

Fasten **Fasten on** 1. [LIT] Attach.
I can't fasten this lid on.
2. [MET] Pick out for a particular purpose, or as the person responsible.
Someone must have broken the plate, but why fasten on me?

Fat **Fat in the fire** [LIT] The splutter and flames made when fat splashes from a frying-pan into the fire. [MET] General excitement, anger, etc., when a sensational piece of news is made known.
The fat of the land The best and most expensive (food, etc.) obtainable.

Fate **As sure as fate** Very certain.
Fate worse than death Serious consequences.
The irony of fate An ironic coincidence. An event, frequently tragic, which defies or defeats what has been intended.

Fault **At fault** Wrong; inaccurate.
Find fault with Grumble at; complain.

Favour **Curry favour** Try to ingratiate oneself.
Find favour Receive approval.

Fear **For fear of** To avoid the risk of.
Never fear There is no need to worry.
Put the fear of God into Frighten severely.
Without fear or favour Impartially.
In high favour Extremely popular.

Feather **Birds of a feather** People of a particular type. [Or. Proverb: *Birds of a feather flock together.*]
Feather-bed Make matters comfortable for.
Feather-brained Foolish. Forgetful.
A feather in one's cap An honour; something to be proud of. [Or. The custom of American Indians adding a feather to their headdress for every enemy that they killed.]
Feather one's nest Gradually acquire extra money, honestly or otherwise, during one's employment. [Or. The habit of birds lining their nests with feathers.]
Feathered friends Birds in general.
Show the white feather Behave like a coward. [Or. The old English sport of cockfighting. No pure-bred gamecock has a white feather in its plumage.]
You could have knocked me down with a feather I was astonished.

Feel **Feel for** Feel pity for; sympathize with.
Feel like Would like.

Feel up to Be ready for.

Feeler **Put** *or* **throw out feelers** *or* **a feeler** Find out by surreptitious or gentle question or hint.
Why not put out a few feelers to see what the rest of the staff think?

Feeling **Fellow-feeling** The sympathy and understanding felt for a sufferer by one who has been through similar trials.
Good feeling Spirit of cooperation, helpfulness, friendship etc.
Ill feeling Animosity

Fell **At one fell swoop** In one blow. At a stroke.

Fellow **Hail-fellow-well-met** Friendly.

Fellowship **The hand of fellowship** The right hand of a friend, clasped as a sign of goodwill and peace.

Fence **Fence with a question** Give a non-committal answer to avoid the question.
Mend fences Restore harmony.
Sit on the fence Refrain from giving one's support to either side; remain entirely neutral (usually from motives of cowardice or discretion).

Fetch **Fetch up** Come to rest.
Wrong *or* **right side of the fence** In these and similar expressions, 'fence' means 'dispute'.

Fettle **In fine fettle** In good condition (applied to person or animal). In good spirits.

Few **Every few days** Once in every group of a few days.
Few and far between Rare, scarce. [Or. Abbreviated quotation from the poet Campbell, 'Like angel visits, few and far between'.]
A good few A reasonable number.

Fiddle **Fit as a fiddle** In excellent health.
Play second fiddle Take subordinate role.

Field **Open field** Many (or unlimited) opportunities.
There's an open field for new industry in this area.
Take the field Enter a playing-field to begin a competition.

Fifty **Fifty-fifty** Equal shares. Halves.
The proceeds of the event will be split fifty-fifty between two charities.

Fight **Fight shy of** Avoid, keep away from.
Fight to a standstill Fight until both sides are too exhausted to make any further effort.
Put up a fight Offer resistance.

Fighting **Fighting chance** Reasonable chance.
Fighting fit In good health.

Figure **Cut a figure** Become prominent (often for being conspicuously well dressed). Make an impression.
Figure of fun Ridiculous; absurd.
Figures of speech Literary forms such as the metaphor, simile, hyperbole, allegory, etc.

File **In Indian file; in single file** Singly, one behind another. [Or. The American Indians used to mislead their enemies as to their number by each man stepping exactly in the footsteps of the man in front of him.]
The path was so narrow that we had to walk in Indian file.

Fill **Fill the bill** Suffice.
I haven't any gin; would whisky fill the bill?
Fill an office Occupy a position or post.
Fill out Enlarge. Become more plump.
Fill up *or* **in documents** Add details which are required.
If you require a passport, will you please fill up this form.
Drink (take) one's fill Take enough to satisfy, all that one is capable of taking.
We took our fill of the sunshine and fresh air.

Filthy **Filthy lucre** Money. Wealth. [Old f.] [Or. Biblical.]

Final **Final touch** The last detail; that which completes the work.

Find **Find oneself in** Supply oneself with.
All found Everything provided.
We are paying five pounds a week, all found.
Find guilty The legal phrase used when an accused person has been tried, and it has been 'found' that he committed the crime.
Find one's feet Obtain and develop the use of one's abilities.
After a year in the job, I'm beginning to find my feet.
Find in one's heart Be firm enough. Be inclined.
I couldn't find it in my heart to refuse her request.
Must take us as you find us Must accept us as we are.

Fine **Cut fine** Leave little room for error.
In fine Stated exactly or briefly.
Fine distinction A difference perceptible only with difficulty.
Not to put too fine a point on it Generally speaking.
One of these fine days Some day (used in prophesying).
I'll do something about it one of these fine days.

With a fine-tooth comb Very carefully, with minute attention to detail.

I've been through my bank-statement with a fine-tooth comb.

Fingers **Fingers are all thumbs** Fingers are clumsy, awkward. Also **all fingers and thumbs**: clumsy.

Burn one's fingers Suffer as a result of some action.

If you buy that business, I think you'll burn your fingers.

Have a finger in the pie Be concerned with, or mixed up with some affair.

Keep one's fingers crossed Hope for a good result. Hope for good luck.

Lift *or* **stir a finger** Make the smallest effort.

Point the finger at Identify.

Put one's finger on Locate. Identify.

At one's finger-tips Immediately available. (Applied to information, knowledge, etc.)

Slip through one's fingers Escape.

Twist person round one's (little) finger Dominate person.

Work one's fingers to the bone Work very hard (usually, with one's hands).

Fire **(Breathe) fire and brimstone** (Utter) angry threats.

Go through fire and water Face all dangers.

No smoke without fire Every rumour has an origin.

Play with fire Take risks.

Set the Thames on fire Do something noteworthy.

Strike fire Arouse enthusiasm.

Take fire [LIT] Become ignited. [MET] Become excited, indignant or enthusiastic.

Through fire and water Through any kind of suffering or discomfort.

First **At the first blush** *or* **glance** Superficially; before examining closely.

First class Top quality. Best available.

First things first A proper order of priorities.

From first to last From beginning to end; all the time.

In the first place Firstly.

Fish **A fish out of water** One out of one's natural element or surroundings.

During my first weeks in the new job, I felt like a fish out of water.

Fish in troubled waters Interest oneself in affairs that are likely to lead to trouble and danger.

Neither fish nor fowl See under *Flesh.*

Other fish to fry Other business to occupy the time.
I can't discuss the matter any longer—I've other fish to fry.
Pretty kettle of fish A thoroughly unsatisfactory state of affairs; general upheaval and excitement; a mixture of muddle and trouble. [Or. 'Kettle' is a corruption of 'kittle', which in turn is a corruption of 'kiddle', a basket arranged in river water to catch fish.]

Fist **Iron fist** Severity. Usually **iron fist in velvet glove** Severity (of action) disguised as gentleness.

Fit In a suitable condition to work, in good health. (Also **fighting fit.**)
Fit in with Co-ordinate with.
Your visit tomorrow will fit in with my cousin's arrival.
Fit to wake the dead Very loud.
Fit up *or* **out** Prepare an expedition, etc.
In fits and starts Irregularly, spasmodically; in a series of spurts.
He does his work in fits and starts.
Not fit to hold a candle to Unworthy to be compared with.
See fit Think to be appropriate. Also **think fit.**

Fix **In a fix** In difficulty.

Flag **Keep the flag flying** Continue fighting. Show defiance.
Put the flag out Celebrate.
Show the flag Make people take note.
Show *or* **hoist** *or* **wave the white flag** Surrender.

Flame **Add fuel to** *or* **fan the flames** Add fresh causes for anger.
An old flame A sweetheart in past days. [Old f.]

Flare **Flare up** 1. As a verb: give way to a sudden burst of anger.
2. As a noun: a violent quarrel.

Flash **Flash in the pan** A brief display producing no useful result. [Or, Military. The 'flash-pan' of the old-fashioned gun was the place at which a small quantity of powder was exploded to fire the larger quantity in the barrel. If it failed to do this, it merely 'flashed' in the pan.]
That brilliant poem he wrote when young was a mere flash in the pan; he has produced nothing since.
In a flash, quick as a flash Very quickly indeed.

Flat **Flat denial, contradiction,** *etc.* Flat (adjective) (or flatly, adverb) is here in the sense of 'complete' and 'absolute'.
He flatly denied that he had stolen the coat.

Flat as a flounder *or* **pancake** Completely flat. [Or. A flounder is a flat fish. A pancake is a thin cake made of batter and fried in a pan.] See **fall flat.**

That's flat Let there be no doubt about that.

Flea **Sent off with a flea in one's ear** Dismissed, after receiving a sharp rebuke.

If anyone wakens me up, he'll get a flea in his ear.

Flesh **Neither flesh** *or* **fish, fowl nor good red herring** With no definite qualities; not worth classifying.

He is extremely vague about his profession; he seems to be neither fish, fowl nor good red herring.

Flesh-pots (of Egypt) The good things of life; rich food, etc. [Or. Biblical.]

Make one's flesh creep Horrify; shock; frighten with some ghastly story or sight.

More than flesh and blood can stand Utterly intolerable.

One's own flesh and blood Near relation. Close family.

Flight **In the top flight** Of the best quality

Put to flight Rout.

Take flight Retreat; flee away rapidly.

Fling **Have one's fling** Indulge freely in one's pleasures.

Float **Float a company** Organize a public company and issue shares in it.

Float an idea Make a tentative suggestion.

Flog **Flog a dead horse** Waste one's energy. Work very hard for little or no result. Persevere with a doomed endeavour.

Flood **Flood tide** Highest degree of success, misery, etc.

Floor **From the floor** from a place in the audience, not the platform, at a meeting.

Take the floor Begin to speak or dance.

Flown **The bird has flown** The person wanted has escaped.

Flowing **Flowing with milk and honey** Filled with all good things to eat and drink. [Or. Biblical.] [Old f.]

Flutter (Applied to playing card games, betting, etc.) A brief period of amusement.

Cause a flutter Cause excitement, as when a flock of birds is disturbed. (Similarly **flutter the dovecotes**: cause excitement in a society or community.)

Fly **Fly a kite** Do something tentatively (in words or deeds) to test people's reactions to an idea or plan.

Fly at Attack violently, physically or verbally.

Fly-by-night Unreliable person. Similar to **here today and gone tomorrow**.

Fly in the ointment The flaw, inconvenience or impediment in an arrangement.

Fly on the wall Unseen observer or listener.

Fly *or* **go off at a tangent** Abruptly abandon one subject for another.

Let fly Throw. Discharge a missile. Use strong, violent or abusive language.

I managed to keep calm for a long time, but finally I just had to let fly at them.

Like flies In large numbers.

Make the fur fly Create a violent quarrel or disturbance, as animals make the fur fly when fighting.

Foam **Foam with rage** [LIT] To foam at the mouth, as mad dogs do. [MET] Indicate a state of extreme and ungovernable anger.

Fob **Fob off** Persuade someone to accept a substitute.

I asked for butter, and will not be fobbed off with margarine.

Follow **Follow one's bent** Follow one's inclination; act in accordance with one's abilities and desires.

Follow the dictates of one's heart Obey one's inward desires and feelings.

Follow one's own devices Amuse or divert oneself as one wishes. Similar to **go one's own way**.

Follow suit Behave similarly; do the same thing. [Or. Card-palying.]

The conductor missed a beat, and the orchestra followed suit.

Follow up Continue a process already begun.

The horse kicked furiously and followed this up by trying to bite me.

Follow-up (noun and adjective.) Continuation.

When the survey is complete, we shall keep a follow-up check on the people we questioned.

Fool **Fool away** Waste (as a fool wastes)

Fool on, play the fool Act stupidly.

A fool's errand A useless journey.

Fool's paradise An entirely false conception; a state of happiness unjustified by the actual facts.

Fool-proof So simple and strong that even a fool cannot use it wrongly or break it.

Fools rush in (where angels fear to tread) It is unwise to be over-hasty. [Or. Proverb.]

Make a fool of Cause someone to appear ridiculous or

contemptible. Similar to **take a rise out of.**

Nobody's fool A sensible person

Foot **Drag one's feet** Show reluctance.

Fall on one's feet Enjoy good luck.

Feet foremost *or* **first** An elaborate evasion of 'dead'.

I shan't leave this house until I'm carried out feet foremost.

Foot the bill Pay whatever charge is involved.

If the Government grants higher pensions, the people themselves will have to foot the bill.

Get off on the wrong foot Begin by making a mistake.

Have foot in both camps Belong to two (sometimes opposing) sides.

Have feet of clay Be weak, and liable to overthrow.

Have one's feet on the ground Be reliable and level-headed.

Keep one's feet Remain standing.

Miss one's footing Slip; stumble.

Not put a foot wrong Do or act correctly.

Obtain *or* **gain a footing** Obtain a status or position ('footing' is constantly used in this sense).

On a firm footing On a sound and stable basis.

Since its reorganization, the business is on a much firmer footing.

On a friendly footing On friendly terms; friends with.

I like to be on a friendly footing with my neighbours.

One foot in the grave So old or diseased that life is nearly finished.

On foot Walking or running.

Put one's foot down Take firm and determined action.

When the girl wanted to stay out until past midnight, her father put his foot down.

Put one's best foot forward Proceed as quickly as possible.

We shall have to put our best foot forward if we are to reach London tonight.

Put one's feet up Rest.

Put one's foot in it Make a blunder; a *faux pas.* Similar to **drop a brick.**

Set foot on Step on to.

My father has never set foot on foreign soil.

Set on foot Initiate; begin any process or action.

Set on his *or* **her feet** Help a person to regain a lost position or lost health.

Stand on one's own (two) feet Be independent.

Under one's feet Obstructing one.

Force **By force of circumstances** Compelled by events.

Come into force Operate; function.

The new laws come into force next month.

Force a man's hand Compel him to show his intentions, or to take definite action. [Or. Card-playing.]

Force of habit Custom.

Force one's way Enter or make one's way by using force.

Force the pace Hurry so as to cause others to hurry.

Join forces Become associated with, or partners with.

The two explorers joined forces, and continued their journey together.

Foreign **Foreign soil** A foreign country.

Foreign substance *or* **body** Any improper and injurious substance—dust, dirt, etc.

Forfeit **Forfeit the good opinion of** Lose the good opinion of a person by bad or foolish conduct.

Forlorn **Forlorn hope** Hope that is very unlikely to be fulfilled. A final effort. [Or. Corruption of the Dutch 'Verlorenhoop'—lost troop.]

I'll try again, but I think it's a forlorn hope.

Form **Good form** The correct convention.

Matter of form Routine.

Off form Not in good health or spirits. Not playing well.

On form In good condition.

Top form Performing well.

Fortune **Make a fortune** Become very wealthy.

Small fortune Large sum of money.

Forty **Forty winks** A slight, brief sleep. [Or. 'Forty' formerly implied an indefinite number, meaning 'a few'. Shakespeare and the Bible so use it.]

The roaring forties Applied to latitude 40 degrees south, where strong winds blow throughout the year.

Foul **Foul play** Unfair, unsporting; frequently applied to criminal action.

The sailor was never seen again; the police suspected foul play.

Found **Ill-founded** Without justification.

Well-founded Justified.

Fountain **Fountain-head** Starting-place; source.

Four **Four-square** [LIT] Facing squarely in four directions. [MET] Facing the world firmly and without fear.
On all fours 1. On one's hands and knees.
2. In agreement with each other.

Fraught **Fraught with** Laden with; bearing.
This whole matter is fraught with difficulty.

Fray **Thick of the fray** Where the fighting is fiercest.

Free **Free and easy** Unconventional; not arranged according to any formal plan.
Free hand *(two entirely separate words)* Complete freedom of action.
I have been given a free hand in arranging the concert.
Free-hand *(one word, or with hyphen)* Applied to drawing in which no mechanical help from instruments is employed.
Free-handed *or* **free** Generous.
Free fight *or* **free for all** A general and indiscriminate dispute in which anyone may join.
Someone in the audience threw a cabbage at the speaker, and the meeting ended in a free fight.
Free-lance Self-employed person, or one who works for a number of organizations, instead of being regularly employed by one employer only. Usually applied to a limited number of trades, e.g. musician, journalist, photographer, artist.
Free translation *or* **rendering** A translation which is not literal, but which conveys the general meaning and effect.
Make free with Take liberties with.
Scot free [LIT] Tax free. [MET] Without any punishment or penalty. [Or. Legal. Scot = tax]
Set free Release.

French **Take French leave** Leave without permission.

Fresh **Fresh as a daisy** Brisk.
Fresh as (new) paint Entirely fresh and unspoilt.

Friend **Bosom friend** A specially close and intimate friend.
Friend at court Someone with private influence.
Make friends *(plural only)* Form friendships; become friendly.

Fry **Out of the frying pan (into the fire)** Out of one difficulty into another equally or more serious.

Full **Full well** Very well (adverb only.)
He knew full well.
In the fullness of time Eventually.

Fun **For the fun of it** Without serious purpose.

Fun and games Exciting happenings.
Make fun of Ridicule.
Poke fun at Ridicule.
Fur **Make the fur fly** Create a disturbance.

G

Gallery **Play to the gallery** Appeal to popular taste.
Game **Fair game** A legitimate target.
Play the game Behave fairly.
Two can play at that game Another's behaviour or misbehaviour may be copied in a way he may regret.
The game's up Further effort is useless. Similar to **all up.**
Garden **Everything in the garden's lovely** All is in order.
Gasp **At one's last gasp** Exhausted.
Gate **Gate-crashing** Entering uninvited to a dance, entertainment, etc.
Gate-crasher—one who so enters.
Gauntlet **Running the gauntlet** [LIT] Driven between a row of persons each provided with sticks, ropes, etc., with which to strike the offender. [Or. Gauntlet = corruption of the French *Gauntelope*, itself of Swedish derivation, a passage between two rows of soldiers facing one another.] A former punishment for sailors, also employed by schoolboys. [MET] Subjected to criticism or attack from an organized body of people.
He ran the gauntlet of criticism from every doctor in the country when he published his book.
Throw *or* **fling down the gauntlet** Applied to any act of defiance or challenge. [Or. The Middle Ages, when a knight who wished to fight with another threw down his gauntlet (or hand-armour) as a challenge.]
Take up the gauntlet Accept the challenge.
After the speech of the Leader of the Opposition, the Prime Minister took up the gauntlet on behalf of the Government.
Get **Get at** Contact; reach.
Getting at Implying, hinting, inadequately communicating.
He spoke so vaguely that I couldn't understand what he was getting at.
Get away Escape.
Get away with Succeed in what one is trying to do.

Get away with murder Succeed by dint of effrontery, or luck.

Get away with you Jocular term of dismissal or refusal.

Get going Make a beginning, a start.

It's past seven—we must get going.

Get hold of Grasp [LIT] and [MET].

I'll explain, and you'll soon get hold of the idea.

Get into Put on (clothes).

Get off to Begin with.

The performance got off to a rather shaky start.

Get on 1. [LIT] Mount; climb on to.

The boy was too small to get on his pony without help.

2. [MET] Agree; be friends with.

I hope Jack and his cousin will get on with each other.

Similar to **hit it off.**

3. [MET] Progress satisfactorily.

Jane works so hard at her job that she is certain to get on.

4. Continue.

I'll get on with cleaning the car.

Get on with you! Expression of disbelief.

Get out of Escape from.

Get out of hand Become out of control.

Get over 1. Recover from.

He soon got over the shock.

2. Overcome by persuasion, etc.

He got over her objections to the marriage.

Get rid of Dispose of something not desired or needed.

We're going to get rid of our old car.

Get round Persuade (person) by cajolery.

Get up 1. Arrange. Begin.

2. Rise from one's bed.

Get oneself up Dress smartly or strikingly.

Get well soon I hope you soon recover from your illness.

Get wind of Hear rumours of.

Get the wind up Become apprehensive.

Ghost **Ghost of a chance** The slightest, the least chance.

Give up the ghost Cease to hope.

Gift **Don't look a gift-horse in the mouth** Do not spurn a present.

Gilt **Take the gilt off the gingerbread** Take away the charm or advantage (sometimes the artificial attractiveness). [Or. In the Middle Ages small gilded gingerbread cakes were sold at fairs.]

The fact that I've got to return to the office in the middle of my holiday takes the gilt off the gingerbread.

Gilt-edged investments Investments—mortgages, debentures, etc.—in which there is no risk of losing one's capital.

Gird **Gird up one's loins** Prepare for an ordeal or combat. [Or. Biblical.] [Old f.].

Give **Give a brass farthing** *or* **a damn** Care in the slightest. (Usually used in negative.)

I don't give a damn what the price is.

Give and take Willingness to compromise.

Give a person *or* **thing the go-by** Ignore; treat as non-existent.

I shall give the whole scheme the go-by.

Give as good as one gets Retaliate sufficiently.

Give away 1. Distribute.

2. Reveal a secret or expose a person.

Give oneself away Unintentionally reveal one's intentions or emotions.

Give ear Listen.

Give ground Yield.

Give in Surrender.

Give notice Make an announcement (often formally, or in writing, etc.) of one's intention. ('Notice' often – statement of intention to quit job.)

Half of the cleaning-staff have given their notice.

Give off Emit.

Give out 1. Issue; distribute (information, verbally or in print).

2. Be finished, all used.

You can't have a hot bath—the water has given out.

Give *or* **yield place to** Be replaced or superseded by someone or something else.

In the nineteenth century gas gave place to electric light.

Give rise to Cause; create.

The Ambassador's disappearance is giving rise to concern.

Give the game away Reveal a secret.

Give up 1. Abandon.

I shall give up smoking.

2. Surrender; cease to fight.

Give it up Cease to attempt.

The puzzle is too difficult; I shall give it up.

Give oneself up Surrender to authority.

Give up the ghost Die; expire. [Or. The ghost or spirit of a person is supposed to leave the body at the moment of death.] The idiom is also used (facetiously) in connection with inanimate things.
My old bicycle gave up the ghost today.
Give way 1. Yield.
2. Break; collapse.

Glance **Glance at** Look at swiftly.
Glance over Read swiftly.

Glass **People who live in glass houses** Abbreviation of proverb *People who live in glass houses should not throw stones.* Those who are vulnerable to criticism should not themselves criticise.

Globe **Globe-trotter** One who travels extensively.

Glory **Glory in** Take great pride in.

Gloss **Gloss over** Try to mimimize by ignoring or excusing.
The lawyer tried to gloss over his client's bad record by saying that his parents neglected him.

Glove **Fit like a glove** Fit exactly.
With kid gloves Gently.
The whole matter needs handling with kid gloves.
With the gloves off With great seriousness. Also **the gloves are off** The argument (controversy, battle, etc.) is in earnest.
See *Velvet.*

Glutton **A glutton for punishment, work,** etc.
A person who is eager for punishment, work, etc.

Go **Go after** Follow.
Go ahead 1. [LIT] Go in front, or before.
You go ahead and tell him that we're coming.
2. [MET] Proceed at once.
If you think you can solve the problem, go ahead.
Go a long way towards Has an important effect in.
Go along with Agree with.
Go back on Reverse a previous promise or pledge.
He said he would help us, and then went back on his promise.
Go-between One who acts as a link between two people or groups of people; a negotiator.
Go-by See under *Give.*
Go by the board Be ignored. Be finished with. [Or. Board = side of a ship, so phrase means 'fall overboard'.]
Caution went by the board as the match neared its conclusion.
Go down with Suffer from.
He's gone down with chicken-pox.
Go far Succeed.

Go fifty-fifty Receive fifty per cent each; share equally.
We'll go fifty-fifty with the profits.
Go for nothing Be without value; have no effect.
All the efforts we have made will go for nothing.
Go-getter Ambitious person.
Go halves Same as **go fifty-fifty.**
Go in for Undertake seriously, as a profession or hobby.
I hear he's gone in for gardening.
Going strong Persisting vigorously.
My grandfather is ninety and still going strong.
Go off 1. Succeed.
I thought her speech went off well.
2. Explode.
The terrorists' bomb went off in the High Street.
3. Deteriorate.
The pianist's playing is rapidly going off.
Go on 1. An expression which may mean, according to
circumstances, an injunction to hurry (*Go on—we shall never
get there!*); an expression of disbelief (*You saw a ghost? Go
on!*); a request for further information (*Please go on with
the story*).
2. Use as guidance.
We have no information to go on.
3. Continue.
If we can't find a hotel, we shall have to go on.
Go on the stage Become an actor.
Go one better Improve upon; prove more skilful, etc.
Go out of one's way Incur extra trouble.
This hotel-keeper goes out of his way to make his guests happy.
Go over Revise.
Go over the ground Examine the facts, survey.
*It is a difficult problem, and I should like to go over the ground
again.*
Go round Visit informally.
Go through fire and water Make any sacrifice;
endure any sufferings.
Go through with Continue to the end.
*He has begun to study for a degree, but I don't think he'll go
through with it.*
Go together Match.
Go to sea Become a sailor.
Go to the country Hold a general election.
Go to the wall Be pushed on one side, passed by; be
ignored.
Go to war Declare or wage war.

Go under 1. Succumb. Fail.
If a supermarket opens here, the small grocers will go under.
2. Be known by.
On the stage, she goes under a different name.
Go without Be without; lack.
I'm afraid you'll have to go without milk in your tea.
Go without saying Be obvious; self-evident.
How are things going? What progress is being made?
Word go Beginning.
He was in trouble from the word go.

Goat **Sort out the sheep from the goats** Distinguish worthy people from unworthy ones.

God **God's truth** The absolute truth.
In the lap of the gods Not subject to human control.

Going **Get going** Begin.
Going concern Business, etc. already working.
Going to happen, occur, *etc*. 'Going to' here is used in the sense 'will'.
(Make) heavy going Difficult progress.
[Or. Horse-riding. A wet or muddy race-track.]
This book is rather heavy going.
To be going on with To serve for the time being.
While the going is good While the circumstances are favourable.

Gold **Worth one's weight in gold** Extremely useful, helpful or valuable.

Golden **Golden mean** The ideal 'middle course'; that which pleases most people because most moderate.
Golden rule The recommended way, because it has been well tried.
The golden rule for frying sausages is to do it slowly.

Good **As good as** Equal to. Practically.
This coat is as good as new.
Be so good as to Will you please.
Do good Show kindness or helpfulness.
For good *or* **for good and all** Permanently; always.
Good-for-nothing Wastrel.
Good for nothing Valueless. Useless.
Good wine needs no bush Things of good quality need no advertisement.
Have a good time Enjoy oneself.
In good time 1. Not late.
2. **All in good time** Wait for the proper time.
Make good 1. Repair. See under *Make.*

2. Reclaim the past. See under **Make.**
Not good enough Unsatisfactory.
A good Samaritan One who helps a needy person.
[Or. Biblical. The Parable of the Good Samaritan,
St Luke x. 30–37.]
On good terms On friendly conditions; in a friendly
way.
We parted on good terms.
Put in a good word for Speak in support of.
Take in good part Not be offended by.
A good turn A kindness; a friendly action.
To the good 1. Profit.
2. General advantage.
Up to no good Committing mischief.
A good while A long time.

Goodness See under **Wish.**

Goose **All his geese are swans** He thinks all his plans, etc.
are better than they are.
Cook one's goose Give one his deserts.
Goose-flesh A cold and roughened condition of the
skin, resembling that of a plucked goose, caused by cold
or fear. People are said to 'go all goose-flesh' when they
are terrified.
Kill the goose that lays the golden egg Do away
with that which brings good fortune.
Say 'boo' to a goose Show courage. (*Note*—This
idiom is always used in the negative.)
**What is sauce for the goose is sauce for the
gander** One must accept even-handed dealing.

Got **Have got to** Must.
I have got to finish this sewing before I go out.

Grace **Airs and graces** Ostentatious behaviour.
Fall from grace Lose good repute.
With a good grace Cheerfully; without protesting.
With a bad grace The reverse.

Grade **Make the grade** Succeed in some specified object. [Or.
American. The literal meaning of 'grade' is a railroad
incline which the engine driver is required to 'make' or
climb.]

Grain **Against the grain** Against one's inclination or wishes.
[Or. The grain or fibre of wood.]

Grape **Sour grapes** Pretending to dislike what one wants but
cannot obtain.

Grasp **Grasp the nettle** Deal with difficulty boldly.

Grass **Not let the grass grow under one's feet** Act swiftly.

Grass widow A woman whose husband is away for a prolonged period.

Grate **Grate on the ear** Sound harsh and unpleasant.

Grave **Dig one's own grave** Cause one's own downfall.

Have one foot in the grave Be old, infirm.

Turn in one's grave Expression used of something which the deceased person referred to would have very strongly resented.

That production is enough to make Shakespeare turn in his grave.

Grease **Grease a man's palm** Bribe him.

Greek **All Greek to me** Incomprehensible. Unintelligible. [Or. Shakespeare, *Julius Caesar*.]

Green **Green-eyed monster** Jealousy. [Or. Shakespeare's *Othello*: 'Beware of jealousy, it is a green-eyed monster.']

Green fingers Skill in making plants, flowers, etc. grow.

Green room The general reception room of a theatre; it is said that such rooms formerly had their walls coloured green to relieve the strain on the actors' eyes after the stage lights.

Grey **Grey matter** Brains.

Grief **Come to grief** Meet with misfortune.

Grievance **Air a grievance** See under *Air*.

Grim **Hold on like grim death** Cling firmly.

Grin **Grin and bear it** Endure as well as one can.

Grind **Keep one's nose to the grindstone** Work without stopping.

Grips **Come (get) to grips with** Try to deal with (in a businesslike or vigorous fashion).

Grist **All's grist that comes to the mill** Everything that is received can be used. [Or. 'Grist' is all corn, etc., which is to be crushed in a mill at one time.]

Groove **Run (be) in a groove** *or* **rut** Function in the same limited and narrow way, or by the same methods.

Ground **Break new ground** Explore new subject.

Cut the ground from under one's feet Anticipate and/or negate one's plans, arguments, etc., by having unexpected information, skill, etc.

Gain ground Advance; progress.

Get off the ground Make a successful start.

Ground swell of opinion Increasing support.

Have one's feet on the ground Be realistic, practical, etc.

Stand one's ground Keep to one's position.

Grow **Growing pains** Difficulties associated with early development of business, plan, etc.

Grown up Adult.

Grow on one Gradually impress its charm and personality.

You may not like Bath at first, but you'll find it grows on you.

Grow out of 1. [LIT] Become too big for, as child *grows out of his clothes.*

2. [MET] Become too mature for, as person *grows out of childish ways.*

Grudge **Bear a grudge** Retain resentful feelings because of a previous dispute.

Grundy **Mrs Grundy** A severely conventional character in a play called 'Speed the Plough'. 'What will Mrs Grundy say?' = 'What will Society and our neighbours think of this?' 'To offend Mrs Grundy' is to commit some social crime, though she is usually a figure of fun.

Guard **Catch off one's guard** Take advantage of someone temporarily distracted or forgetful.

On one's guard Alert; prepared.

Guess **Anybody's guess** An uncertain thing.

Gun **Blow great guns** Blow tremendous winds; a gale.

It was blowing great guns when the ship left harbour.

Go great guns Make excellent progress.

Stick to one's guns Firmly maintain one's standpoint.

H

Habit **Creature of habit** Person who acts predictably.

From force of habit Because one's behaviour is normally governed by one's habits.

Get out of the habit of Stop doing regularly.

Hackles **Make one's hackles rise** Make one angry.

Hail **Hail from** Come from.

Hail-fellow-well-met Person on familiar and friendly terms with everybody one meets. (Also adjective.)

Hair **Hair standing on end** Indicative of extreme terror and astonishment. [Or. There is a legend of one prisoner whose long grey hair rose and stood stiffly upright, and then gradually sank down.] Also used more jocularly.

Hair-raising Frightening. Very surprising.

Splitting hairs Arguing or disagreeing over extremely trivial matters. (Also **hair-splitting.**)

(Not) turn a hair Show (no) signs of fear or embarrassment.

Hair's breadth A minute distance. E.g., a hair's-breadth escape is a very narrow escape, an event which only just missed disaster.

Halcyon **Halcyon days** A time of happiness and prosperity. [Or. An ancient belief that the kingfisher, called in Greek 'halcyon', laid and hatched its eggs on the sea just before the coming of winter (mid-December), when the waves were smooth and unruffled.]

Half **At half cock** Imperfectly. Usually **Go off at half cock** Take place in a desultory way.

By half Expression of exaggeration, e.g. **too clever by half; too cheeky by half.**

By halves Incompletely.

Go halves Share equally.

Half-and-half Divided into two equal parts or portions.

Half-hearted Without energy or enthusiasm.

Halfway house Half the distance.

No half measures No compromise.

The half of it The remaining and more important part.

Hallmark [LIT] The official marking (after testing) of all gold and silver goods with the 'hall' or standard mark as a guarantee of purity. [MET] A sign of good quality (in conduct, manners, ability, taste, etc.).

Hammer **Hammer and tongs** With much noise and/or vigour and enthusiasm.
He may have no skill as a golfer, but he certainly goes at it hammer and tongs.

Hammer out Arrive at a decision or solution by examining and discussing every detail of the subject.
We spent all day hammering out our plans for the holiday.

Under the hammer By public auction. [Or. The auctioneer's hammer (technically a 'gavel') with which he raps on his table each time an object is 'knocked down' to a buyer.]

Hand **All hands to the pumps** Assistance from everyone available. [Or. Nautical. When a ship is leaking so badly that she is likely to sink, all 'hands' (members of the crew) are summoned to work the pumps.]

They'll need all hands to the pumps if the business is to be saved.

(At) first hand Directly; straight from the person concerned.

I heard the story of the match first hand from the captain.

At hand; close at hand Near; available.

At the hands of Under the control or direction of.

By hand 1. By messenger.

2. By the use of manual labour.

High-handed Insolent. Overbearing. Supercilious.

Change hands Pass from the ownership of one person to that of another.

Clean hands Innocently; honestly; without fraud.

Do a hand's turn Do the slightest piece of work.

From hand to mouth (Live) in poverty.

Give one's hand to Marry (used of females only). [Old f.]

Hand in glove In partnership; intimately associated.

Hand in hand [LIT] Clasped hands. [MET] In close association.

Hand to hand One person to another.

Hand to mouth From day to day, without any provision for the future. Also **hand-to-mouth** (adjective).

Hand over Surrender; give to someone else. Similar to **turn over.**

Hand over hand *or* **fist** Rapidly. [Or. Nautical.]

He's overtaking us, hand over fist.

Hands off Leave (it) alone.

Have a hand in Take a part or share in.

Have one's hands full Be completely occupied, very busy.

We shall have our hands full when the visitors arrive.

Have on one's hands Be responsible for; have to dispose of.

When the house is sold I shall have the furniture on my hands.

High-handed Presumptuous. Arrogant.

Hold one's hand 1. [LIT]

2. [MET] Act as guide to one (person).

In hand *or* **well in hand** 1. Under one's control.

There was a little rioting, but the police soon had the situation well in hand.

2. In one's possession.

When all our debts are paid, we shall have over £10 in hand.

In the hands of Being dealt with by.
The contract is in the hands of my solicitor.
Keep in hand Retain; keep under control.
Keep one's hand in Keep practising.
Lay hands on Find.
Lend a hand Help.
All the packing has to be done; perhaps you'll lend a hand?
Lift *or* **raise one's hand against** Strike; attack;
threaten to hit.
Off-hand See under *Off.*
Off one's hands No longer as one's responsibility.
An old hand A person with considerable experience.
Let me help—I'm an old hand at chopping wood.
On all hands; on every hand Universally.
On hand Same as **at hand.**
On one's hands As one's responsibility.
I've a lot of work on my hands at the moment.
On the one hand Said to introduce the first part of a
contrasting expression.
On the other hand Otherwise; alternatively.
We may leave London; on the other hand, we may remain.
Similar to **on the contrary.**
Out of hand Uncontrollable; beyond restraint.
*The crowd became so excited that it was soon completely out of
hand.*
Out of one's hands No longer in one's control.
Show one's hand Reveal one's real intentions. [Or.
The 'hand' of cards held by a player.]
*If he asks you to name a price, don't show all your hand at
once.*
Sleight of hand See under *Sleight.*
Stay one's hand Refrain from action.
Take a hand Share; play a part in.
The State ought to take a hand in building new houses.
Similar to **have a hand.**
Take in hand Take immediate charge of; assume
responsibility for.
The upper *or* **whip hand** The chief power; the real
control.
Throw in one's hand Abandon any further effort.
[Or. Card-playing.]
*I'm so disgusted with the whole thing that I'm going to throw
in my hand.*
Try one's hand at Attempt; test one's powers.

Have you ever tried your hand at cooking?
Turn one's hand to Undertake.
Wash one's hands of Have no further connection with; refuse to accept any further responsibility for.
Win hands down Win easily.
Upper hand Dominating position.

Handle Deal with; direct.
I think the plumber is the best man to handle this.
A handle to one's name A title.

Hang **Get the hang of** Understand.
Hang about Loiter.
Hang back Hesitate to proceed; show reluctance to agree or assist.
Hangdog Untrustworthy. (Sometimes used as noun, meaning 'a suspicious-looking person'.)
Hang fire Fail to produce results when expected. Wait. [Or. A gun or pistol in which the cartridge fails to explode 'hangs fire'.]
Hang in the balance Be undecided.
The future of this school hangs in the balance until the Council next meets.
Hang heavy Pass slowly. (Usually applied to time.)
Hang it Expression of irritation or dismissal.
Hang by a thread Be in an extremely delicate and precarious state. [Or. The story of the sword of Damocles, which see under *Sword*.]
The negotiations are hanging by a thread.
Hang in the balance Be uncertain.
Hang one's head Show shame.
Hang together Collaborate closely; support one another. Be a unified whole.
The plan needs more details if it is to hang together.
Hang upon Depend upon.
I'll be hanged Expression of annoyance or astonishment. Also **hang it all!** See under *Blow.*
I'll be hanged if I'll pay that much for a pair of shoes.
Thereby hangs a tale There are consequences to that.

Happen **Happen what may** Whatever may occur. [Old f.]
Happy **Happy-go-lucky** Careless; gaily reckless; relying on good luck for help out of difficulties.
Happy medium Compromise that suits both parties.
Hard **Go hard with** Involve punishment or suffering for.
Hard and fast Strict. Rigidly organized.

In view of the weather, we'd better not make any hard and fast arrangements.

Hard as nails Uncompromising.

Hard at it Working hard.

Hard bargain One without concessions.

Hard-boiled 1. [LIT] (Of food) boiled so that it is hard. 2. [MET] (Of person) rough; uncompromising; made unyielding by experience.

Hard by Near. [Old f.]

Hard cash Real money, not cheques, promises, etc.

Hard drinker One who drinks beer, wine, etc., frequently and in large quantities.

Hard-earned Earned with difficulty.

Hard facts Indisputable ones.

We have to face the hard fact that we can't afford it.

Hard-featured Severe-looking; grim.

Hard-headed Tough. Practical, not sentimental.

Hard-hearted Unfeeling. Unsympathetic.

Hard-hitting Vigorous.

Hard lines *or* **luck** Harsh; undeservedly severe.

Hard nut to crack Difficult person, problem, situation, etc., to deal with.

Hard of hearing Unable to hear well.

Hard pressed 1. Busy. 2. Closely pursued.

Hard put to it In difficulty.

Hard times Difficult circumstances to bear.

Hard up With insufficient money.

Hard words See under *Word.*

See also **plain speaking** (under *Speak*) and **not to mince matters** (under *Mince*).

Hare **Hare-brained** (= **scatter-brained**) Foolish and irresponsible.

Mad as a March hare See under *Mad.*

Hark **Hark back** Revert (e.g. to topic previously mentioned).

Harm **Out of harm's way** In a safe position.

Harness **In harness** Actively engaged in regular work.

Harp **Harp on; harp on the same string** *or* **subject,** *etc.* Talk about the same subject until the listener becomes bored or irritated.

Hash **Make a hash of** Make a muddle of.

Colin made rather a hash of trying to lay the carpet.

Hat **At the drop of a hat** Swiftly.

Eat one's hat Expression used to add emphasis.

If the train arrives on time, I'll eat my hat.
Keep something under one's hat Keep something secret.
Perform the hat-trick In cricket, a bowler is said to do this when he dismisses three consecutive batsmen in three consecutive balls. Loosely used in connection with any similar triple success.
Take off one's hat to [MET] Express unusual approval of some action of another's.
I don't expect him to succeed, but I'll take my hat off to him if he does.
Take *or* **send** *or* **pass the hat round** Ask for contribution.
Throw one's hat in the ring Put oneself forward as contestant.
Wear two hats Act in two capacities.

Have **Have anything** *or* **nothing to do with** Be (not) concerned or connected with.
He's the kindest person I've ever had anything to do with.
If I were you, I'd have nothing to do with that laundry.
Have done Finish; stop.
Have you done with the washing-up?
Have it out 1. Have extracted.
I'll have this tooth out tomorrow.
2. Discuss a subject (usually a dispute) openly and frankly.
I am going to have the whole thing out with the garage.
Have on 1. Wear.
Are you sure you had gloves on when you arrived?
2. Deceive. Trick.
If he said he was a frist-class snooker-player, he was having you on.
Have (got) to Must.

Hay **Make hay of** Ruin; render confused and muddled.
Make hay while the sun shines Take advantage of a good opportunity, or a specially suitable occasion.

Hazard **Hazard an opinion** (*or* **guess**) Risk expressing an opinion or view.

Head **Above one's head** Beyond one's comprehension.
Come *or* **enter into one's head** Occur to one.
Come to a head Reach a crisis.
Count heads Count people (present, etc.).
Give person his head Allow him to act freely.
Go to one's head Excite; intoxicate; make irresponsible.
Hang one's head See under *Hang.*

Have a (good) head for heights Not be troubled by giddiness, etc. when standing at a high point.

Have a head on one's shoulders Possess intelligence and common sense.

Have one's head Go one's own way without any interference [Or. Riding or driving a horse. To let a horse 'have his head' is to allow him to travel at his own speed unrestrained by the reins.]
He's the sort of man who works best if you let him have his head.

Have one's head screwed on the right way Be intelligent and shrewd.

Head and shoulders above Far above or superior to.
He's head and shoulders above the rest of the candidates.

Head off 1. Intercept; prevent escaping. Divert.
2. **Laugh, eat**, etc. **one's head off**. Laugh, eat, heartily. See under *Bite.*

Head on Directly; frontally.
The two cars collided head on.

Head-over-ears (*in love, debt, etc.*). Utterly and completely.

Head-over-heels Turned upside down; complete inversion.
Similar to **topsy-turvy.**

Heads or tails A coin is frequently 'tossed' (or thrown in the air) by one person to decide which of two alternatives shall be followed. The other competing person 'calls' either 'heads' or 'tails'; if what is called falls uppermost, that person is considered the winner. If not, the one who tossed the coin succeeds.

Heads I win, tails you lose An arrangement which ends in the challenger remaining the winner, whatever happens; a hopelessly unfair agreement.

Heads will roll People will be dismissed.

Hold one's head up *or* **high** Show pride or defiance

Keep one's head above water Live within one's income; avoid bankruptcy. Just manage to avoid difficulty. [Or. Swimming.]

Keep one's head down Behave unobtrusively; act so as not to be conspicuous.

Let person have his/her head Allow person to act freely without interference.

Lose one's head Momentarily lose self-control; behave wildly and senselessly.

Make head or tail of Understand; comprehend. (Always used in the negative.)
I cannot make head nor tail of the argument.
Off one's head Mentally weak; unbalanced; mad; so excited as to be entirely irresponsible.
Old head on young shoulders Wisdom or experience unexpected in so young a person.
On one's own head One's own personal responsibility. (The phrase is generally used as a warning.)
If you insist, it will be on your own head.
Standing on one's head Very easily.
She can repair car-engines standing on her head.
Put into one's head Suggest.
Put *or* **lay our heads together** Consult together; discuss.
If they would only put their heads together, I'm sure they could reach an agreement.
Take into one's head Take a sudden and unexpected action.
The boy took it into his head to play truant.
Toss one's head Raise it with a jerk of pride or contempt.
Turn one's head *or* **brain** Render one vain, self-conscious, irresponsible, etc.
Two heads are better than one It is an advantage to have a second person's opinion; collaboration is valuable.
Over one's head 1. Beyond one's comprehension.
Most of his speech went over my head.
2. In preference to one having a prior claim.
He was appointed manager over his boss's head.

Headway **Make headway** Progress; go forward.
Hear **Hear from** Receive message from.
Hear of 1. Be told about.
2. **Will not hear of** Refuse to consider.
Hear tell of Be told about.
Hearing **A fair hearing** Opportunity to state one's case while being listened to impartially.
Hard of hearing Partially, but not completely, deaf.
Lose one's hearing Become completely deaf.
Out of hearing Too far away to be heard.
Heart **After one's own heart** Such as one could like and appreciate. In accordance with one's tastes.
At heart As one's concern.

Break one's heart Cause one extreme distress or disappointment.

Change of heart Change of feelings.

Do one's heart good Make one happy and pleased. *It did my heart good to see the children's delight.*

Find it in one's heart Be firm or hard-hearted enough (usually used in the negative).

From the bottom of one's heart Most sincerely.

Have a heart Be personally concerned or interested in. *Her parents naturally have the girl's happiness at heart.*

Have one's heart in one's mouth Be in a state of extreme nervousness.

Have the heart to See **find it in one's heart.**

Heart and soul With all one's force.

Heart in the right place In spite of imperfections, possessing good and sensible ideas. Well-meaning. *He's rather unapproachable, but his heart is in the right place.*

Heart is not in it Interest is not really devoted to it.

Heart's content Complete satisfaction; as much or as long as one desires. *We can swim in the river to our heart's content.*

Heart goes out to Feelings of sympathy are with.

Heart of the matter The essence, or most vital part, of something.

Heart-rending Extremely distressing.

Heart stands still One experiences momentary fear.

Heart-strings Deepest feelings or affections.

Heart-to-heart Frank and intimate.

In good heart In good spirits.

Know (off) by heart Know, literally and every word.

Learn (off) by heart Memorize.

Lose heart Become too depressed to continue.

Lose one's heart to Fall in love with; be charmed.

Set one's heart upon Desire intensely.

Take heart Be encouraged. *We may take heart from the fact that the illness isn't getting any worse.*

Take to heart Take very seriously.

Wear one's heart on one's sleeve Exhibit one's intentions for all to see; be completely frank. [Or. The old custom of a lover tying a ribbon given him by his sweetheart on his sleeve.]

Win the heart of Gain the affection of.

Heat **In the heat of the moment** During a brief time

of confusion, anxiety, excitement, panic, etc.

Heaven Used in numerous mild exclamations such as
Good heavens, Heavens above, For heaven's sake. Also emphatic phrase **In heaven's name.**
What in heaven's name does he think he's doing?
Heaven forbid I hope that does not happen.
Heaven only knows I do not know.
More heaven and earth Act vigorously (to achieve something).
Seventh heaven A state of great happiness and contentment.
The heavens opened It rained very heavily.

Heavy **Make heavy weather of** Find great difficulties in.
You seem to be making heavy weather of that job.

Heel **Heel of Achilles** See **Achilles' heel.**
Clean pair of heels Superior speed.
Come to heel. Obey humbly and completely, as a dog comes obediently to the heels of his master.
(Left to) cool one's heels Be kept waiting, usually by a superior.
Dig one's heels in Be stubborn.
Down-at-heel Shabby and untidy, like one whose shoe-heels are worn down.
Kick one's heels Waste time.
I had to kick my heels for an hour before he would see me.
Similar to **cool one's heels** and **twiddle one's thumbs.**
On the heels of Immediately behind, or very soon afterwards.
Show a clean pair of heels Run away from and escape.
Take to one's heels Run away.
The boy broke the window and took to his heels.
Turn on one's heel Turn sharply away.
She turned on her heel, and disappeared in the crowd.

Helm **At the helm** In control.
Take the helm Take charge.

Help **Help oneself to** Select and take away without formality or waiting to ask permission.
The guests helped themselves to the refreshments at the buffet.

Helter-skelter
Hurriedly and in confusion.
They dashed helter-skelter out of the room.

Hem **Hem in** Restrain; restrict.

Hen **Hen-pecked** Constantly faulted, nagged, scolded, etc., by one's wife.

Here **Here and there** Scattered; distributed. In various places.

They looked down upon fields and woods, with a farmhouse here and there.

Here, there and everywhere In very many places.

Here today and gone tomorrow Merely temporary; staying for a short time in any place.

Neither here nor there Immaterial to a matter, etc.

Hero **Hero's welcome** Welcome with acclamation (as for hero returning from war).

Herod **Out-Herod Herod** To be excessively wicked. [Or. Shakespeare, *Hamlet*.]

Hide **Hide one's light under a bushel** Conceal one's merits because of modesty. [Or. Biblical: 'Neither do men light a candle and put it under a bushel.'] The phrase is generally used in the negative.

High **High and dry** Stranded.

High and low Everywhere.

High and mighty Arrogant.

Highbrow Of cultured tastes.

Highdays, holidays and bonfire nights An old-f. facetious phrase applied to celebrations in general.

High-falutin' High-flown; absurdly elaborate and fantastic (generally applied to speech).

High-flown Extravagant.

High-flyer Ambitious person with the ability to succeed.

High-handed See under *Hand.*

High life Life of luxury.

Highlight Most prominent part.

Highly (probable, *etc.***)** To a great extent.

High-minded Serious in moral attitudes.

High places Senior ranks (of Government, organisation, etc.).

High-sounding Pompous; magnificent.

He's talking a lot of high-sounding nonsense.

High spot Outstanding attraction.

The high spot of the evening was the firework display.

Highly strung Tense. Unusually sensitive.

High table The end table, usually at right-angles to the others and raised, at which the masters and other important personages of a college dine.

High tea An early evening meal which combines meat or some similar extra dish with the usual tea.

High time Fully time; applied to an event already due, if not overdue.

Look at the clock; it's high time you went to bed.

Highway **Queen's highway** All public roads and thoroughfares along which the public has a right to travel (but, legally, only to travel, not to linger upon, or to obstruct).

Hill **Old as the hills** Very old.

Hinge **Hinge upon** Depend on.

The whole play hinges upon the success of his performance.

Hint **Broad hint** A stressed, an obvious hint.

Drop *or* **throw out a hint** Hint in a casual manner.

I still haven't received the boss's reply; will you drop a hint to her secretary?

Hit **Hit back** Retaliate.

Hit below the belt 1. [LIT] Commit foul in boxing. 2. [MET] Behave unfairly.

Hit it off Agree.

Similar to **see eye to eye** and **get on.**

Hit the (right) nail on the head Guess or judge correctly.

Hit upon Discover (usually unexpectedly).

Hither **Hither and thither** Here and there; in this direction and in that direction. [Old f.]

Hive **Hive off** Take away (responsibility, work, etc.) and give to another.

Hoary **Hoary age** Age when one's hair has turned white, or hoary; very old.

He died at the hoary age of ninety.

(Note—Hoary is often used to mean 'very old' in connection with other matters, e.g. *a hoary joke*.)

Hobby See under **Horse.**

Hobson **Hobson's choice** See under *Choice.*

Hocus-pocus

The words traditionally uttered by a conjuror as he performs a trick; hence, a cheat, a swindle. [Or. Obscure. Perhaps the name of a famous French conjuror, Ochus Boshus, or the Welsh *Hocca pucca*.]

Hog **Go the whole hog** Go to the fullest possible extent. Complete a matter.

If we're going to the cinema, why not go the whole hog and have a meal out as well.

H

Hoist **Hoist with one's own petard** Beaten with one's own weapons; caught in one's own trap. [Or. The medieval 'petard', an engine designed, when filled with gunpowder, to blow in a city gate. There was extreme risk of those who fired it being destroyed too.]

Hold **Hold aloof** Remain deliberately apart; isolated.
Hold cheap Regard as having little value.
Hold dear Cherish.
Hold it against (one) Blame (one).
Hold the fort [LIT] Defend a fortress. [MET] Remain on duty, in charge, at work, in supervision, etc.
Hold forth Discourse; orate.
Hold good Remain unaffected and unaltered.
My promise to visit you next summer holds good.
Hold off Delay.
Hold *or* **stand one's ground** Not yield.
Despite the Opposition's abuse, the Minister stood his ground.
Hold (oneself) in Restrain (oneself).
Hold on 1. [LIT] Continue one's grasp.
2. [MET] Wait.
Hold one's own Maintain successfully one's opinion, argument, or position.
Hold out 1. As **hold on** (1).
2. Extend, offer.
Hold over 1. Keep back; reserve.
2. Use some knowledge as a threat.
Hold to Adhere to.
Hold together Remain undivided; not separated.
Hold up 1. Delay.
2. Support.
3. Exhibit.
Hold water See under *Water.*
Hold with Concur; agree with.
I don't hold with allowing children too much freedom.
No holds barred Without restraint.
There's no holding one One is difficult to restrain.

Hole **Be in a hole** Be in an awkward situation.
Hole-and-corner Furtive; secret.
Pick holes in Find fault with.
Square peg in a round hole Person not suited for his or her position.

Hollow **Hollow laugh** Mirthless laugh.
Hollow promises False promises.

Holy **Holier-than-thou** Sanctimonious.

Homage **Pay** *or* **give homage to** Show respect and reverence.

Home **At-home** An evening party, usually informal.
Bring a thing home to a person Compel him to realize it.
Perhaps the accident will bring home to him his stupidity in driving so fast.
Come home to roost Recoil disadvantageously against originator.
Home from home Place which is not one's home but where one feels at home.
Make oneself at home Behave informally, as though the house was one's own.
Do sit down and make yourself at home.

Honest **Earn (turn) an honest penny** Earn money honestly.
Honest broker Impartial mediator.

Honour **A debt of honour** A debt which cannot be legally enforced—e.g. a gambling debt, or one which is purely moral.
Do the honours Act as host or hostess.
Honour among thieves Mutual help or trust even among people normally considered incapable of either. Similar to **dog doesn't eat dog.**
Honours are even Neither side has won or lost.
In honour of To celebrate.
(In) honour bound Compelled by one's sense of duty or correctness.
A point of honour Conduct arising from one's own particular sense of self-respect.

Hook **By hook or by crook** By any method, right or wrong; without scruples.
Hook, line and sinker Completely and utterly. [Or. Parts of a fishing-rod.]
I put the plan a different way, and they fell for it (swallowed it) hook, line and sinker.
Off the hook Out of a difficulty. [Or. Fishing.]
It's his own fault for getting himself into this situation, but we'll have to think of a way to get him off the hook.

Hoop **Go** *or* **be put through the hoop(s)** Suffer an ordeal.

Horizon **On the horizon** [MET] Likely to occur in the remote future.

Horn **Draw in one's horns** Withdraw, alter or abandon (plans, etc.). [Or. A snail's 'horns', which are drawn in if it senses danger.]

Hornet's nest
Stir up *or* **put one's hand in a hornet's nest** Create trouble by interfering unwisely.

Horse **A dark horse** A person whose qualities and possibilities are unknown. [Or. Racing.]

Eat like a horse Have a good appetite.

Flog a dead horse Make useless effort.

Hobby-horse 1. Favourite notion or private idea which one is constantly referring to.
The foreman's been riding his hobby-horse about efficiency again.
2. Abbreviation **hobby.** Spare-time occupation. Pastime. [Or. Wickerwork horse worn round waist of folk-dancers. Child's toy: stick with horse's head. Both are 'ridden'.]

Look a gift horse in the mouth Examine too critically anything which is a present. [Or. The proverb, 'Never look a gift horse in the mouth.' A horse's age is judged by the condition of its teeth.]

On one's high horse Assuming a haughty or superior attitude. Stand-offish. Also **trying to ride the high horse.**

Put the cart before the horse Do things in the wrong order.

(Straight) from the horse's mouth (Of information received) direct, not through an intermediary.

Take a horse to the water Only go so far. [Or. Proverb, 'You can take a horse to the water, but you can't make him drink.']

Wild horses wouldn't (make one) Nothing would.
Wild horses wouldn't make me go swimming in the sea today.

Hot **Hot air** Excited, boastful, meaningless talk.

Hot and bothered Flustered.

Hot favourite Very popular. Strongly recommended.

Hot under the collar Angry.

Hot water See under *Water.*

Hour **Improve the shining hour** Take advantage of an opportunity. [Or. Abbrev. quotation from child's poem, 'How doth the little busy bee improve each shining hour.']

Keep regular hours Always go to bed and get up at the same times, usually early ones.

The small hours The early hours of the morning, i.e. between 1 and 4 a.m.

The witching hour Midnight. [Or. The time when witches are said to exercise their powers.] [Old f.]

Till all hours Until very late.

House **Bring down the house** Give a tremendously popular performance, not necessarily in a theatre, of any type.

[Or. Theatrical, to receive so much applause that the building shakes.]

House-warming A dinner-party, etc., given to celebrate the settling down in a new house, a return after a long absence, or any similar occasion.

Keep open house Welcome visitors, without invitation, at any time. Be generous and frequent with hospitality.

Like a house on fire Vigorously. Extremely well. Successfully.

On the house Free.

Put one's house in order Organise one's affairs in an orderly way.

How **How are you?** Same as **how do you do?**

How comes it?; how is it? How or why does it happen?

How comes it that you are always late on Monday?

How do you do? The usual formal greeting.

[Or. 'Do' = 'du', from the Anglo-Saxon 'dugan', 'to go'.]

How is —— ? Abbrev. for How (= in what state) is the health of ——?

Hue **Hue and cry** Noise of pursuit. Outcry (**against**). [Or. Old legal name for official cry when calling for assistance, e.g. in pursuit of escaping criminal. Old French = *huer*, to shout.]

Some M.P.s are raising a great hue and cry about the amount of money being spent on defence.

Hum **Hum and haw** Hesitate; procrastinate.

Hunt **Hunt down** Find after careful search.

Hunt up Search for.

You'll have to hunt up the word in the dictionary.

Hurl **Hurl defiance** Openly and loudly defy. Frequently used facetiously.

Hurly-burly

Tumult; the noise and struggle of crowds.

Hurry **Hurry on with; hurry up** Hasten.

Hurry up, or we shall miss the train.

In a hurry Hastening. Not reluctantly.

We won't go to that restaurant again in a hurry.

Husband **Husband one's resources** To 'husband' is to take care of, to use economically. 'Resources' are all the means one has.

Hush **Hush up** Suppress mention of.

I

Ice **Break the ice** Overcome reserve.
Cut no ice Fail to impress.
On ice In reserve. Waiting for later attention.
On thin ice Taking risks.

Idea **What's the big idea?** What folly have you in mind?

Ilk **That ilk** The same name. The same nature.

Ill **Ill-assorted** Incompatible; badly matched.
Ill-at-ease Uncomfortable; in a state of embarrassment.
It's an ill wind that blows nobody good It is a specially disastrous matter if nobody whatsoever derives any benefit from it.
Speak ill of Disparage.

Image **The image; the very image; the spit and image** (incorrectly **the spitting image**) Exactly alike.
The baby is the image of his father.

Imagination
Flight *or* **stretch of imagination** Imaginative effort.

Impression **Give** *or* **create a false impression** Mislead by a statement or action.
The story she has told gives a totally false impression of what really happened.
Make a good impression Behave in a manner which will create admiration and respect.
He made a very good impression when he applied for the job.
Under the impression Having the notion or (vague) belief.
I was under the impression that today was Friday.

In **In at** Present at.
In with On intimate or friendly terms with.
Ins and outs Details.
Not much in it Little difference (between various arguments, competitors etc.).

Inch **Every inch** Completely; entirely.
John looks every inch a golfer.
Inch by inch See **little by little**.
Within an inch of Close to.

Incline **Be inclined to** Have a tendency to; be in favour of.
I am inclined to forgive him because of his youth.

Incumbent **Incumbent upon one** An essential duty for one.

Inference **Draw an inference** Assume; infer.
From his manner, we drew the inference that he was satisfied with the results of his visit.

Influence **Under the influence** In full, 'under the influence of intoxicating liquor'.

Iniquity **Sink of iniquity** Any place with a bad reputation. (Frequently used facetiously).

Initiative **On one's own initiative** Without prompting.

Take the initiative. Be the first (to do something).

In-laws The relations of one's husband or wife—**mother-in-law, sister-in-law,** etc.

Innings **Have a good innings** Spend a long time. (E.g. said of someone who has lived to old age.)

Ins-and-outs

The ins-and-outs All the details.

Instance **For instance** As an example; to explain or elaborate one's meaning.

Similar to **for example.**

In the first instance To begin with.

Intent **To all intents and purposes** Apparently. As far as one can see.

Interim **In the interim** Between now and some specified event.

We leave next week; in the interim we shall be visiting friends.

Interval **At intervals** At irregular periods of time.

The discussion continued; at intervals the speakers stopped for refreshment.

Iota **One iota** The smallest possible quantity. [Or. The iota is the smallest letter of the Greek alphabet.]

(*Note*—This idiom is always used in the negative.)

Iron **Iron out** Remove difficulties from.

Irons in the fire Matters of interest or importance which may prove profitable.

Strike while the iron is hot Act promptly, and while the conditions are in one's favour.

Issue **Confuse the issue** Confuse the final analysis or result; bring forward irrelevant arguments.

Force an issue Compel a decision to be reached.

Join issue (with someone) (on something) Proceed to argue.

Take issue Disagree.

It **This is it** What has been expected has arrived.

J

Jack **Every man jack** Every single man.

Jack of all trades (and master of none) One

J

capable of undertaking a variety of jobs (but who is
expert at none of them).
Before you can say Jack Robinson Extremely
quickly.
*He knocked, and before you could say Jack Robinson the door
opened.*

Jaundice **View with a jaundiced eye; take a jundiced view
of** Regard with jealousy, envy, suspicion or distrust.
[Or. Janudice is a disease which turns the skin
temporarily yellow, and yellow is the colour associated
with jealousy.]

Jib **The cut of one's jib** One's personal appearance and
manner.

Job **A good job** Fortunate.
It's a good job it's not raining.
Job's comforter One who comes nominally to console
and comfort a person, but who actually adds to his
distress by being pessimistic and reproachful. [Or.
Biblical.]
Make a good job of Succeed at.
Make the best of a bad job Do one's best in
unfortunate circumstances.
Try the patience of Job Be vexatious.

Jog **Jog along** To 'jog' is to proceed at a slow, regular
pace. Used almost always metaphorically to indicate
quiet, routine and unexciting progress.
Jog-trot Progress as above.
Jog a person's memory Remind, in order to prevent
something being forgotten.

Joke **Crack a joke** Make a joke; tell a humorous story.
It's no joke It is a serious matter.
Practical joke Trick played on a person to gain a
laugh at his expense.

Jones **Keep up with the Joneses** Try to reach same
standards (especially of material comfort) as everyone
else, or one's neighbours.

Jot **Jot or tittle** 'Jot is a corruption of 'iota' (which see);
'tittle' also means something tiny. (The expression is
always used negatively.)
Jot down Note briefly and quickly.

Judgement **Against one's better judgement** Contrary to what
one really feels to be best.
Sit in judgement on Judge.

Juggle with Rearrange. Misrepresent.

114

Juice **Stew in one's own juice** Endure the consequences of one's own actions.

Jump **Jump at** Take a quick advantage of; seize an opportunity.

The house is a bargain, and you should jump at the offer.

Jump down one's throat Speak with unexpected violence to one.

I only asked him if I could use his telephone, and he jumped down my throat.

Jump in Get in (car).

Jump the queue Take place in queue ahead of others already there.

The high jump Serious trouble.

When David comes back home, he's for the high jump.

Jungle **Law of the jungle** Lawlessness. State of vicious competition.

Just **Just in case** As a precaution.

Justice **Do justice to** Treat justly or fairly; appreciate fully (used frequently in reference to food).

Do oneself justice Show one's abilities to their good advantage.

Did you do yourself justice in the driving-test?

Poetic justice Justice that is specially pleasing.

Rough justice Justice that is not impeceable.

K

Keen **Keen as mustard (on)** Very enthusiastic (about).

Keep **Keep abreast of** Keep level with.

We do our best to keep abreast of modern improvements.
Similar to **keep pace with.**

Keep aloof Remain distant from, physically or in manner.

Keep at Persist or continue with.

You'll never learn to paint unless you keep at it.

Keep back Conceal. Slow down the progress of.

Keep company Associate with.

Keep cool Remain calm.

Keep dark Conceal; refrain from mentioning.

Keep one's counsel Remain silent and reticent.

Keep one's distance (Originally) Maintain one's correct and formal attitude. (Now more frequently) Remain away from.

The dog's rather wild, so I should keep your distance.
Keep one's end up Not slacken. Acquit oneself well.
Keep an eye on Watch; act as temporary guardian to.
I would be glad if you'd keep an eye on the children while we're away.
Keep at arm's length Avoid familiarity with.
Keep going Continue (at one's work or routine, etc.).
He looks ill; I don't know how long he'll be able to keep going.
Keep guard Watch; act as sentinel.
Keep one's hand in Continue to practise, in order to retain one's skill.
Keep one's head Not allow oneself to become flustered.
Keep house Act as the manager of a household.
When his wife died his sister went to keep house for him.
Keep in touch (with) Remain in contact or in communication (with).
Keep in with Remain on good terms with, usually with some definite motive.
Keep it up Continue in the same manner.
Keep off Avoid.
Keep on Persist in; repeat one's present actions.
Keep one's word Do as one promises.
Keep order Control.
Keep out Refuse admittance to.
Keep out of the way Absent or efface oneself.
Keep pace with Move at the same speed as.
1. [LIT].
My horse couldn't keep pace with the rest of the field.
2. [MET].
I can't keep pace with all the changes in tax law.
Keep the ball rolling Maintain impetus.
Keep the peace Maintain peace.
Keep secret Similar to **keep it dark.**
Keep to Adhere to.
Keep to oneself Remain alone.
Keep something to oneself Fail to disclose or share something.
Keep a stiff upper lip Not allow one's lip to tremble with emotion; be firm and brave.
Keep a straight face Refrain from laughing.
Keep track of Follow the progress of.
Keep up Continue.
We wrote frequently at first, but I hadn't enough time to keep up

the correspondence.

Keep up with Similar to **keep pace with** [LIT] and [MET]

I can't keep up with you—you walk too fast.

It is difficult to keep up with all these new inventions.

Keep watch Act as look-out.

In keeping with (negative form = out of keeping with) Appropriate to; suitable to.

Key **Low key** Subdued.

Kick **Kick over the traces** Be insubordinate. Act independently.

Kick up a fuss Cause a violent disturbance; quarrel.

Kill **Dressed** *or* **got up to kill** Dressed in a manner designed to attract maximum attention.

Kill oneself Exert oneself unduly.

Kill the fatted calf Entertain lavishly.

Kill two birds with one stone Achieve two purposes with a single act.

Kill with kindness Harm with too much kindness.

Kin **Next of kin** Nearest relations.

Kind **Nothing of the kind** Nothing like that.

Two of a kind Two similar people or things.

Kindly **Take kindly to** Be well disposed towards.

Kiss **Kiss goodbye to** Regard as lost.

Kitchen **Everything but the kitchen sink** Everything that can be imagined.

Kite **Fly a kite** Act so as to test people's opinion, reaction etc.

Kith **Kith and kin** Acquaintances and blood relations. (Used loosely to refer to members of same race.)

Knee **Bring person to his knees** Cause him to submit.

Knife **Get one's knife into** Behave vindictively to.

Knight **Knight errant** In medieval days, an armed knight who roamed about the countryside, prepared to defend oppressed and helpless maidens. The phrase is today applied to any chivalrous man who, without expecting reward, helps and protects a weak or helpless person.

Knit **Knit one's brows** Frown; regard in a puzzled way. ('Knit' here means to draw towards one another.)

Knock **Knock about** 1. Wander, gaining experience in the process.

I've knocked about the world for forty years.

2. Injure physically. Treat roughly.

I got knocked about a bit playing football yesterday.

3. **Knock-about** (Adjective) Noisy, boisterous, rowdy.

Knock down Strike a person so violently that he falls.
Knock-down prices The cheapest possible. The best available (as in an auction. See **knock down to**).
Knock down to Sell to a person who has made a final bid at an auction sale. (An auctioneer gives a sharp rap with his hammer when the highest and final bid has been made, and the article or 'lot' is then legally the property of the bidder.) See **under the hammer** (under *Hammer*).
Knock into a cocked hat Defeat easily. Be very much superior to.
Knock off 1. Cease work for the day.
2. Steal.
Knock on the head 1. [LIT] Kill [Old f.]
2. [MET] Destroy.
We'll soon knock his scheme on the head.
Knock out (Verb) Render incapable of further fighting. [Or. Boxing.]
Knock over 1. [LIT] Overturn; upset.
2. [MET] Completely overwhelm.
Knock the bottom out of Destroy.
Knock together Create hastily.
Knock up Rouse from sleep by knocking at the door.
Take a knock 1. Receive a slight injury.
2. Suffer (slightly).

Knot **Tie (up) in knots** Baffle. Confuse.
Know **I don't know him from Adam** Exaggeration for 'I don't know him'.
Know the ropes See under *Ropes*.
Not want to know Be uninterested or unconcerned.
Knuckle **Knuckle down** Work hard. Begin to work.
If I can get a chance to knuckle down to it, I'll soon finish painting the bathroom.
Knuckle under Surrender. [LIT] Kneel for pardon. ('Knuckle' here means the knee).
Rap on the knuckle See under *Rap*.

L

Labour **Labour of love** Work performed from affection or regard, and without expectation of payment.
Labour a point Over-stress a point in one's argument.
Labour under an affliction Suffer from some

L

handicap or inconvenience, usually permanent.

Labour under a delusion *or* **illusion** Be influenced by some false idea.

Lady **Lady Bountiful** A generous and kindly woman; now often applied derogatorily to a person who is too prominent in works of charity. [Or. Character in Farquhar's *Beaux' Stratagem*.]

Ladies' man One who makes special efforts to charm or please women.

Laid **Laid up** 1. In bed through illness or accident.
2. Nautical. In harbour for repairs, etc.

Lamb **Like a lamb** Without resistance.

Might as well be hanged for a sheep as (for) a lamb As one is taking risks (in trouble, doing wrong, etc.) one might just as well be bold.

Lame **Lame duck** Person or business unable to function effectively.

Land **Land on one's feet** Enjoy fortunate success.

Land up Find oneself in certain place.

See how the land lies Discover the state of affairs; make discreet enquiries.

The land of the living Among living people.

The lie of the land How matters are.

Landslide (*political*) A sudden complete change of political popularity and, as a result, political power in an election. (Hence **landslide victory**.)

Language **Speak the same language** Have similar outlook.

Lap **Lap of luxury** Extreme richness.
This flat is hardly the lap of luxury, but it suits us.

Large **At large** 1. Free after escaping.
2. In general.

Lark **Rise with the lark** Get up early.

Last **At last** Eventually; after a long time has passed.

At long last As above, but more emphatic.

At one's last gasp In an utterly exhausted, or almost dying, condition.

Last but not least Last to be mentioned, but not last in importance.

Last out Survive, be available or serviceable, for as long as is necessary.

On one's last legs Almost, though not quite, exhausted. (The idiom is also applied to any affair, etc., which is on the verge of failing.)

Stick to one's last Confine oneself to what one does

119

well. Not meddle in another's business.

The last straw See under **Straw**.

The last word 1. The final contribution to an argument.

He's a difficult man to negotiate with—always insists on having the last ward.

2. [MET] The culminating achievement, than which nothing can be better. (Usually exaggeration).

This is the last word in electric cookers.

Late **Sooner or later** Eventually.

Laugh; Laughter **Convulsed with laughter** Laughing so excessively that one is practically helpless.

Laugh away *or* **off** Dismiss (or conceal) something by laughing.

Laugh in person's face Show open contempt for person.

Laugh on the other side of one's face Be the reverse of amused; be depressed or unhappy.

Laugh out of court Fail to be taken seriously.

Laugh up one's sleeve Be amused secretly; hide one's laughter in contempt.

No laughing matter A serious matter.

Launch **Launch out** Depart from one's normal habits or occupation.

Laurels **(Win) laurels** (Acquire) honour. [Or. The Roman custom of crowning a victor with laurel wreaths.]

Look to one's laurels Beware of losing one's place.

Rest on one's laurels Cease to strive further.

Law **Arm of the law** Criminal law, personified by the police.

The eyes *or* **eye of the law** A legal stand-point.

In the eyes of the law, you are now an adult.

Have the law on Prosecute in a court of law.

Law-abiding Observing the law.

A law unto himself One who follows his own inclinations, regardless of custom.

Law-abiding One who obeys the law.

Lay down the law Speak very firmly; use one's authority; insist on proper observance.

The doctor laid down the law, and told me to eat less.

Take the law into one's own hands Ignore the legal method of obtaining justice, and act entirely as one considers suitable and just.

Lay **Lay about one** Strike out violently in every direction.
Lay *or* **put aside; lay by** 1. Abandon, usually for a short time.
2. Put away for future use.
Lay bare Reveal.
Lay a bet Place a bet or wager.
Lay at one's door *or* **to one's charge** Place the blame or responsibility on one.
The death of the patient was laid at the hospital's door.
Lay off Cease to employ (person).
Lay one's hands on Find. Obtain possession of.
I can't lay my hands on my umbrella.
Lay hold of Grasp.
Lay in *or* **up** Store for future use.
We must lay in some candles in case there's an electricity strike.
Lay on thick Exaggerate greatly (usually blame, or praise).
Lay oneself open (to) Expose oneself (to); lead to an unfavourable assumption.
If this party goes on much longer, we'll lay ourselves wide open to complaints from the people next door.
Lay out 1. Spend.
2. Present to view.
I'm going to lay out £500 in fittings for my shop.
Lay stress (weight, emphasis) on Emphasize.
The Chancellor laid stress on the need for economy.
Lay waste Ravage.

Lead **Give a lead** 1. Provide an example by doing something first.
2. Provide a clue.
Lead a dance Cause considerable trouble and activity.
The chicken led us a dance before we caught it.
Lead astray Mislead. Encourage to do wrong.
Lead by the nose Control a person as completely as if he were a horse being led by a rope.
Lead off Act as the leader in beginning any function (dancing, singing, etc.); start.
Lead on Encourage to go further than was intended.
He's normally go, but sometimes others lead him on.
Lead one a dog's life Make one's life miserable.
Lead the way Similar to **lead off,** but also frequently used in the literal sense of going first to point the way.
Lead up to Progress gradually towards.

Leading light Prominent person.

Take the lead *or* **leading part** Act the most important part. Show initiative.

Someone will have to take the lead in forming a committee.

Leaf **Take a leaf out of a person's book** Copy; take as an example.

I wish you'd take a leaf out of Peter's book, and get up early.

Turn over a new leaf Alter; change; make a fresh and better beginning.

She has promised to turn over a new leaf, and be more punctual.

Lean **Lean over backwards** Use all one's best endeavours.

Leap **By leaps and bounds** With extreme rapidity.

National prosperity is increasing by leaps and bounds.

A leap in the dark An action the result of which is uncertain or unknown.

Learn **Learn by heart** Memorize. Similar to **commit to memory.**

Lease **A new lease of life** Fresh reserves of energy.

Leash **Straining at the leash** Keen to start.

Least **At least** As the minimum.

If we can't afford a new car, at least we can get the old one repaired.

In the least In the smallest degree.

Least said, soonest mended The less one says, the better.

To say the least of it To minimize; express as mildly as possible.

His bluntness was, to say the least of it, unlikely to make him popular.

Leave **Beg leave** Ask permission. [Old f. Formal.]

Leave alone Do not interfere with.

Leave behind 1. Forget.

John has left his spectacles behind.

2. Deliberately discard.

I've left my umbrella behind; it isn't going to rain.

Leave in *or* **out in the cold** Ignore; to take no notice of, or interest in.

Leave in the lurch Abandon in circumstances of danger and difficulty. [Or. The card-game called cribbage, in which the 'lurch' is a hopeless position.]

Leave it at that Take no further action. Make no further comment.

Leave much to be desired Be far from satisfactory.

Leave off 1. Cease to wear a garment.

2. Cease; stop what one is doing.

Leave out Omit.

Leave over Defer.

I can't do it now; I'll leave it over till tomorrow.

Leave a person to it Leave a person alone to continue in his own way.

If you think you can finish it on your own, I'll leave you to it.

Leave at the post See under *Post.*

Leave one cold Fail to excite, interest, etc.

That sort of book just leaves me cold.

Leave to oneself Leave in solitude, without interference.

If you leave him to himself, he'll be quite happy.

Similar to **leave a person to it.**

Leave word Leave a message, verbal or written.

Take French leave Abandon one's work or post without obtaining the necessary permission from one's superior.

Take leave Venture.

Take leave of one's senses Go mad.

Take one's leave Depart; say farewell to.

Without so much as a by your leave Without even asking permission.

Leeway **Make up leeway** Compensate for time which has been lost. [Or. Nautical. 'Leeway' is the distance which a ship has drifted from the position in which she should have been.] Also, escape from a difficult position. 'Leeway' is often used to mean 'room for manoeuvre'.

Left **Have two left feet** Be clumsy.

Left-handed compliment One which is the reverse of complimentary.

Leg **Give a leg-up** [LIT] Help a person to mount horse, etc. [MET] Help generally.

Not a leg to stand on Having nothing effective in support of an argument.

On one's last legs Close to exhaustion or to the limits of usefulness.

Pull one's leg Deceive jocularly. Trick. Befool.

He takes everything so seriously: I can't resist pulling his leg.

Stretch one's legs Take a walk for exercise.

Lend **Lend a hand** Help.

Length **At great length** For a long time.

She spoke at great length about nothing at all.

At length After considerable time; eventually.

Go to any lengths Ignore every impediment that may get in one's way.

Leopard **Leopard cannot change its spots** Person's nature cannot be altered. [Or. Biblical.]

Less **In less than no time** Very quickly.

Lesson **Teach one a lesson** Do something which will act as a reprimand to one and show up one's fault.

Let **Let alone** 1. Refrain from interfering with.

2. In addition to being (or having).

Let be Same as **let alone** (1).

Let the cat out of the bag Reveal a secret (usually accidentally). Create trouble (usually by tactlessness).

Let down Betray; fail to support when support was needed.

My brother promised to give me a lift, but he let me down.

Let fall *(applied to speech)* Remark casually.

Let fly 1. [LIT] Propel swiftly.

2. [MET] Abandon control.

He lost his temper, and let fly.

Let go Release one's hold.

He let go of the rope, and crashed to the ground.

Let someone in 1. Admit.

John knocked, and I let him in.

2. Involve a person without his or her knowledge or consent; make responsible for.

His tactlessness lets me in for a lot of embarrassment.

Let loose Release.

Let off 1. Allow to go free and unpunished.

The prisoner was let off with some good advice.

2. Explode.

We let off fireworks on November 5th.

Let oneself go Give way to one's impulses, enthusiasms, etc.

Let out 1. Release; set free.

I'll open the cage and let out the bird.

2. Disclose; reveal.

I'll tell you a secret, but you mustn't let it out.

Let pass Ignore.

What the newspaper said isn't at all accurate, but let that pass.

Let sleeping dogs lie Avoid anything (usually people) which might stir up trouble.

Let slip Inadvertently release (e.g. a remark). Miss (an opportunity).

Let well alone Refrain from interfering, because it may do more harm than good.

Letter **To the letter** Exactly; precisely.

His report was correct to the letter.

The letter of the law Exactly in accordance with the rules and regulations of the law.

Level Do one's level best Do one's utmost; use all one's efforts.
I'll do my level best to be at the concert.

Keep a level head Remain calm and sensible. Keep control of oneself.
In these exciting times, it isn't always easy to keep a level head.
Level-headed Sensible.
On the level Truth(fully), honest(ly).

Liberal Liberal education One planned on broad principles. The phrase is entirely non-political, 'liberal' here meaning 'ample, abundant'. The opposite of a specialized education.

Liberty At liberty Free; unrestrained. Permitted or invited to do something.
You are at liberty to wander anywhere in the park.

Take the liberty Act as though one possessed a right which in fact one does not; presume.
I have taken the liberty of switching off your car-lights.

Take liberties Go beyond the normal limits of convention or good manners. Be unduly familiar **(with)**.

Lick Lick into shape Make efficient or presentable. Mould [Or. The licking by its mother of a new-born bear or similar cub.]

Lick one's boots Be sycophantic to one.

Lick one's wounds Consider consequences of one's defeat.

Lid Take the lid off Expose.

Lie Give the lie to Completely deny; disprove.

Has made one's bed and must lie on it Must endure the consequences of one's action.

Lie at one's door Become one's responsibility.

Lie in one's teeth Tell serious lies.

Lie low Remain unobtrusive.

Lie up Lie in bed as the result of an illness or accident. See under *Laid*.

White lie A harmless lie told only with the object of helping or comforting someone.

Lieu In lieu of Instead of; in place of.

Life As large as life [LIT] In person. [MET] Prominent. Unmistakable. (This idiom is used in a general rather than an exact and literal sense, as emphasis.)

Breath of life Absolutely essential.

Come to life Become alive; give an indication of being alive.

I seldom come to life before mid-morning.

For the life of me. For dear life. [LIT] 'Even if what I am saying meant the loss of my life.' Used merely for emphasis.

For the life of me I can't understand what you're worrying about.

Have the time of one's life Enjoy oneself thoroughly.

Large as life In person.

Life and soul A vivacious person.

Matter of life and death Desperately serious matter; of crucial significance.

New lease of life Fresh possibilities of continued existence.

Since he got back from holiday he's taken on a new lease of life.

Prime of life The most fully developed period of life (usually supposed to be about forty).

Take one's life in one's hands Take bold risk.

To the life Exactly; with complete realism.

True to life Accurate.

Lift **Lift a finger** Make a slight effort. (Usually used in negative.)

He never lifted a finger to help me.

Lift one's hand against Strike.

Light **Come to light** Be revealed, exposed.

In a good light Favourably.

In the light of In view of. With the help given by.

Light-fingered Thievish.

Light upon Discover by chance.

Make light of Treat as of little consequence.

Shed *or* **throw (a flood of) light on** 1. [LIT] Light brilliantly.

2. [MET] Make clear and plain. Help to explain.

Strike a light Ignite a match.

The lighter side The more enjoyable or amusing aspect.

Like **Like; the like** A similar object; anything strongly resembling another of the same class.

Apples, pears, and the like.

Like father, like son The son is like (or as bad as) his father.

Like-minded Similar in their attitudes, views, etc.

Nothing like 1. Emphatic form of 'unlike'.

That picture is nothing like him.

2. Not nearly.

There were nothing like as many people as we expected.

Likelihood **In all likelihood** Very probably.
Similar to **in all probability.**

Likely **Likely enough** Fairly probable.

Lily **Gild** *or* **paint the lily** Improve what is already satisfactory.

Limit **Within limits** To some extent.

Line **All along the line** In every way. [Or. Military, the 'line' being the line of battle.]
Come into line Agree. Co-operate.
End of the line Point beyond which it is useless to go.
Hard line Uncompromising attitude.
In line for Likely to receive.
In line with In accordance with.
In the line of duty As part of one's duty.
In one's line Within one's knowledge, experience or interests.
Toe the line Conform.

Linen **Wash one's dirty linen in public** Reveal discreditable matters about oneself.

Lion **The lion's share** The greatest or most valuable portion.

Lips **Lick one's lips** Express pleasure in anticipation of something.
Smack one's lips Show eager anticipation.
Stiff upper lip Fortitude.

Little **Little by little, inch by inch,** *etc*. A small amount or distance, repeated until a large total is reached.
Little by little the truth is being made public.

Live **Live down** By good conduct, etc., enable people to forget some past failure.
If I fail, I shall never live it down.
Live and learn Way of greeting some new fact or piece of knowledge, etc.
Live and let live Be sympathetic to the failings of others.
Live up to Prove oneself worthy of.
Within living memory Within the memory of people still alive.

Lo! **Lo and behold!** An exclamatory introduction expressing surprise ('Lo' is a shortened form of *loke*, Anglo-Saxon for 'look'.)
And lo and behold, he changed his mind.

Load **Take a load off one's mind** Relieve one of anxiety.

Lock **Lock, stock and barrel** Entirely; wholly. [Or. Military. A gun or pistol consists of three principal parts—the lock, containing the mechanism; the stock, or wooden portion; and the barrel.]

Under lock and key Secure.

Log **Sleep like a log** Sleep very soundly.

Loin **Gird up one's loins** Prepare.

Loggerheads

At loggerheads Disagreeing; quarrelling.

Long **In the long run** At the end; after a number of other things have happened.

In the long run, honesty is always the best policy.

Long ago A long time ago; in the distant past.

Long arm of coincidence Applied to coincidences in general, the 'long arm' referring to the surprising and abnormal way in which they occur.

I hadn't seen him for years, but by the long arm of coincidence we met on a train journey.

Long-drawn (out) Long continued or sustained.

A long-drawn cry sounded across the sea.

Long duration *or* **short duration** A long (or short) period during which some event continues.

Their journey was not, however, of long duration.

Long odds Unfavourable chances; an improbable event. [Or. Betting.]

The long and the short of it The whole position or situation briefly stated.

Long shot See under *Shot*.

Long-standing Existing for a long time.

Long-suffering Patient and enduring.

Long-term plans Plans which extend a long way into the future.

Long-winded Verbose; wearingly talkative.

Look **Look about** *or* **around one** Study one's surroundings and prospects.

I want to look around for a month or two before I start at university.

Look after Take care or charge of.

We promised to look after the cats while the family was abroad.

Look back Contemplate the past.

If we look back, we realize the changes war has made.

Look bad Appear discreditable.

Look before you leap Take care before committing yourself to action.

Look daggers Regard fiercely and bitterly; look at with fury and hatred.

Look down upon *or* **down one's nose at** Scorn; regard with contempt.

Look for 1. Search for.
She looked for the missing money.
2. Expect.
I look for a number of improvements when the Government changes.

Look for a needle in a haystack Look for a small object in a large place, or for one person among many, etc.

Look forward to Regard some future event with pleasure.
I look forward to your visit next week.

Look a gift horse in the mouth See under *Horse.*

Look good Appear creditable.

Look into Examine; scrutinize.
He promised to look into my complaint.

Look on the bright side Regard cheerfully; see the best in any situation.

Look one in the eye *or* **face** Not be ashamed.

Look one's age In appearance to give impression of being as old as one actually is.

Look the other way [LIT] Turn one's head. [MET] Refrain from noticing.

Look out! (*exclamation*) Beware, be careful!
Look out, or you'll be run over!

Look out; keep a sharp lookout for Watch for.

Look-out (Noun) Affair; concern; business.
Joan has decided to go to South America. What happens there is her own look-out.

Look over 1. [LIT]
He looked over the wall.
2. [MET] Scan; examine.
I'd be glad if you'll look over these letters.

Look small Appear insignificant.

Look to it Note; take careful action.

Look up 1. Refer to books, etc., to ascertain some fact.
I'll look it up in the encyclopaedia.
2. Visit an acquaintance whom one hasn't seen for some time.
3. Improve; appear more cheerful.
The business is beginning to look up.

Look up to Regard with awe or respect.

Not to like the look of something Find something alarming.

Loose **(Play) fast and loose** Act irresponsibly.

At a loose end Idle; having no definite object.

Loosen person's tongue Make person talk freely.

Lord **Drunk as a lord** Very drunk.

Lord it over Behave arrogantly, as a person of importance.

Lose **Lose face** Be humiliated. Lose reputation or credibility. Hence **loss of face.**

Lose ground Suffer, by degrees, loss of reputation, health or position.

Lose heart Become discouraged.

Lose one's head Suffer panic or loss of control.

Lose one's hearing Become deaf.

Lose oneself in Be preoccupied by.

Losing battle A hopeless cause.

Loss; Lost **At a loss** 1. For less than the cost price.

I sold the goods at a loss.

2. Temporarily unable to act or reply; undecided.

I was at a loss to answer him.

A lost cause A movement, project or agitation, etc., which has no longer any chance of becoming effective.

Lost in admiration So overcome with admiration that one cannot express one's emotions.

Lot **Throw** *or* **cast in one's lot with** Decide to join, or to share the fortunes of.

Draw lots *or* **cast lots** Decide by throwing dice or by some similar method of chance.

The whole lot The whole number.

Love **Calf-love** Adolescent love; a young man's first love affair; usually not very serious.

Labour of love Work done out of love for someone or something, rather than for money.

For love or money By any means.

I've tried all the shops, but I can't get any cream for love or money.

No love lost Dislike, unfriendliness.

Lovely **Lovely and** Very.

The sun's lovely and warm.

Low **At a low ebb** [LIT] A condition existing when an ebbing tide has left the water in a river at its lowest point. [MET] Feeble, almost exhausted.

In low spirits Depressed.

Luck **As luck would have it** Unfortunately.

Down on one's luck In an unfortunate state.
Hard luck Unfortunate.
Push one's luck Take more risks than necessary.
Run of luck A series of lucky events. Used also in the opposite sense—**a run of bad luck.** [Or. Gambling].
Take pot luck Accept impromptu hospitality without a definite invitation. Dine on whatever happens to be cooking in the pot. Take any sort of risk.
Try one's luck Attempt success.
With luck If all goes well.
Worse luck Exclamation meaning 'Unfortunately'.

Lump **A lump in one's throat** A sense of pity, producing a desire to weep.
Lump sum The whole amount at once.
They paid him in a lump sum all that was owing.
Lump together Merge.
If we lump all our money together, we shall have over £5.

Lying **Refuse to take something lying down** Object strenuously to something. Resist something strongly.

M

Mad **Drive** *or* **send mad** Cause to become mad.
The noise of that radio is driving me mad.
Like mad With tremendous energy.
He ran like mad.
Mad as a march hare Utterly and completely mad. [Or. Hares are supposed to be particularly wild and shy during March, their mating-season.]
Mad about Infatuated with.
Mad on Extremely or wildly interested in.
My daughter's mad on dancing.

Maiden **Maiden name** The surname of a woman before she was married. (Fr. *née*.)
Maiden speech The first speech made in Parliament by a member.
Maiden voyage The first voyage made by a vessel in the sea or air.
(*Note* that in all the above cases 'maiden' is used in the sense of 'first'.)
Maiden over An 'over' (or six consecutive balls) in which no runs have been made. [Or. Cricket.]

Main **In the main** Chiefly.

Main chance; have an eye to the main chance Be alert to one's own interests.

Majority **Attain one's majority** Reach the age at which one is legally regarded as an adult.

Made **Made for** Ideally suited to.

Self-made man *or* **woman** One who has made own success (in life, business).

Make **Make after** Follow quickly.

Make as if Pretend.

Make-believe Pretence.

Make the best of it Accept misfortune or discomfort cheerfully.

We got soaked to the skin, but we made the best of it.

Make a clean breast See under *Breast.*

Make a clean sweep See under *Sweep.*

Make do Use as the best substitute available.

We hadn't time for lunch, but we made do with sandwiches.

Make an example of Punish as warning to others.

Make eyes at Gaze at lovingly or longingly.

Make fast Secure; fasten firmly.

They made fast the boat to the pier.

Make a fool of Cause to appear ridiculous.

Make for 1. Set out, usually quickly, in a particular direction.

The ships made for the harbour because of the storm.

2. Help to make or maintain.

The minister's speech does not make for peace.

Make free with Use freely, without asking permission.

Make friends with Become friendly with.

Make fun of Ridicule; joke about.

Make a fuss of Treat with unusual and excessive courtesy and kindness,

The family made a tremendous fuss of John when he came back from his year abroad.

Make good 1. Repair; put back something that has been destroyed; restore.

2. Recover a lost reputation.

Make a habit of doing Become accustomed to do.

Make headway *or* **head (against)** Proceed, usually in spite of any difficulties or obstructions. [Or. Nautical.]

Make head or tail of See under *Head.*

Make it up Become friendly again after a quarrel, or

agree after a dispute.

Make light *or* **little of** Treat as something of little importance.

The athlete made light of his injury.

Make money Earn money. Show a profit.

Make the most of Put to the best use possible.

Make much of Make special efforts to please; treat with conspicuous kindness and respect.

Very similar to **make a fuss of.**

Make a name for oneself Create one's reputation.

Make no bones Show no hesitation or fear of the consequences.

Make nothing of 1. Treat as trivial or of no importance. Similar to **make little of.**

2. Completely fail to understand.

What do you make of it? What do you deduce from it? Do you understand it?

Make off Run away (usually as the result of some guilty act).

Make oneself scarce Disappear quickly; efface oneself.

We decided that it would be tactful to make ourselves scarce.

Make or break Succeed or fail. Also **make or mar.**

Make out 1. Comprehend; decipher.

2. Inscribe, write.

3. Imply; indicate.

Make over Make a formal gift of property.

Make a point of doing something Be careful to do something.

Make room for Allow space for person or thing by removing or crowding others.

Make so bold as to Take the liberty of. [Slightly formal and old f.]

May I make so bold as to suggest a compromise?

Make a splash See under *Splash.*

Make sure Ensure.

Make time for Act to provide an opportunity for discussion of, attention to, etc.

Make up 1. Invent; originate.

2. Complete.

3. Compensate for.

See **make it up.**

Make-up Cosmetics.

Make up to Flatter, attempt to please, in order to obtain favours.

Make a virtue of necessity Treat something one is obliged to do as if it were being done from choice.

Make way for Move away to allow something else to fill the place.

Makeshift **Makeshift** Inferior or temporary; substitute.
We will put up a makeshift roof till the other is mended.

Making **Be the making of** Will cause the success of. **In the making** Being made.

Man **As one man** Unanimously.

Every man-jack Everyone.

Man and boy Since childhood.

Man in the street Ordinary man.

A man of letters An author; one whose profession is that of a writer.

A man of straw A worthless person.

A man of his word One who is truthful and trustworthy, who does not break promises.

A man of the world One with worldly knowledge and experience.

Man-to-man Without prevarication.

Sort out the men from the boys Determine who is mature, brave, competent etc. and who is not.

To a man Everyone, without exception.

Manner **All manner of** All kinds of.

By no manner of means See under *Means*.

In a manner of speaking So to say. As it were.

To the manner born As if naturally or instinctively fitted for a position, etc.

Many **A good** *or* **great many** Very many.

Many a long day A long time.

Many's the time Frequently.

Mare **Mare's nest** Something which does not exist; a mere effort of the imagination. (A mare—female horse—has obviously no nest.)

Mark **Beside the mark** Unconnected with the subject being discussed.

Make one's mark Establish a reputation.

Mark down Reduce price.

A marked man One who has become notorious through his connection with some particular incident.

Mark my words Take particular note of what I am saying.

Mark time Deliberately wait, without progressing. [Or. Military. At the command 'Mark time' soldiers raise and lower their feet as if marching, but do not move forward.

Mark-up Sum added to ensure profit.

Overstep the mark Go beyond what is proper. Also **overshoot the mark**.

Up to the mark In a normal state of health; well. (This idiom is generally used in the negative.) See also under *Par*.

Wide of the mark Very inaccurate.
His guesses were all wide of the mark.

Market **Be in the market for** Be interested in buying.

Be on the market Be available for sale.

Put on the market Offer for sale.

Marrow **To the marrow** All the way through.

Martyr **Be a martyr to** Suffer severely from.

Mass **Masses of** A large number of.

Master **Master mind** (Noun) Chief planner, thinker or originator.

Master-mind (Verb) To be in control as master mind.

Master of oneself Capable of self-control; able to think and act coolly and logically.

Master-stroke An exceptionally shrewd or clever action.

Matter **For that matter** As far as that is concerned.

Matter of course An affair of normal routine; regularly.

Matter of fact Something which is established as truth (as opposed to opinion). Hence **as a matter of fact**: emphatic phrase stressing truth of an expression.

Matter-of-fact (Adjective) Commonplace; ordinary.

A matter of life and death Of vital and extreme importance.

The matter in question The affair being discussed or referred to.

No matter 1. In spite of.
I shall go, no matter what the weather may be.
2. Immaterial; having no importance.
I had something to say, but it's no matter (it doesn't matter).

What's the matter? What is concerning or occupying you?

What's the matter with it? What is wrong with it?

May **Be that as it may** Even so.

That is as may be That may be so.

Meal **Make a meal of** Find or create undue difficulties in; take a long time doing.

Square meal A full, complete meal.

Mealy **Mealy-mouthed** Applied to one who is a hypocrite or coward, and is afraid to speak honestly.

Mean **Mean well** Possess good intentions.

Means **By all means** 1. Indication of cordial assent.

Shall I ask him to come in? By all means.

2. By exerting every effort.

Try by all (or every) means to persuade him to come.

By all *or* **no manner of means** Indicating emphatic assent (or dissent).

By fair means or foul In any way possible.

By no means; not by any means Elaborated forms of 'not'.

By what means? By what method? How?

Means to an end An action merely leading to one's real object.

Meantime; **In the meantime; meanwhile** The period during
Meanwhile which an event has occurred; while this was happening; during the intervening time.

Similar to **for the time being** (under *Time*).

Measure **For good measure** To add something more than necessary.

In some measure To some extent.

Measure one's length Fall flat.

He staggered, and measured his length on the pavement.

Take measures to Take suitable action to.

Take person's measure Estimate the sort of person someone is.

Measure up to Reach the level or standard of.

Does the scenery measure up to your expectations?

Meat **Meat and drink** Very easy. Very enjoyable.

One man's meat is another man's poison What one person enjoys may be disliked by another.

Medicine **A dose of one's own medicine** Treatment that one is accustomed to give (rather than receive).

Take one's medicine 1. [LIT].

2. [MET] Suffer one's just deserts.

Meet **Meet half-way** Compromise.

Meet the case Suffice.

Meet with 1. Receive.

2. Be received with.

More than meets the eye Something suppressed or hidden.

Melt **In the melting-pot** Under reconsideration, and likely to be completely changed.

Melt away 1. [LIT] Disappear or change form by melting. 2. [MET] (Of person) Depart unobtrusively.

Melt down Reduce to a single mass by heating until it becomes fluid, and then allow to harden.

Memory **Burden one's memory** Cause to become a weight or burden on one's memory.

Commit to memory Similar to **learn by heart** (under *Heart*).

Within living memory During the lifetime of people now alive.

Mend **On the mend** Recovering from illness, injury or a period of weakness.

Mention **Not to mention** In addition to; distinct from.

Don't mention it A polite dismissal of apology or thanks. *'I am sorry to have troubled you.' 'Don't mention it.'*

Mercy **At the mercy of** Dependent upon; controlled by; in the power of.
The ship was at the mercy of the waves.

Left to the (tender) mercies *or* **mercy of** Abandoned to the (unpleasant) effect of.

Merry **Make merry** Rejoice.

Make merry at Make fun of. Laugh at.

Merry-making Rejoicing and festivities upon some special occasion.

Play merry hell with Cause considerable upset to.

Mess **Make a mess of** Bungle.

Mess up Bring muddle to.

Mete **Mete out** Distribute; give out. (Frequently applied to justice, punishment, etc.)

Method **There's method in his madness** What he says, plans, does (etc.) is not as mad as it appears.

Mettle **On one's mettle** Roused to the use of one's best efforts; prepared to do one's utmost.

Midsummer

Midsummer madness [LIT] Temporary madness, brought on by the conjunction of the full moon at midsummer and the heat of the season. [MET] Applied to any sort of crazy idea or plan.

Midway Halfway; half the distance.
He started to cross the road, but stopped midway.

Might **Might and main** All one's powers or strength.

Mildly **Put something mildly** Make a deliberate or ironic understatement.
When the telephone rang in the middle of the night, I was rather irritated, to put it mildly.

Mile **A mile away** *or* **off** Easily.
You could see a mile off that the accident would happen.

Milk **Milk-and-water** Feeble; weak.
Also **Wishy-washy.**
Milk of human kindness Genuine and natural kindness towards one's fellow-creatures.
No use crying over spilt milk Useless to bewail mistake that cannot be put right.

Mill **Go** *or* **be put through the mill** Undergo any rigorous experience, usually at someone's hands.
Mill-stone round one's neck Liability.

Mince **Not to mince matters** *or* **words** Not to speak tactfully or politely; to be plain and direct.
I told him, without mincing matters, that I wasn't satisfied.
Make mincemeat of 'Mincemeat' consists [LIT] of ingredients chopped (or minced) into very small pieces for cooking. The phrase is used [MET] to indicate the destruction of arguments, plans, etc.

Mind **Apply** *or* **give one's mind to** Consider carefully; concentrate one's attention upon.
Bear *or* **keep in mind** Retain in one's memory; remember.
Be in two minds Be undecided.
Be of the same mind Agree.
Bring to mind Recollect. Remember.
Call to mind Recollect. Remember.
Cast one's mind back Recall the past.
Change one's mind Adopt new opinion.
Come into one's mind Be remembered.
Do you mind? Don't do or say that.
Go out of one's mind 1. Forget.
2. [LIT] Go insane. [MET] Become intensely irritated, confused, etc.
Give one's mind to See **apply one's mind.**
Give a piece of one's mind Blame; express one's opinion candidly (and, usually, critically or adversely).
Have a good mind to Be much inclined to.
Have a mind of one's own Be able to form one's own opinions.

Have half a mind to Be strongly disposed to do something, but unlikely to do it.

Have it in mind to Intend to.

Have on one's mind Be preoccupied by.

In one's right mind Sane. Generally used negatively, an alternative being **out of one's mind.**

Keep one's mind on Think constantly about.

Know one's own mind Have clear and fixed opinions.

Make up one's mind Come to a decision.

Mind 1. Take into one's care or charge.
The mother asked the girl to mind the baby for an hour.
2. Show care about; be careful of.
Mind the wet paint.
3. Regret; object to.
I hope you won't mind my going out.

Mind's eye Imagination.

Mind one's own business Do not concern oneself in other people's affairs.

Mind (out for) Be on one's guard against.

A mind to A liking or desire to.

Of one *or* **the same mind** Having the same opinions.

One-track mind A mind, or personality, exclusively committed to one preoccupation (e.g. money, work, sex, etc.).

Out of one's mind See **in one's right mind.**

Out of sight, out of mind That which cannot be seen may be forgotten.

Presence of mind Mental alertness and an immediate response to an emergency.

Prey on one's mind Cause deep and prolonged mental distress.

Put one's mind to Concentrate on.

Put out of one's mind Take no account of.

Put person in mind of Make person remember.

Read one's mind Know what one is thinking.

Set one's mind on Wish to attain.

Speak one's mind Give one's frank opinion.

To my mind In my opinion. According to my judgment.

Mine **Mine of information** Source of much information.

Mint **Mint of money** A very large sum of money. [Or. The Royal Mint is where English coins are made.]

Mischief **Make mischief** Intentionally cause discord and
unhappiness.

Miss **Give a miss** Avoid.

Not miss much 1. Be absent from something
uninteresting.

2. Be alert.

Mistake **And** *or* **make no mistake!** An idiom used entirely
for emphasis.

There's no mistaking It is impossible to mistake.

Mix **Mixed blessing** Having advantages and disadvantages.

Moment **At the moment** At present.

Half a moment A very short time.

In a moment In a short while.

Unguarded moment A moment in which one
has forgotten to be careful in speech or action.

Money **Hush-money** Money paid to prevent a secret being
revealed.

Money is no object The shortage of money is no
hindrance.

Pin-money Money supplied for minor pleasures and
amusements. [Or. Pin-money was the term originally
applied to money supplied to women to purchase the
ornate and beautiful pins that jewellers were allowed
to offer for sale on the first two days of the year.]

Pocket-money Small sums given to children, usually
each week, for their personal expenditure.

Month **Month of Sundays** A long and indefinite period.

Moon **Moonshine** Unreal, fantastic and untrue statement,
ideas, plans, etc.

Moon-struck Dazed, incapable of thought.

Once in a blue moon Very infrequently.

Morning **Morning coffee** Coffee drunk halfway through the
morning, i.e. about eleven o'clock.

Morning dress Official and formal clothing worn by
men during the day (as opposed to evening dress), i.e.
black coat with short 'tails', black waistcoat and dark
grey trousers.

Morning tea Tea drunk in one's bedroom before
dressing in the morning.

Most **At the most; at most** At the highest; as the
limit.

For the most part In most circumstances; usually.
For the most part, we go away at weekends.

Mother earth The ground.

M

Mother of pearl The shining inner lining of oyster and similar shells, extensively used for ornamental purposes.

Mother-tongue The language spoken in one's native land.

Motion **Go through the motions** Do something without serious purpose.

Set in motion Begin.

Mount **Mount up** Increase; accumulate.

I'm afraid our expenses are mounting up rather fast.

Mountain **Mahomet and the mountain** Several expressions include these terms: Mahomet = person who can't get his own way; mountain = something inevitable, unavoidable, fixed.

Make a mountain out of a molehill Make much out of very little; greatly exaggerate.

Move mountains Make every effort.

Mouth **By word of mouth** By speech; orally.

Down in the mouth Depressed; despondent.

Make one's mouth water Create pleasurable sense of anticipation.

Take the words out of someone's mouth Say what someone was about to say.

Move **Make a move** Go.

Move heaven and earth Make every possible effort; use every available means.

Move off Depart.

Move on Change one's position.

Mow **Mow down** Cut, with wide sweeping strokes, as wheat, etc., is cut with a scythe. Gunfire is frequently said to 'mow down' advancing troops.

Much **Not come to much** Have little success.

Not much to look at Insignificant. Not striking or attractive.

Muddle **Muddle through** Achieve one's objectives without showing very much skill in doing so.

Music **Face the music** Be prepared to accept criticism, usually as consequence of one's own actions.

Music to one's ears A pleasure to hear.

Must **It must needs be** It will inevitably be. [Old f.]

It must needs be some weeks before we receive a reply from Australia.

Needs must when the Devil drives If this is inevitable, I must accept it as such.

Mustard **Keen as mustard (on)** Very eager (about).
Muster **Pass muster** Be accepted as adequate.

N

Nail **Hard as nails** Very tough. (Applied to people.)
Hit the nail on the head See under *Hit.*
Nail-biting Such as to cause nervous anxiety.
Nail in one's coffin Something that will shorten life—drink, anxiety, etc.—or destroy one's reputation.
Nail one's colours to the mast Publicly demonstrate one's allegiance. Refuse to surrender or modify one's opinions or principles. [Or. Naval. During a battle the colours, or flag, of a ship were in the past frequently nailed to the mast to make it impossible to lower them as a signal of surrender.]
On the nail Promptly; immediately.
He pays his debts on the nail.

Namby-pamby
Feeble; effeminate. Insipid. [Or. The seventeenth-century poet Ambrose (sneeringly nicknamed 'Namby' as a baby would pronounce it) Phillips.]

Name **Have to one's name** Own.
Make a name for oneself Gain a reputation.
Take one's name in vain Refer to one lightly.
You name it No matter what.

Nap **Catch napping** See under *Catch.*

Narrow **A narrow escape, majority,** *etc.* One which nearly did not occur.
I had a narrow escape from being run over by a bus this morning.
A narrow margin Very little (space, etc.).
John passed the examination by a narrow margin.
A narrow squeak A success or escape only just attained.
We won the game, but it was a narrow squeak.

Nature **In the nature of things** Part of normal circumstances, routine, instinct, etc.
It's in the nature of things for children to behave in that way.

Near **Near by** *or* **near at hand** Close; a short distance away.
Near the mark Nearly or approximately correct.
Near miss Narrow failure to strike, hit, collide etc.

A near *or* **close thing** A success which was very nearly a failure.

I ran all the way and caught the train, but it was a near thing.

Necessity **Make a virtue of necessity** See under **Make.**

Necessity is the mother of invention New ways of doing things are usually contrived because of a pressing need.

Of necessity Unavoidably.

Neck **Neck and crop** Entirely. [Or. The 'crop', or gorge, is the lower part of a bird's neck.]

Neck and neck Side by side; level.

It was a neck and neck race.

Neck or nothing Desperate; risking everything. [Or. Racing. To win by the length of the horse's neck, or not at all.]

Needle **Needle in a haystack** Thing impossible to find because of its concealment among many other things.

Sharp as a needle 1. [LIT] Very sharp.
2. [MET] Acute.

Needless **Needless to say** It is unnecessary to say.

Negative **In the negative** No.

Neither **Neither here nor there** See under **Here.**

Nerves **Bundle of nerves** Very nervous person.

Get on one's nerves Irritate (usually by the repetition of some annoying action, usually slight).

Have the nerve to Have the courage, or impertinence, to.

Nest **Feather one's nest** See under **Feather.**

Nest egg [LIT] An artificial egg left in the nest to encourage the hen to further laying. [MET] Money saved for one's old age or for some specific purpose in the future.

Never **Never mind** Do not trouble or concern yourself.

Never say die! Never give up hope of success.

Well I never! Expression of surprise.

New **New broom** A newcomer who intends to demonstrate his efficiency, ideas, etc. [Or. The proverb 'A new broom sweeps clean'.]

New-fangled A slightly contemptuous term applied to any new invention or method, usually of a minor type.

Next **Next door to** [LIT] In the adjoining house. [MET] Any form of nearness.

Her statements are next door to lying.

Next to nothing Practically nothing.

What (ever) next? Expression of surprise, literally

suggesting 'What can occur subsequently which can possibly be more absurd, surprising, shocking, etc.?'

Nicety **To a nicety** Precisely; exactly.
The coat will fit you to a nicety.

Nick **In the nick of time** Just in time, at the right and vital moment. [Or. The old custom of marking long sticks with 'nicks' or notches at intervals to indicate numbers.]

Night **Have a good** *or* **bad night** Sleep well (or badly).
Night out Evening (not night) away from home, for enjoyment.
Overnight [LIT] The period between one day and the next. [MET] In a very brief time.
He became famous overnight.
Stay the night Remain until following day.

Niminy-piminy
Irritatingly affected and trivial.

Nine **Nine day's wonder** See under *Wonder*.
Nine times out of ten Nearly always.
Nine to five Normal hours of work.
Nineteen to the dozen Very vigorously.
Up to the nines Magnificently; gorgeously. [Or. The Oriental regard for the number nine as indicative of the highest splendour and generosity, e.g. presenting a guest with nine camels, nine cases of jewels, etc.] Usually **dressed up to the nines.**

Nip **Nip and tuck** Same as **neck and neck.**
Nip in the bud End any project before it has a chance of maturing.

Nit **Nit-picking** Trivial and irritating fault-finding.

No **No one else** No other person.
No such thing An emphatic negative.
He said I had promised to go, but I told him I had done no such thing.
There's no accounting for taste Some people have very unexpected or odd likes and dislikes.
Will not take no for an answer Persist, despite refusals.

Nod **Nodding acquaintance** Slight acquaintance with person, or slight knowledge of thing.
On the nod Without objection.
The committee approved the whole plan on the nod.

Noise **Noise abroad** Cause to be widely known.

Nose **Cut off one's nose to spite one's face** Commit, through revenge or spite, some foolish action which injures oneself.
Follow one's nose Go straight forward.

Keep one's nose clean Avoid trouble or risk.

Keep one's nose to the grindstone Make one work incessantly.

Lead by the nose See under *Lead*.

Look down one's nose at Scorn.

Pay through the nose Pay far too much; pay extortionately.

You'll have to pay through the nose if you stay at that hotel.

Plain as the nose on one's face Very obvious.

Poke one's nose into Interfere with, pry or intrude into.

Rub person's nose in it Punish person (excessively). Humiliate person by reminding him of mistake.

Thumb one's nose at Express or show scorn for.

Turn up one's nose at Sneer at; scorn.

Under one's nose A near and obvious place.

Not **Not in the least; not a bit** Not to any degree whatever.

I was not in the least afraid.

Not so No; a general negative.

Note **Strike a wrong note** Be inappropriate.

Strike the right note Act suitably.

Take note (of) Pay attention (to).

Nothing **Can make nothing of** Cannot understand.

Count for nothing Not be appreciated. Carry no influence

For nothing 1. Without payment
2. Without result.

Have nothing to do with Not be concerned with.

Nothing to choose between them; nothing in it Practically equal.

Both brothers are clever; there is nothing to choose between them.

Nothing for it No option; no other choice.

If I fail to get this job, there'll be nothing for it but to emigrate.

Nothing like as *or* **so good as** In no way as good as.

Nothing more nor less; nothing short of Completely; absolutely.

The film was nothing more nor less than a disaster.

There's nothing to it It is easy.

To say nothing of Not to mention.

Notice **At short notice** At the end of an unexpectedly short period.

We have to leave for America at short notice.

Till further notice Until a future time to be decided.

Now **(Every) now and again** *or* **and then** From time to time

For now Until later.

Just now Almost, but not quite at the present time.
Now or never The unique opportunity.
Null **Null and void** Non-existent and consequently non-effective. [Or. Legal.]
Nut **A hard nut to crack** A difficult problem or person to deal with, or matter to decide.
Nutshell **In a nutshell** Stated very briefly.
This book will explain the whole problem in a nutshell.

O

Oar **Put in one's oar** Intervene; interfere.
Rest on one's oars Cease work for a time.
Oats **Sow one's wild oats** Commit the usual follies of youth.
Obligations **Discharge one's obligations** Repay what is due.
Under an obligation Compelled, either by law or by one's sense of duty.
Please don't feel under any obligation to come.
Oblivion **Fall** *or* **sink into oblivion** Become completely forgotten.
Occasion **Have occasion** Have need, reason, justification.
If the occasion arises If there is reason, opportunity.
On occasion Sometimes; when necessary.
Rise to the occasion Show the required qualities.
Take the occasion to Seize the opportunity to.
Occupy **Occupy one's time, energies, talents,** *etc.* 'Occupy' here used in the sense of 'employ', 'use'.
Occur **It occurs to me; it has just occurred to me** The idea has come to me; I have just realized.
It occurs to me that if we go to the concert tonight we won't get back in time.
Odd **Odd** is added to numbers to indicate additional unspecified amounts of lower denomination. Thus *Forty-odd chairs* means any number between forty and fifty; *five pounds odd* means five pounds and some pence.
Odd man out Person unlike others in a group.
Odds The terms upon which one may bet. **'Long odds'** means that the chances of winning are considered very slight, and the phrase is used to indicate improbability.
It's long odds against Arthur coming home from Australia this year.
'The odds', on the other hand, may imply the reverse, a probable event.
The odds are that Jim will be able to come.

What's the odds! What does it matter!

Odds and ends Small, unclassified objects; what remains when more important things have been dealt with.

Odds-on Likely to succeed.

Over the odds More than the normal price.

Odour **In bad odour** Unpopular; regarded unfavourably.

Odour of sanctity (Disagreeable) sense of one's holiness.

Off **Badly off** Poor.

Be off 1. An imperative order to depart.

2. Depart.

I must be off to catch my train.

3. Be unfit to eat or drink; stale. (Also **go off.**)

Don't eat that meat—it was bought last week, and must be (have gone) off by now.

Off and on From time to time.

Off colour Slightly unwell.

Off one's food Disinclined to eat; without an appetite.

Off one's guard In a state of relaxation and unawareness.

Off one's hands Disposed of.

Off-hand 1. Without preparation; impromptu.

I can't give you the figures off-hand; I shall have to look them up.

2. Casual and irresponsible.

Offshoot A branching-off; a lesser concern or business which has developed from the original one.

Off the beaten track In a remote place.

Off the map Vanished. Not existing.

Off the point Irrelevant.

Well off 1. Rich.

2. In comfortable and satisfactory circumstances.

You shouldn't grumble about the house; you don't realize when you're well off.

On the off chance In the hope (usually faint).

Often **As often as not** Occurring on about half of the possible occasions.

Every so often Occasionally

More often than not Usually.

Once too often In a way bringing failure.

Oil **Burn the midnight oil** Stay up late to work or study.

Oil and water Applied to two dissimilar or irreconcilable things, people, points of view, etc.

Oil the wheels Make things work well.

Pour oil on trouble waters Speak or act soothingly and tactfully in order to bring a quarrel to an end. [Or. It is stated that a young eighth-century priest was given by his bishop a bottle of oil to pour on the sea if it became rough, and actually calmed the waves by this means. It has been proved that oil sprayed upon the surface does help to calm a high sea.]

Ointment **Fly in the ointment** See under *Fly.*

Old **Of old** Belonging to the distant past.

An old hand Person very skilled or experienced at something.

Old hat Out of date. Well known.

Old head See under *Head.*

Old as the hills Very old indeed. Frequently applied to an out-of-date object.

Old maid An elderly spinster, or one with fixed habits. [Old f.]

Old stager Similar to **old hand.**

Olive **Olive-branch** A gesture of peace. [Or. The olive-branch was, in the past, a symbol of peace.]

On **On and off** Intermittently; occasionally.

Once **All at once** 1. Suddenly.
2. All together.

At once Immediately.

Just this once On this occasion (and no other).

Once and for all Finally.

Once bitten, twice shy Pain, loss, etc., teaches caution.

Once in a blue moon Very rarely. Similar to **a month of Sundays.**

Once in a way *or* **while** Occasionally, but not often.

Once or twice A few times.

Once upon a time At some period in the past.

One **One and all** Everyone.

One by one Singly.

One-sided (**agreement, treaty,** *etc.*) Made from one point of view and for the advantage of one party only. (Present-day official equivalent, 'unilateral'.)

Open **Open and above-board** Enitirely frank and candid. *He was entirely open and above-board in his statements.*

Open (**a discussion, proceedings**) Begin.

Open one's eyes to Make one aware.

Open the door to Lead to; encourage; result in.

Open-mouthed Showing surprise.

Open secret A fact supposed to be secret, but known to everybody; no secret at all.

Open sesame Any simple and miraculous method of

solving a problem. [Or. From the story of 'Ali Baba and the Forty Thieves', in which a cave containing immense treasure could be entered only by the utterance of those words.]

The Chancellor thinks that taxing the rich is the open sesame to universal prosperity.

Open to Ready to receive

Open with Frank and honest in dealings with.

With open arms Enthusiastically. Heartily.

The hotel welcomed us with open arms.

With (one's) eyes open Aware of the consequences, implications, etc.

Opinion **Be of the opinion** Believe; consider.

Golden opinions Very great admiration; general praise.

The new President has already won golden opinions, even from his political opponents.

In my opinion I think.

Matter of opinion Subject for dispute. Opposite of **matter of fact.**

Pass an opinion Express an opinion or view.

I don't know enough about paintings to pass an opinion.

Opportunity

Take *or* **seize the opportunity** Make use of a particular moment.

May I take this opportunity of expressing our gratitude for your kindness.

Opposition **Meet with opposition** Be opposed.

Option **Have no option but to** Must.

Keep *or* **leave one's options open** Refrain from committing oneself.

Order **Order about** Domineer by giving orders.

Order of the day The current fashion.

In good order Fit for use.

In order 1. In succession; as pre-arranged plan.

The candidates will be interviewed in alphabetical order.

2. Tidy, neat.

Please see that this room is in order when the visitors arrive.

3. Officially correct.

You will be in order if you speak after the chairman.

In working order Ready for use.

On order Requested from the manufacturer but not yet supplied.

Our new cooker has now been on order for five weeks.

Out of order 1. The reverse of **in order** (2).
All these papers are out of order.
2. The reverse of **in order** (3).
You will be out of order if you interrupt the Chairman.
Take orders from Obey orders given by.
Take (**holy**) **orders** Become a clergyman.

Ordinary **In the ordinary way** Normally.
Ordinary run of things (*or* **course of events**)
Events which may be expected to happen normally.
In the ordinary run of things I play tennis nearly every weekend.
Out of the ordinary Unusual; exceptional.
It is quite out of the ordinary for snow to fall during the summer in Britain.

Other **On the other hand** On the contrary.
The other day Recently; not long ago.

Out **All out** Using all one's speed or effort.
Be out 1. Be mistaken in one's judgment.
2. Not at home.
I am sorry we were out when you called.
Flat out At full speed. Using all one's energies.
Have it out See under *Have.*
Out and about Outside, in motion.
Out-and-out Thoroughly, completely.
Out-at-elbows Shabby; wearing torn and ragged clothes.
Out for Engaged in seeking.
He's out for all the credit he can get.
Out of 1. From.
He did it out of kindness.
2. Without any (applied to something normally available).
The grocer was out of coffee.
See **out of stock.**
3. Having no share or part in.
Out of breath Breathless.
Out of character Not typical.
His behaviour yesterday was very out of character.
Out of condition 1. As **out of sorts,** but applying particularly to animals.
2. Unfit for special exertion, because untrained.
Out of date Belonging to the past; unfashionable.
This guide-book is completely out of date.
Out of doors In the open air; exposed to the weather.

Out of joint Restless, uncomfortable, and generally unsatisfactory.

Out of one's mind [LIT] Insane. [MET] Extremely foolish or rash.

Out of place See under *Place.*

Out of pocket See under *Pocket.*

Out of print Term applied to a book when all copies are sold and no more will be printed.

Out of sight Invisible.

Out of sorts See under *Sort.*

Out of the question See under *Question.*

Out of stock Not available, owing to supplies being exhausted.
I am sorry, but that brand of cigarettes is out of stock.
Similar to **out of** (2).

Out of training Similar to **out of condition** (2).

Out of one's way 1. On a detour.
It's a little out of my way, but I'll drive you there.
2. To some trouble, inconvenience.
The neighbours went out of their way to be helpful when we first came to live here.

Out of the way 1. Unusual.
It was an out-of-the-way request.
2. Remote.
The house was in an out-of-the-way village
3. In a position which causes no obstruction.
Please put the cushion out of your way.

Out of the wood Freed from one's trouble and difficulties.

Out of work Without employment.

Out to Striving to.

Will out Will be discovered.

Over **All over** See under *All.*

Over and above In addition to; extra to.
I've been given a week's holiday over and above my normal entitlement.

Over and over (again) Repeatedly; many times.

Over one's head Beyond one's comprehension.

Overshoot; overshoot the mark Go too far; exceed; exaggerate.

Owe **Owe it to oneself** Consider it necessary to one's self-respect or happiness.
I owe it to myself to explain how it all happened.

Owing to Because of.

Own **Come into one's own** Reach position where one is properly appreciated.

Get one's own back on Revenge oneself on.

Hold one's own Maintain one's position.

He can hold his own in most sorts of argument.

On one's own By oneself; without companionship or assistance.

Off one's own bat On one's own initiative or responsibility.

Own up Make a confession.

P

Pace **Keep pace** Keep level; go at the same speed [LIT] and [MET].

Put through one's paces Test a person in order to discover his knowledge or ability. [Or. Horsemanship. A purchaser of a horse 'puts it through' its various 'paces'—walking, trotting, etc.]

Set the pace Establish speed of progress.

Stand the pace Maintain equality with others.

Pack **Packed like sardines** Crowded as closely together as sardines are in the tins in which they are sold.

Packed out Very crowded.

Pack of lies Many lies.

Pack one's bags Get ready to depart.

Pack up Finish. Go out of action.

Send packing Dismiss peremptorily.

Paddle **Paddle one's own canoe** Manage one's own affairs without help or interference.

Pain **Be at** *or* **take pains to** Take trouble to.

I was at great pains to make the occasion a success.

Get for one's pains Receive for one's exertions or trouble.

All he got for his pains was ingratitude.

On pain of Incurring punishment by.

Paint **Not so black as is painted** Not as bad as represented.

Pale **Beyond the pale** Outside the normal limits of acceptable behaviour.

Palm **Grease one's palm** Bribe one.

In the palm of one's hand Under one's control.

Palm off on Substitute something of inferior value. (A conjurer 'palms', or conceals in the palm of his hand, a card or other small object he does not wish the audience to see.)
I asked for butter, but they palmed off margarine on me.
Palmy days Times of great prosperity.

Paper **Commit to paper** Write, with the special object of keeping a record.
On paper By report. Hypothetically. To judge from what is written down, as distinct from what is known in practice.
On paper, these policies seem very sound.
Put pen to paper Begin to write.

Par **Below par** Below the expected standard.
On a par with On the same terms as.
That remark is on a par with his normal behaviour.
Up to par At the expected level.

Parallel **Draw a parallel** Compare to indicate similarity.

Parcel **Parcel out** Divide and distribute in portions.

Pare **Pare down** Reduce by degrees. ('Pare' is to peel or shave off the surface.)
We have pared down expenses to the limit.

Parlour **Parlour tricks** Minor social accomplishments—amateur singing, playing, etc. Now used ironically to mean minor roguery or incompetence.

Parrot-fashion
As a parrot talks; from memory, with little or no regard to the real meaning.

Part **For my part** As far as I am concerned.
For the most part In most cases.
Many parts Many abilities.
On the part of Coming from.
Part and parcel An essential and necessary part.
Part with Surrender.
Take in good part Not be offended at.
Take the part of Support. Back up.

Parthian **A Parthian shot** A parting retort. (Or. The Parthians used to fire arrows as they galloped away from their enemies.)

Partial **Be partial to** Like; enjoy.
I am rather partial to duck and green peas.

Particular **In particular** Especially.

Parting **Parting shot** Remark made when one is leaving (usually sign of defiance, or so that no response is possible).

Parting of the ways Point at which people disagree.

Partner **Partner in crime** 1. [LIT] Person with whom one commits crime.

2. [MET] (Usually jocular) Companion. Friend.

Sleeping partner Fellow-owner (of firm) who does no work (i.e. is merely investor).

Pass **Make a pass** Make a threatening movement or gesture towards.

Pass *(at cards)* Refrain from playing at that particular moment of the game.

Pass away, over Formal and rather old-f. phrase for 'die'.

Pass by Go past.

Pass for Be accepted as.

Pass one's comprehension Be more than one can understand.

Pass judgment Express a final and definite opinion.

Pass muster Be regarded as up to the necessary standards; just good enough. [Or. Military. Soldiers are 'mustered' and examined for correctness of uniform, etc., before going on parade.]

Pass off 1. Ignore; treat as if it were unimportant.
She hated his familiarity, but passed it off as a joke.
2. Intentionally convey a false impression concerning some person or object.
The boy was only twelve, but liked to pass himself off as much older.
3. Disappear by degrees or stages.
There was a thick mist at first, but it soon began to pass off.

Pass on 1. Go on. 2. Die. 3. Hand on.

Pass one's eye over Read quickly.

Pass out Finish military training successfully.

Pass over 1. Ignore.
2. Forgive; excuse.
3. Die.

A pretty pass *or* **mess!** A fine state of affairs! (Always used ironically.)
Things have come to a pretty pass!

Pass the time Spend or use up time.

Pass the time of day Spend a few moments in conversation.

Pass a remark Utter; make a remark.

Pass up 1. Hand over.
2. Ignore. Refuse.

Past **Not put it past (a person) to do** Not be surprised if (a person) did. Regard (a person) to be (normally) capable of doing.

Past-master An expert; a highly experienced person. [Or. A past-master in any guild or Association is one who has in the past achieved the position of Chairman or Master.]

Pat **Pat on the back** Expression of congratulation.

Patch **A good** *or* **bad patch** A period of good (or poor) luck, success, etc.

The school's football is going through a bad patch this season.

Hit *or* **strike a bad patch** Experience period of difficulty

In patches In places or at certain times.

Patch up (a quarrel, *etc.***)** Repair. Set to rights (usually hastily or temporarily).

Patience **Out of patience; having lost patience** With no patience left; exasperated.

Pave **Pave the way to (for)** Lead to; result in.

This treaty will pave the way to peace.

Paved with good intentions Well-meaning. [Or. Old saying, 'The road to hell is paved . . .']

Pay **The devil to pay** Tremendous trouble; a general up-heaval; serious consequences.

If you don't post that letter tonight, there'll be the devil to pay

Pay attention Listen and observe intently and carefully.

Pay attention to your teachers, and don't waste your time.

Pay back 1. Return what has been lent or given. 2. Punish, in return for some injury.

Pay for 1. Hand over money in payment for. 2. Be punished for.

Pay off 1. Pay the whole of what is due.
2. Naval. A ship is said to be 'paid off' when she returns to port and discharges her crew.
3. Succeed.

Pay out 1. [Nautical.] Slacken or loosen a rope.
2. Pay; disburse money.

Pay the piper Pay whatever the cost, financial or otherwise, may be. Be in a position of power because one has the authority (especially financial) to demand obedience. [Or. Abbrev. of 'He who pays the piper should call the tune'.]

Pay one's way Pay expenses out of one's income.

I doubt if that shop will ever pay its way.
Pay up Pay what one owes.
Put paid to Finished. Settled.
A broken leg put paid to his walking holiday.

Peace **Hold one's peace** Remain silent.
Keep the peace Refrain from quarrelling, or causing any other disturbance.
Make one's peace with Re-establish friendly relations with.
Pipe of peace American Indians celebrated the end of warfare between two tribes or two individuals by smoking a pipe as a symbol of their being at peace with their recent enemies. See **bury the hatchet.**

Pearl **Cast pearls before swine** Present or introduce something of value or beauty to those who are entirely unable to appreciate it. [Or. Biblical.]
Pearls of wisdom Wise sayings, advice, etc.

Peck **Pecking order** Hierarchy. [Or. Habit of birds in establishing order in which they eat.]

Pedal **Soft-pedal** Refrain from stressing.

Pedestal **Put on a pedestal** Admire. Respect.

Peg **Off the peg** Ready-made.
Peg away Continue steadily; persevere.
If you peg away long enough, you'll be able to learn any language.
Peg down Confine to a certain level.
Take one down a peg *or* **two** Humble someone

Penalty **Pay the penalty** Suffer what is due and inevitable as the result of an action.

Penny **In for a penny, in for a pound** (Frequently abbrev. to 'In for a penny'.) Being slightly involved, one may as well as involved still further.
In penny numbers In small quantities.
Like a bad penny Occurring or reappearing frequently when not wanted.
Penny-dreadful An old-f. term for cheap and sensational magazines.
A penny for your thoughts A facetious offer, made to arouse someone who has been silent and withdrawn.
Penny-pinching Mean(ness).
Penny wise Careful in saving small sums, but wasteful in large matters. [Or. Abbrev. of the proverb 'Penny wise and pound foolish'.]
A pretty penny A large sum of money.
Take care of the pennies (and the pounds will

take care of themselves) Care of small matters will reduce problems with large ones.

Turn *or* **earn an honest penny** Earn money (usually by extra work, or unusual methods).

Two (ten) a penny Common.

Period **At no period** At no time; never in the past.

Perish **Perish the thought** I do hope that that will not happen.

Person **In person** Personally.

Perspective **Put something in perspective** Place it in its context; view it in relation to other factors.

Pet **Pet aversion** Person or thing disliked all above.

Peter **Rob Peter to pay Paul** Take from one to give to another, thus not improving matters.

Pick **Pick and choose** Select carefully.

Pick holes in Criticize. Show the faults in.

Pick-me-up A quick restorative, after weakness or fatigue.

Pick of the bunch Best of those available.

Pick on Select from others, for special treatment.

Pick someone's brains Ask for his ideas or knowledge, with a view to using them oneself.

Pick a quarrel Deliberately begin a quarrel.

Pick up Acquire by chance; obtain casually.

Pick one's way *or* **one's steps** Walk deliberately and carefully among difficulties and obstructions.

Pick one's words Select carefully what one says.

Piece **All of a piece** All part of, or connected with.

A piece of one's mind One's candid opinion. A rebuke.

Go to pieces Deteriorate completely. Opposite, **pick up the pieces**: correct a damaged situation.

In one piece 1. [LIT] Unbroken.

2. [MET] Unharmed.

Pull to pieces Analyse; examine closely with the object of finding fault. Similar to **pick holes in.**

Say one's piece Say what one must say.

Pig **Make a pig of oneself** Eat too much.

Pig in a poke Something acquired without knowing its value, and without previous examination or knowledge. Usually used with the verb 'buy'. (The word 'poke' here means a pocket or small sack.)

Pigs might fly Wonders might occur. (Used ironically.)

Pile **Pile it on** Exaggerate.

Pile on the agony Increase or intensify distress or discomfort.

Pill **A bitter pill** An unpleasant, humiliating or intensely disappointing fact.

Sugar *or* **sweeten the pill** Do something to make an unpleasant task, statement, piece of news, etc., less so.

Pillar **From pillar to post** From one predicament or resource to another.

Pin **Pin down** 1. [LIT] Fix; fasten firmly.

2. [MET] Compel to deal with some particular fact or substantiate a statement.

The plumber promised to come, but it was difficult to pin him down to an exact time.

Pin one's faith on Believe in completely; trust absolutely.

Pin one's hopes on Attach one's hopes to; concentrate one's hopes on.

We are pinning our hopes on having a longer holiday next year.

Pin-money See under *Money.*

Pins and needles The tingling sensation felt in a limb which has become stiff and numb.

Pin-prick Small irritation.

Pinch **At a pinch** In an emergency; if absolutely necessary.

Where the shoe pinches Where the difficulty lies.

Pink **Pink of perfection** Absolutely and completely perfect. [Old. f.]

Pipe **Pipe up** Speak. Interrupt.

Piping **Piping hot** [LIT] Hot as water that is 'piping' or singing in a kettle just before reaching boiling-point.

Pistol **Hold pistol to one's head** Threaten one.

Pit **Pit against** Place in competition against; compel to fight.

Pit one's wits against Set about planning to defeat one by exercise of wits.

Pitch **Pitch black** Very black.

Pitch darkness Extreme darkness.

Pitch one's tent [LIT] To 'pitch' a tent is to erect it, usually for a limited period. [MET] To settle anywhere.

Pity **What a pity** *or* **shame!** A general expression of regret.

What a pity that you won't be able to come to the party.

More's the pity That makes matters worse.

Take pity on Feel sympathy for.

Place **In the first place** Firstly, at the beginning.

In the first place, I must explain that I can't speak English very well.

(Similarly second, third, etc., place.)

In place In the correct position.

In place of Instead of.

In places At some points (but not at others).

Out of place Unsuitable; in the wrong surroundings.

Take place Happen; occur.

The wedding will take place next week.

Plague **Like the plague** As much as possible. Usually **avoid person** *or* **thing like the plague.**

Plain **Plain dealing** Honest and open business methods.

Plain as a pikestaff Obvious; unmistakable. [Or. The pikestaff or long stick carried by pilgrims and on which was fastened a statement of their devotion to Christ.

Plain sailing A course of action without any difficulties.

Plain speaking Frank and honest speaking.

Play **Child's play** Extremely easy to perform or solve.

This crossword is child's play.

Play about *or* **around with** Fail to take seriously.

Play one's cards well *or* **badly,** *etc*. Make good (bad) use of one's opportunities.

Play down Reduce the importance of.

Play by ear 1. Perform on a musical instrument without having been taught or without using music. 2. Follow a course of action without any advance planning.

Play false Betray; cheat. See **double-cross** and **double-dealing**

Play fast and loose Act irresponsibly, without consideration for others, and regardless of one's promises.

Play fair Act honestly.

Play for time Act so as to gain time (to one's advantage).

Play to the gallery Try to achieve popularity; degrade one's abilities in order to obtain popularity [Or. Theatrical.]

Play the game [LIT] Observe the rules. [MET] Behave honourably.

Play into the hands of Behave so that one's actions are an advantage to someone else, usually an opponent or enemy.

Play off Use two opponents, one against the other, to one's own advantage.

Play safe Act cautiously.

Play second fiddle Be in a subordinate position. (The first fiddle is the most important member of an orchestra.)

Play truant Remain away from school.

Play upon Take advantage of.

Play upon words A pun; a verbal joke.

Play with fire Act dangerously.

Played out Exhausted; finished; out of date.

Plead **Plead the cause** Speak favourably for; help by supporting.

Please **Please oneself** Do as one desires.

I am going home—you can please yourself.

Pleased as Punch Extremely pleased.

Pledge **Pledge oneself** Make a solemn and formal promise.

Sign *or* **take the pledge** Formally undertake never to drink intoxicants—wine, spirits, beer, etc.

Plentiful **Plentiful as blackberries** Extremely plentiful. (Blackberries grow in large numbers in the English hedges in autumn.)

Plight **Plight one's troth** Make a formal promise to marry. [Or. Troth = truth.] [Old f.]

Plot **The plot thickens** The affair becomes more complicated and exciting.

Plough **Plough back** Reinvest (e.g. profits in a business) in order to increase further.

Plough a lone furrow Act without help.

Put one's hand to the plough Undertake a task.

Pluck **Pluck at one's heart strings** Appeal to one's deepest feelings.

Pluck up courage Acquire confidence and conquer fear.

Pocket **In one's pocket** In one's control.

Out of pocket Poorer financially.

I am ten pounds out of pocket as a result of the arrangement.

Out-of-pocket expenses Expenses incurred and paid in transacting business.

Put one's hand in one's pocket Spend or give money.

Pocket an insult Submit to an insult without protest; ignore it.

Pocket one's pride Become humble under compulsion or necessity.

Point **At the point of** On the verge of.

Beside the point Irrelevant.

Carry one's point See under *Carry*.

A case in point An example.
Many politicians make memorable speeches; Sir Winston Churchill was a case in point.

Come to the point Arrive at the crux, or what is really important.

Culminating point Climax.
The culminating point of the opera is the magnificient duet in the second act.

I take your point I accept what you say (but).

Make a point Contribute something to an argument.
I was able to make my point before the discussion ended.

Make a point of Take special care and trouble about.
She made a point of phoning her mother every week.

A moot point A point or detail which is unsettled and open to discussion or argument.

Not to put too fine a point on it To speak bluntly.

Off the point Irrelevant.

On the point of *On the verge of.*

The point The object.
The point of these discussions is that they enable the ministers concerned to get a clear idea of what is happening.

Point blank Direct; without any qualification. [Or. Gunnery. Fr. *point-blanc*—the white centre of the official target.]
He denied point-blank that he had ever entered the house.

Point a moral Emphasize some moral truth.

Point of honour Matter affecting one's honour

Point out Indicate; remind a person.
May I point out that you have not yet paid your bill.

Possession is nine points of the law If one possesses something, one is almost entitled to it. (Nine points = nine-tenths = virtually the whole.)

Score points off Win in parts of argument, discussion, debate etc.

A sore point A subject upon which one is sensitive.
The fact that he is only five feet tall is a sore point with him.

Stretch a point Concede a certain amount.

Strong point Distinctive characteristic; special skill.
Golf is not my strong point.

To the point Directly relevant. Relevantly.
He spoke bluntly and to the point.

Point of view Personal opinion or aspect.
From the smokers' point of view the tobacco tax is too high.

Up to a point To some extent.

Poke **Poke fun at** Mock.

Poke one's nose in Interfere.

Poker **Poker-face** Expressionless face.

Stiff as a poker Very stiff (e.g. in manner).

Pole **Pole to pole** i.e. From the North to the South Pole. All over the world.

Poles apart A very great distance apart.

The management and the trade union are poles apart on the matter of working conditions.

Polish **Polish off** Finish quickly.

I can polish off the job in five minutes.

Polish up Improve. Smarten.

Poor **Take a poor view of** Regard with disfavour.

Possess **Like a man possessed** With furious energy.

What(ever) possessed you. . .? How could you have been so rash as to . . .?

Possession **In possession of** Possessing; having.

See under *Point.*

Post **At one's post** At one's appointed place, or official position.

Beaten at the post Defeated at the last moment.

Deaf as a post Completely deaf.

Left at the post Hopelessly beaten in competition. [Or. Racing, the 'post' being the starting-post, the point at which a race begins.]

Post-haste Very quickly.

Pot **Keep the pot boiling** Enable any kind of enterprise, etc., to remain in an active condition.

Pot-boiler Any literary or artistic work turned out merely to provide money for necessities.

The pot calling the kettle black One person accusing another of faults of which he or she is also guilty.

A pot-shot A deliberate shot at some stationary object.

Take pot luck See under *Luck.*

Pound **Pound away** [LIT] Strike heavily and repeatedly. [MET] Work vigorously.

Pound of flesh Full and complete payment, regardless of circumstances. (Usually jocular.) [Or. Shakespeare's comedy *The Merchant of Venice*, in which Shylock, the moneylender, claims a pound of flesh rashly promised by a man who cannot pay his debts.]

Pour **It never rains but it pours** Troubles never come singly.

Pour oil on troubled waters Sooth a disturbed situation (usually with calming words).

Power **More** *or* **all power to your elbow**! Good luck to your efforts.

The powers that be Those in command; the authorities.

Practice **In practice** In the sphere of action (as distinct from theory).

Sharp practice Dealings which are dishonest or very nearly so.

Pray **Past praying for** Impossible to alter, to repair or to improve.

This old suit is past praying for.

Premium **Put a premium on** Prize.

Preparation **In course of preparation** Being prepard.

Present **At present** At the present time; now.

Present company excepted Excluding people who are here now.

Press **Be pressed for** Have scarcely enough.

Get a good *or* **bad press** Receive favourable (unfavourable) publicity.

Press forward *or* **on** 1. [LIT] Push in a forward direction.

The crowd pressed forward to see his arrival.

2. [MET] Hasten.

I want you to press on with that work.

Go to press (i.e. the printing-press) Usually applied to a periodical, or to a book.

Pretty **Pretty good, active,** *etc.* 'Pretty' here is used in the sense of fairly, moderately, comparatively.

He is in pretty good health, considering his age.

Pretty well *or* **nearly** Almost.

A pretty pass *or* **mess** See under *Pass*.

Prevail **Prevail upon** Persuade.

Prey **A prey to** Suffering from.

Price **At any price** In any circumstances.

Prick **Prick up one's ears** Become suddenly alert and attentive (as an animal raises its ears at hearing an unfamiliar sound).

Pride **Pride of place** Exalted position.

Put one's pride in one's pocket Same as **pocket one's pride.** See under *Pocket.*

Take pride in Derive satisfaction from. Be proud or careful of.

Primrose **The primrose path** The pleasant, easy-going, unthinking way of living. [Or. Shakespeare's *Hamlet*, 'The primrose path of dalliance'.]

Prison **Commit to prison** Formally order to be sent to prison.

Pro **Pro's and con's** Arguments for and against.

Probability **In all probability** *or* **likelihood** Very probably; very likely.

Profile **Keep a low profile** Remain inconspicuous.

Progress **In progress** Being done or undertaken.
Repairs to many of the houses were in progress.

Proof **Child-proof** Made so that childrem are unable to harm themselves by it.

Foolproof See under *Fool.*

Proof against Able to resist.
This coat is proof against the coldest weather.

Proof positive Definite proof.

The proof of the pudding is in the eating The value or wisdom of any action can only be discovered by actual experience.
[Or. Proverb.]

Put *or* **bring to the proof** Test.
I think the plan will work, but let us put it to the proof.

Proportion **Out of all proportion** Far more than is deserved.
The cost is out of all proportion to the benefits we should get.

Prospect **In prospect** Being considered.
I have a much better job in prospect.

Prove **Prove oneself** Show oneself capable.

Public **In the public eye** Known to the general public.

Puff **Puffed up** Proud.

Pull **Pull a (long) face** Express disagreement, disgust, etc.

Pull one's leg Tease.

Pull together Work together unitedly. [Or. The game of 'tug-of-war' in which each 'side', pulling opposite ends of a rope, tries to drag the other across a line between them.]
If we pull together, success is certain.

Pull one's punches [LIT] Fail to give the fullest force to one's blows (in boxing). [MET] Speak (or act) gently. (Usually used in negative.)

Pull one's weight Use all one's efforts in support.

Pull oneself together Make an effort to regain one's normal mental state.

Pull out 1. Move away.

2. Move to side.

3. Withdraw.

Pull rank Use one's superior position to achieve something.

Pull strings Use influence (usually covertly).

Pull through Survive.

Pull up 1. (Noun) A stopping-place where drivers, etc., may stop for rest, food, etc.

2. (Verb) Halt; stop.

3. Reprimand.

Pull up short Stop abruptly, and before one intended.

Punch **Pleased as punch** Very pleased.

Pup **Sell one a pup** Swindle one.

Purpose **On purpose; purposely** Intentionally.

Serve no purpose Be useless

To the purpose Direct to the subject, practically and sensibly.

To no purpose Uselessly; without success. See under *Serve.*

To some *or* **little purpose** With some (or little) result.

Put **Not put it past someone** Not be surprised if someone (does something).

Put about 1. Worried; anxious. [Old f.]

2. Nautical. Turn in the opposite direction.

The ship put about and returned to port.

3. Circulate; make publicly known.

It was put about that the Cabinet was in disagreement.

Put across Successfully narrate, convince or influence.

He is a good teacher, who puts his subject across very well.

Put all one's eggs in one basket See under *Basket.*

Put in an appearance Arrive and be present.

I am glad you were able to put in an appearance at the meeting.

Put it on Pretend. Feign or exaggerate an emotion, etc.

He says he's unwell, but I think he's putting it on.

Put one's back up See under *Back.*

Put by Save, usually for a special purpose.

Put to death Execute; kill.

Put down 1. Cease to hold.

Please put the shopping-bag down on the table.

2. Suppress.

The General put down the rebellion in six weeks.

3. Store for future use (wine, etc.).

We've put down two dozen bottles of port.

4. Write; record.

Please put down the following facts.

5. (Of animals.) Painlessly kill.
The dog was very old and we had him put down.
6. Ascribe. Attribute.
I put his irritability down to his ill-health.
Put to flight Compel to run away.
Put one's best foot *or* **leg foremost** See under *Foot.*
Put one's foot down Act firmly, decisively.
Put one's foot in it Behave tactlessly.
Be put in *or* **into force** Same as **come into force,**
under *Force.*
Put one's nose out of joint See under *Nose.*
Put off 1. Delay. Postpone. Evade.
Never put off till tomorrow what you can do today.
2. Repelled. Discouraged.
I meant to go, but was rather put off by the snow.
Put on airs; put on side Try to impress people by one's
superiority.
Put on the screw *or* **screws** Compel a person by
pressure (as a screw increases pressure) to do what is
desired.
Put on steam Make a special effort to progress.
Put out 1. Extinguish.
He put out the light.
2. Remove from a house or other building; eject.
He put out the cat.
3. Annoy; perturb. Inconvenience.
The old lady seemed put out.
4. Dislocate. Strain.
I put my back out by moving the piano.
Put over Communicate.
Put oneself out Take extra trouble.
Put a spoke in one's wheel Thwart one's intentions,
plans, etc.
Put a stop *or* **an end to** Terminate; end.
The Government ought to put a stop to official waste.
Put to it; hard put to it Tested; confronted with
difficulties. Pressed.
*He was hard put to it to decide whether to stay in England or go
abroad.*
Put two and two together (and make four) Deduce
from obvious facts.
*Putting two and two together, he realized that the firm would soon be
bankrupt.*

Put up 1. Receive as a temporary guest; provide with a bed.

We can easily put you up for the night.

2. Provide for a definite purpose, usually an investment.

Put up at Reside; live at temporarily.

We put up at my brother's when we go to Oxford.

Put up with Endure.

I can't put up with this toothache any longer.

A put-up affair A previously arranged affair; a plot.

Put upon Impose upon.

Put in a (good) word Speak in favour of; recommend.

Q

Qualms **Have qualms** Have doubts; feel uneasy.

Quantity **Unknown quantity** Thing or person having unpredictable influence or importance.

Quarrel **Pick a quarrel** Take occasion to make complaint; provoke someone.

Quart **Fit** *or* **put a quart into a pint pot** Make something fit into an inadequate space, time, etc.

Quarter **Give no quarter** Refuse to show mercy.

In every quarter; in all quarters Everywhere; in every direction.

Queer **In Queer Street** In an uncertain position; in difficulties. [Or. The custom of writing *Quere* (enquire) against a person's account when it was considered advisable to make enquiries before trusting him.]

Queer card *or* **customer** An eccentric and unusual type of person.

Queer one's pitch Spoil one's chances beforehand, usually by secret dealings.

I'd rather speak to him myself: if anyone else sees him first, it may queer my pitch.

Quest **In quest of** In search of; to search for.

Question **Begging the question** (Usually) Avoiding an argument or decision by bringing forward some immaterial point. But see *Beg.*

Beyond all question Without doubt; certain.

Burning question A matter requiring an immediate examination and prompt action.

Call in question Express doubt about; challenge.

Come into question Be considered.

In question Mentioned; referred to.
The person in question has a very good reputation.

Is the question Is what is relevant.

It is a question of What is involved is.

Open question Not certain; debatable.

Out of the question Utterly impossible.

Put a question mark against Query.

Put the question Ask for an opinion or vote.

Vexed question A problem or question very difficult to decide.

Without question Without doubt.

Quick **To the quick** See **cut to the quick**.

Quiet **Keep quiet** Say nothing.

On the quiet Unobtrusively.

Quit **Be quits (with)** Be equal (with). Be revenged (on). See **cry quits**.

Quite **Quite a few** A considerable number.

Quite a different *or* **another matter** Not at all the same thing.

Quite so I agree.

Quite something A noteworthy matter.

R

R **The three R's** Reading, (w)riting and (a)rithmetic— the first elements of education.

Rack **On the rack** In a condition of acute mental tension; intensely anxious. [Or. Rack = old instrument of torture.]

Rack one's brains Similar to **cudgel one's brains**

(Go to) rack and ruin Complete decay; destruction.

Rag **Glad rags** Best clothes. Formal dress.

Rags to riches From poverty to success.

Rag-tag and bobtail Disreputable people.

Rage **All the rage** Immensely popular or fashionable.

Ragged **Run ragged** Exhaust(ed).

Rails **Off the rails** Disorganized. Confused. (Usually applied to behaviour of people under strain.)

Rain **It never rains but it pours** Events, fortunate or unfortunate, rarely occur singly.

Rain cats and dogs Rain violently.

(Come) rain or shine [LIT] Whatever the weather. [MET] Whatever happens.

A rainy day Time of need, especially financial.

Raise **Raise a laugh** Cause amusement.

Raise one's eyebrows Express surprise.

Raise one's glass to Toast the health of.

Raise one's hat to Express admiration for.

Raise one's voice 1. Speak.
No one raised his voice in opposition.
2. Speak loudly, usually in anger.
Please don't raise your voice to me.

Raise the wind Obtain sufficient funds.

Rake **Rake's progress** Progressive deterioration as a result of wickedness, over-indulgence, etc.

Rake up Recall unnecessarily from the past.

Ram **Ram home** Express or be felt very forcibly.

Random **At random** By chance; without deliberate selection.

Range **Within range** Within an effective distance or area. Near enough to be heard, seen, controlled, etc.

Rank **Break ranks** Depart from agreement with others.

Close ranks Show solidarity with others.

Pull rank Use the influence attaching to one's seniority.

Rank and file The ordinary working members of an organization. [Or. Military. Technically, soldiers under the rank of lance-sergeant comprise the rank and file.]

Rise from the ranks See under *Rise.*

Ransom **Hold a person to ransom** Threaten a person in order to gain concessions.

Worth a king's ransom Extremely valuable.

Rap **Not worth a rap** Worthless. [Or. A 'rap' was a halfpenny issued in Ireland in 1721 and actually worth about half a farthing.]

Rap on *or* **over the knuckles** A sharp reproof.

Rap out Speak sharply; snap.

Rare **Rare bird** Very unusual (and valuable) person.

Rat **Like a drowned rat** Very wet.

Smell a rat Entertain suspicion.

Rate **At any rate** In any circumstances; whatever has happened or may happen.
The Government, at any rate, is not to blame.

At this *or* **that rate** If this (that) is true.

Rave **Raving mad** Out of one's mind.

Reach **Out of reach** Beyond the furthest distance to which one can stretch, or [MET] communicate.
Within reach Accessible.

Read **Read between the lines** Grasp the hidden significance of something spoken or written.

Ready **At the ready** Prepared to act.

Reality **In reality** Actually; in fact.

Reap See under *Sow.*

Rear **Bring up the rear; be in the rear** Travel behind; be at the back, as the last member of the party.

Reason **Hear** *or* **listen to reason** Allow oneself to be persuaded.
Listen to reason Be persuaded.
See reason Be persuaded.
Stand to reason Be obviously reasonable or logical.
Within reason Within the bounds of moderation.

Reckon **Reckon among** Include among.
Reckoning That which is due, or owing, financially or otherwise.
Reckon on Rely upon. Similar to **count upon**.
Reckon up Count. Summarize.
Reckon with Include in one's plans (usually as a difficulty).

Reconcile **Reconcile oneself** Subdue one's dislike or objections.

Record **Off the record** Unofficial(ly) because not written down or openly acknowledged.
On record In a position of acknowledging openly and publicly.
Put the record straight Correct a mistake or misunderstanding.

Red **In the red** In debt. [Or. Banks' practice of registering overdrawn accounts in red ink on customers' statements.]
Like a red rag to a bull An exasperation; an intense annoyance. [Or. The belief (widespread but erroneous) that the sight of any red article infuriates a bull.]
Red-handed In the act of doing something wrong. [Or. Probably reference to a murderer with his hands still stained with the blood of his victim.]
Red herring An attempt to divert attention from the chief facts by introducing some detail of no importance. [Or. The old trick of drawing a red (dried) herring across the path by criminals when they are being followed by bloodhounds, to destroy the scent.]

Red-letter day Day of rejoicing. [Or. The custom of indicating holidays and important saints' days in red lettering.]

Red tape Official and frequently trivial formalities. [Or. The old custom of Government officials and lawyers tying up their papers with red tape.]

We have given up trying to build a house—there is too much red tape involved.

To see red To become enraged.

To see the red light To have warning of difficulty or danger.

Reference **In** *or* **with reference to** Referring to; in connection with.

With reference to your letter of yesterday, we cannot accept the offer.

Without reference to Irrespective of. Without consulting or taking into account.

He acted without reference to his superior.

Reflection **Due reflection** Appropriate time for considering the matter.

After due reflection, we have decided to refuse.

On reflection After reconsideration.

On reflection, I think I was wrong.

Refresher **Refresher course** An additional course of studies, following an earlier one, taken to refresh one's memory.

Refusal **The first refusal** The first chance of buying an object before it is offered elsewhere.

I like the house, and the owner has given me first refusal.

Regard **As regards** Concerning.

With regard to In respect of.

Regular **Keep regular hours** Do the same thing at the same time every day.

Regular as clockwork Regular as the movements of a clock.

He comes home at six every night, regular as clockwork.

Rein **Give (free) rein to** Allow to escape without restraint.

She is a child who likes to give rein to her imagination.

Keep a tight rein on Control strictly.

Relish **No relish for** No liking for.

I've no relish for long walks in wet weather.

Render **Render an account** Present a bill for payment.

Repeat **Does not bear repeating** Is too disgraceful to repeat.

Reproach **Above or beyond reproach** So good that criticism is impossible.

Resistance **Take the line of least resistance** Take the action that is easiest.

Resolution **Form** *or* **make a resolution** Determine; definitely decide.

I've made a resolution never to go to bed later than eleven.

Resort **In the last resort** When everything else has failed.

Respect **In all respects; in every respect** In every way.

The new washing-machine is better in all respects than the old one.

Pay *or* **send one's respects** Present (or convey) one's polite greetings.

With respect If I may say so without giving offence.

Rest **Rest assured** Be satisfied.

Rest on one's laurels Having earned distinction or honours, to remain satisfied and do nothing further.

Rest on one's oars Remain passive, after making progress. [Or. Rowing.]

Retreat **Beat a retreat** Depart defeated; go away ignominiously. [Or. Military, from the signal to retreat being given by drum-beats.]

Rhyme **Neither rhyme nor reason** Nonsense; rubbish. [Or. The author of a worthless volume took it to Sir Thomas More, who told him to turn it into verse. When this had been done, More said, 'That will do. 'Tis rhyme now; before it was neither rhyme nor reason.']

No rhyme or reason No reason whatever.

There's no rhyme or reason why I shouldn't go.

Rich **Strike it rich** Discover means of becoming wealthy or successful.

Rid **Get rid of; rid oneself of** Dispose of; remove permanently.

Ride **Let something ride** Ignore or accept it.

Ride for a fall Behave rashly.

Ride high Enjoy success.

Ride one' hobby-horse See under *Horse.*

Ride out Survive (difficulty, etc.).

Ride roughshod Proceed without consideration or regard for other people's views or feelings. [Or. A horse is 'roughshod' when it is wearing specially roughened shoes, to prevent slipping.]

Riff-raff Worthless members of society. [Or. Riff = sweeping, raff = rags. Both words are obsolete Anglo-Saxon.]

Right **By rights** Rightly; justly.

By rights, this house belongs to my father.

Put to rights Correct. Make good.

Serves you right See under *Serve.*

Right as rain *or* **a trivet** In satisfactory condition. [Or. A trivet is a metal plate on three legs on which toast, etc., is stood to keep hot.]

Come right See under *Come.*

Right and left *or* **right, left and centre** On all sides. In all ways.

The home team were beaten right, left and centre.

Right-hand man Chief assistant or supporter.

Right of way Pathway, road, etc., established over private property by long-standing usage.

Ring **Ring back** Make telephone call in answer to a prior one.

Ring the changes Change the order of a limited number of items, so as to produce variety, e.g. mutton, beef, lamb, etc., for dinner. [Or. The variations produced by ringing Church bells in varying order.]

Ring off End a telephone call.

Run *or* **make rings round** Do something very much better than.

He can run rings round me at tennis.

Ring up Contact by telephone.

Riot **Run riot** Behave in disorderly way.

Rip **Let rip** Throw off restraint.

Rise **Rise from the ranks** Be promoted from a private soldier to a commissioned officer. The phrase is also used in connection with anyone who has risen from a very inferior position to an important one in the same organization.

Rise in the world Become socially or financially more important.

Rise to Succeed in acting in a manner appropriate to.

The hotel rose to the occasion by producing a magnificent wedding-breakfast.

Rise with the lark Get up early—strictly speaking at sunrise, when the lark begins to sing.

Take a rise out of anyone Make a person look ridiculous, generally by deceiving him or her.

Risk **Run** *or* **take risks** Expose onself to hurt.

Rob **Rob Peter to pay Paul** Take from one person (or thing) to pay another. (The origin of this phrase goes back to the twelfth century.)

Rock **(At) rock-botton** (At the) lowest possible (point).

Public confidence in the Government is at rock-bottom.

Rod **Make a rod for one's own back** Prepare trouble for oneself.

Rule with a rod of iron Govern or control with great severity.

Their father ruled the children with a rod of iron.

Roll **Roll-call** The list of names of those who should be present at some assembly. See **call the roll.**

Rolling in money Very rich.

Roll up 1. [LIT]

2. [MET] Assemble; appear.

Rolled into one Combined in one thing or person.

Rolling **Rolling stone** One who never settles long in one place. [Or. Proverb: 'A rolling stone gathers no moss', i.e. a wanderer gathers no riches.]

Rome **Rome was not built in a day** Achievements take some time to bring about.

When in Rome Adapt yourself to the habits and customs of those among whom you are living. [Or. Proverb: 'When in Rome, do as the Romans do' or 'as Rome does'.]

Roof **A roof over one's head** A place to live or stay.

Room **Make room for** Create space for thing or person by removing or compressing others.

Not room to swing a cat in Very little space.

Prefer a person's room to his company Prefer that person were absent, somewhere else.

Room for improvement Less than satisfactory state of affairs, and capable of being better.

Room and to spare Plenty of space.

Roost **Come home to roost** Return to cause difficulty to whoever started the operation.

Root **Put down roots** Settle happily (in a place).

Root and branch Every part; the whole organization.

The root of the matter, trouble, *etc*. The base; the foundation of.

The root of the whole trouble is that teachers are underpaid.

Root out Remove completely; extract from its surroundings.

Rope **Give one enough rope** Allow one to continue in error until he brings the consequences upon himself. [Or. Proverb: 'Give a man rope enough, and he'll hang himself.']

(Know) the ropes (Be familiar with) the method and procedure.

Rose **Bed of roses** Pleasant and easy condition.
Through rose-coloured spectacles Cheerfully, optimistically.
Rot **Stop the rot** Halt deterioration.
The rot has set in Deterioration has begun.
Rotten **Rotten to the core** Utterly bad.
Rough **Rough and ready** Sufficient, but not elaborate.
Rough and tumble 1. (Adjective) Disorderly.
2. (Noun) Jostling behaviour.
Rough diamond An uneducated or unsophisticated but worthy person.
Rough edge of one's tongue Angry remark. Usually **feel the rough edge of one's tongue**.
Rough edges Minor features (in thing or person) needing to be corrected.
Rough house Disturbance, row.
Rough it Live primitively.
If you go camping, you must be prepared to rough it.
Roughly 1. In a rough manner.
The police handled the prisoners roughly.
2. Approximately.
There are roughly half a million people in the city.
Sleep rough Sleep out of doors, on park-benches, etc.
Take the rough with the smooth Be prepared to tolerate inconvenience, hardship, etc., as well as to accept the more agreeable aspects of life, etc.
Round **Ask person round** Invite person to visit one's home, usually for hospitality.
Get round to Attend to after a time.
Going the rounds A 'round' is a regular tour which a watchman makes to ensure that all is well, or a tradesman to deliver goods. [MET] Circulating; travelling around.
There's a curious rumour going the rounds.
Roundabout way, route, *etc.* A straggling, indirect way.
We came into Liverpool by a roundabout way.
Round down Reduce to nearest or to a convenient whole number.
Round numbers Strictly speaking, this idiom should refer to complete hundreds, thousands, etc. It is, however, constantly used in the sense of 'approximately'.
There are in round numbers 2000 people in the village.
Round off Complete; add a final finish to.

He rounded off the performance with a song.

Round on Upbraid unexpectedly. Blame violently, and frequently undeservedly.

Round robin A letter or other document, usually of complaint, upon which all those concerned sign their names in a circle, so that everyone has the same responsibility and the leader remains anonymous. A petition passed from hand to hand for signature.

Round-table conference A meeting at which representatives of all parties to a dispute meet on equal terms to discuss matters.

Round trip Journey which ends at its starting-point.

Round up 1. Gather together.

2. Increase to nearest whole number.

Rub **Rub down** 1. Make (wood, plaster, etc.) smooth by friction.

2. Dry, clean or massage by rubbing.

Rub off 1. Remove by rubbing.

2. Transfer or be transferred by contact or influence.

Some of the father's arrogance has rubbed off on the son.

Rub one's hands Express glee.

Rub shoulders with Meet or associate with (people).

Rub up 1. Polish.

2. Revive one's knowledge of a subject.

Rub up the wrong way Irritate; annoy. [Or. From annoying a cat by rubbing its fur in the wrong direction.]

Her tactlessness always rubs people up the wrong way.

Rule **As a rule** Usually. More often than not.

Golden rule Basic, most important rule which ought never to be forgotten.

In golf, the golden rule is to keep one's eye on the ball.

Rule of the road The general rules governing traffic.

Rule the roost *or* **roast** Be in the position of one who issues orders, and is in command.

(*Note*—Rule the roost.—Derived from the cock who is master of the farmyard 'roost', or hen house.

Rule the roast.—Derived from the cook whose duty it was to regulate the cooking of the meat on the kitchen fire.)

Rule of thumb [LIT] Measuring lengths by one's thumb. [MET] Measuring by guesswork based on experience.

Rule out Exclude.

Ruling passion The chief incentive in one's life.

Work to rule Observe every rule and regulation in precise detail, thus making efficiency impossible. (Device used as alternative to open strike in industrial disputes, having the advantage of qualifying the employee for wages.)

Run 1. (Verb) Manage.
They run a grocery business.
2. (Noun) An extended number of performances or issues.
The play had a run of 500 nights.
A good run A successful sequence.
In the long run Eventually.
In the long run, crime does not pay.
On the run Being pursued from place to place.
One's blood runs cold One is filled with horror.
Run across Meet casually and unexpectedly.
I don't often run across such an interesting pub.
Run after Seek; pursue.
He runs after every pretty girl he meets.
Run against Similar to **run across.**
Run amuck *or* **amok** Dash about wildly and senselessly.
Run off *or* **away with** 1. Steal and depart with.
The assistant has run off with the week's takings.
2. Win easily.
We expect to run away with the Cup.
Run away with the idea Assume hastily and incorrectly.
I don't want you to run away with the idea that I'm dissatisfied.
Run a chance of being May be.
Run close Be very near in race, competition, merit, etc.
St Helens is probably the ugliest place in England, but Runcorn runs it close.
Run counter to Be in opposition to.
Your suggestions run counter to what we arranged yesterday.
Run its course Follow its own natural development.
Run down 1. Collide with and injure or kill. Similar to **run over.**
2. Overtake, and frequently capture as well.
3. Speak ill of.
4. Visit.
5. In poor health, through overwork, etc.
Run dry Cease to flow.
Run for 1. Run in an attempt to reach (bus, etc.).

2. Be candidate for (office, etc.).

Run to earth Find after a search. [Or. Fox-hunting, from following a fox to its den, or 'earth'.]

I ran the quotation to earth in Shakespeare's Othello.

Run for it Run for some especially urgent reason.

A run for one's money Time and opportunity in which to be free, or enjoy oneself.

Run the gauntlet See under *Gauntlet.*

Run high Become heated; excited.

Feelings always run high during an election.

Runs in the family Is an inherited trait or characteristic.

Twins run in my family.

Run into See **run across,** also **run down** (1) and **run over** (2).

Run into debt Incur debt.

Run into the ground Exhaust.

Run it fine Leave little room for error.

Run like mad See under *Mad.*

Run low Become scanty.

Our oil-supplies are running low.

Run mad Become fantastically exaggerated and unreal.

The plans for rebuilding the City show capitalism run mad.

Run messages Carry messages.

Run of the mill Ordinary. Unexciting. Average.

Run on Hasten ahead. Also **a run on** A heavy (unexpected) demand for.

Run out 1. Come to an end.

My patience has completely run out.

We ran out of coal, and had to burn wood.

2. Cricket. A batsman is 'run out' when the ball is thrown against the wicket before he has had time to complete a run.

Run over 1. Flow over.

The water ran over the edge of the jug.

2. Drive over; collide with.

The train ran over the man as he was crossing the line.

3. Glance over; read through and check.

You'd better run (your eye) over these instructions before you go.

Run ragged Exhaust by ceaseless effort.

Run rings round See under *Ring.*

Run riot Behave in a completely undisciplined way.

Run a risk Incur a risk or danger.

You'll run a risk of cutting your feet if you don't wear shoes.

Run a temperature Have temperature higher than usual, signifying illness.

Run to Reach; have sufficient money or ability for.

This novel runs to over four hundred pages.

I think I can run to another round of drinks.

Run to earth Find after search.

Run to seed 1. [LIT] Grow rank and straggling. As a plant does after it has blossomed. 2. [MET] Deteriorate, with an effect of neglect and decay.

A house will soon run to seed if left unattended.

Run short of Be left without a sufficient supply.

I ran short of milk because the cat knocked over the jug.

Run through 1. Exhaust; squander.

I ran through my pocket money very quickly.

2. Read quickly.

I'll just run through these letters, and then we'll go out.

3. Pierce completely.

The needle ran through her finger.

Run up Stitch rapidly.

Run up a bill Incur debts, usually recklessly.

Run up against Encounter as obstacle.

Run wild Similar to **run riot.**

Runner up The competitor immediately after the winner.

Running **In the running** With a chance of victory.

He's in the running for promotion.

Make the running Take the leading part.

Out of the running With no chance of winning.

Running Consecutive.

We met several days running.

(*Note*—This adjective invariably follows the noun.)

Running fight A fight throughout which the defenders are running away and the attackers pursuing them.

Rush **Rush at** 1. Move rapidly towards.

2. Deal with (task, etc.) impetuously.

Rush off one's feet Exhaust with rapid sequence of tasks.

Rush one's fences Be in too great a hurry for results. [Or. Hunting.]

Rush headlong Rush recklessly, with all one's energy.

S

Sabre **Sabre-rattling** Threat of retribution (by military force or by other means).

Sackcloth **In sackcloth and ashes** Deeply penitent. [Or. Biblical. To dress oneself in sackcloth and put ashes on one's head was an indication of mourning and sorrow.]

Sacred **Sacred cow** Thing (especially idea or institution) that is (sometimes unreasonably) felt to be beyond criticism. [Or. Hindu belief in cow as holy.]

Saddle **In the saddle** [LIT] Riding a horse. [MET] In office; in control of an enterprise.
Saddled with Burdened with.
He was saddled with the responsibility of educating three small children.

Safe **Better safe than sorry** It is wise to take no risks.
It is safe to say One may say without fear of misleading.
On the safe side Leaving room for error.

Safety **Play for safety** Show caution.
Safety first Caution above all else.
Safety in numbers No (or less) risk if there are sufficient amounts, quantities, etc.

Said **No sooner said than done** Accomplished as soon as requested; finished very soon after being ordered, mentioned, etc.
When all is said and done After all.

Sail **Full sail** [LIT] With all sails spread. [MET] Without hindrance.
Sail near *or* **close to the wind** Go very near to something which is improper, illegal, dangerous, etc. [Or. Nautical.]
Sail under false colours Pretend to be something that one is not. [Old f.] [Or. Nautical. Pirate ships used to hoist the flags of friendly nations to deceive other vessels.]
Set sail Start on a sea voyage.

Sake **For God's** *or* **Heaven's** *or* **goodness' sake** Expression of exasperation.
For old times' sake In memory of former days.

Sally **Sally forth** Go forth; come out (often in numbers, and suddenly or dramatically).

Salt **Rub salt into wound** Exacerbate (trouble, etc.).
Salt away Save (money, etc.).

Salt of the earth Person(s) who are valuable members of society. [Or. Biblical: 'Ye are the salt of the earth'; St Matthew, ch. 5, v. 13.]

Not worth one's salt *or* **keep** Worthless; not worth the cost of the salary one is paid. (*Note*—The word 'salary' is derived from the Lat. *salarium*, salt. Originally 'salt money' was money paid to Roman soldiers in lieu of salt.)

Take with a grain *or* **pinch of salt** Accept a statement, but with some doubt as to its complete truth. *We take most of what he says with a grain of salt.*

Salvation **Work out one's own salvation** Discover, by experience, the solution to one's problems.

Sand **Happy as a sandboy** Very happy. [Or. Sandboy = boy who hawked sand for sale.]

Have one's head in the sand Be unobservant or unaware.

The sands are running out There is not much time left. [Or. The grains of sand running through the hourglass, once a common substitute for the clock.]

Sardines **Like sardines** Very close together. [Or. Sardines packed in tins.]

Satisfaction **Give satisfaction** Satisfy; be what is required.

Sauce **Sauce for the goose** What is suitable for one person is equally suitable for another; the same rule applies to all people in similar circumstances. [Or. Proverb: 'What's sauce for the goose is sauce for the gander.']

Save **Save appearances** *or* **one's face** Prevent or minimize embarrassment; deal tactfully with any embarrassing situation.

Save one's breath (to cool one's porridge) Say nothing; keep one's advice to oneself. *I warned her, but I might just as well have saved my breath.*

Save oneself the trouble Refrain from doing something.

Save the mark Expression used to emphasize a statement (usually one expressing surprise or irony) or to apologize for mentioning something unpleasant. [Or. Archery. When anyone shot especially well, the cry was 'God save the mark!', i.e. 'May God prevent the arrow being displaced by a later shot'.]

Save the situation Find or provide a way out of difficulty. *I ran out of petrol, but a passing motorist saved the situation.*

Saving grace Feature that redeems (person's or thing's) faults.

Say **Does not say much for** Does not indicate quality in.

Have one's say Say all that one wishes to say in one's own words. (Opposite: **have no say.**)

Go without saying Be too obvious to deserve mention.

I say An introductory phrase to a remark conveying surprise or special interest.
I say, look at the view from over here.

Not to say And moreover.

To say nothing of Even disregarding.

That is to say In other words.

What do you say to? Would you like?

Saying **As the saying is; as they say** A half-facetious, half-apologetic excuse for using a hackneyed phrase or cliché.
Well, hard work never hurt anyone, as the saying is.

There is no saying It is not known.

Scales **Hold the scales** Be an impartial judge.

Scales of justice The scales traditionally held with each side exactly level by the blindfolded figure of Justice. (The figure is erected over the Central Criminal Court in London, as an emblem of the Law's fairness towards all who are tried there.)

Tip *or* **turn the scales** 1. Weigh.
The boxer turned the scales at 14 stones.
2. Bring about a decisive change in fortunes.
Rain on the second day of the Test match turned the scales in Australia's favour.

Scatter **Scatter-brained** Careless; easily distracted; unable to concentrate on one thing.

Scene **Behind the scenes** [LIT] Backstage in a theatre. [MET] Not in the public eye.

Change of scene(ry) Move to different surroundings.

Come onto the scene Become noticeable.

Create *or* **make a scene** Cause any violent emotional disturbance.

Scent **False scent** Course (of action, etc.) that will not lead to good result.

On the (right) scent Following course that will lead to good result.

Throw off the scent Mislead.

Scent (a mystery, scandal, *etc.***)** Suspect.

School **Of the old school** Of a type characteristic of former times.

Score **On that score** As far as that matter is concerned.
Pay off *or* **wipe off** *or* **settle old scores** Cancel an old injury or injustice by inflicting another adequate punishment. [Or. Score = Anglo-Saxon: a cut or scratch; debts used to be recorded by making such marks in long sticks. When such debts were paid, the 'score' was removed.]

Scorn **Point the finger of scorn** [Old f.] Sneer at; speak about with contempt.

Scot **Scot free** See under *Free.*

Scrape **Get into a scrape** Get into trouble; commit some foolish action leading to trouble.
Scrape acquaintance with Take special trouble to become acquainted with; deliberately set out to become friends with.
Scrape through Succeed by a narrow margin (usually applied to examinations).
Scrape together Succeed, with difficulty, in accumulating something.
Scrape up Same as **scrape together.**

Scratch **Bring to the scratch** Reach a definite decision; decide to take definite action. [Old f.] (See **up to scratch.**) [Or. Prize-fighting. The 'scratch' is the line marked in the prize-ring to which the boxers were led at the beginning of a fight.]
Come up to scratch Reach a required standard.
Scratch the surface Not penetrate deeply into.
The Minister's speech only scratched the surface of the problem.
Scratch team, crew, *etc.* A number of people collected casually, not regular members.
Although we'd only a scratch team, we won all three matches.
Starting from scratch Starting from the beginning, without benefit of other people's or one's own previous work.
Up to scratch Fit to deal with one's work; equal to what is required.
I've had influenza, and am still not up to scratch.
You scratch my back and I'll scratch yours If you help me, I will help you. [Vulgar.]

Screw **Have one's head screwed on** Have good sense.
Put on the screw(s) See under *Put.*

Screw up one's courage Force oneself to be brave.

Scruple **Make no scruple; have no scruples** Have no hesitation. [Frequently applied to some action which might involve some 'scruple' or sense of what is right and wrong.]
The soldiers had no scruples about robbing their prisoners.

Sea **At sea** Unaware; confused.

Get one's sea-legs Learn to walk successfully on the moving deck of a ship; accommodate oneself to the rise and fall of the waves.

Put to sea Leave the shore to start on a voyage.

Sea of blood Scene of extensive bloodshed.

Seal **One's lips are sealed** One is completely silent.

Sealed book A subject completely unknown.
Fifteenth-century art was a sealed book to him.

Set the seal on Conclude. Formally end. Give distinction to.
His fourth goal set the seal on the match.
The presence of numerous international golfers set the seal on the tournament.

Seam **Bursting at the seams** Very full, crowded or packed.

Seamy side More disagreeable feature (of life, etc.).

Sear **The sear and yellow** Old age.

Season **For a season** For a short time.
The play will run for a short season at Stratford before transferring to London.

Close season Period during which certain sports are not played.

Compliments of the season Christmas greetings.

In season Ready for eating and in plentiful supply.˙ (Used of foodstuffs.) See **a word in season.**

In season and out of season At all times, whether suitable or unsuitable.

Out of season Unseasonable; at a wrong or inappropriate time.

A word in season Advice given at an appropriate time.

Second **(At) second hand** 1. Not new.
2. By hearsay.

Come off second-best Be beaten by superior force.

Second childhood Childish behaviour at an age when it is not expected.

(Play) second fiddle (Be of) secondary importance (usually to another person).

Second to none Better than all others.

Second nature Instinctive; an action which has already taken place so many times that it has become automatic.

Second thoughts Later, more mature consideration.
On second thoughts, I won't go to the theatre tonight.

Second wind In exercise, easy breathing after initial breathlessness. Also applied to other circumstances in which continued practice, experience, etc., makes them easier, more pleasant, etc.
After a year in this job, I'm just finding my second wind.

Secret **In the secret** Among those permitted to know something that is kept from others.

Keep a secret Not reveal a secret.

Make no secret of State openly, without concealment.

Open secret Supposed secret which everyone knows about.

Security **Hold as security** Retain, in case of loss or failure to repay.

See **I'll see** I'll consider the matter before deciding.

See about it Decide later.

See better days Enjoy greater prosperity.

See eye to eye Agree.

See with half an eye See immediately, with no effort at all.
One could see with half an eye that she was very ill.
Similar to **see at a glance.**

See fair play Make sure that the rules are obeyed, that there is no cheating.

See fit Choose; decide.

See how the land lies Discover the state or condition of affairs.

See life Experience many things.

See off Accompany to the starting-place.
We saw him off at the station.

See one's way Manage. Contrive. Also **see one's way clear.**
Can you see your way to repairing it immediately?

See over Examine by walking round and looking.

See reason Understand what is reasonable.

See red Become infuriated.

See the back of Get rid of.

See the light Come to understand the truth.

See the light of day Come to public view.

See things Have hallucinations.
See through 1. [LIT] Perceive through something transparent.
I saw him through the window.
2. [MET] Perceive the truth, in spite of attempts to deceive.
Any idiot can see through most television advertising.
3. Ensure that a job is completed.
We are going to see the work through.
(Note alteration in order of words.)
See to Give one's attention to.
See to it that Make sure that.
Seeing is believing One's own observation is the best proof.
Not see the wood for the trees Be unable to see the general picture, the full overall effect, because of impeding detail.

Seed **Run to seed** See under *Run*.
Sow the seeds Bring into being, and thus be responsible for future development.

Sell **Sell off** Sell rest of.
Sell out Sell whole of stock.
Sell up 1. As **sell out.**
2. Sell everything prior to removal, going out of business, etc.

Send **Send down** Suspend or expel from university.
Send for Send message asking person to come or for thing to be brought.
Send off 1. Have (message, etc.) dispatched.
2. Be present at (person's) departure. Also used as noun.
Send on Dispatch onwards.
Send packing Dismiss peremptorily. Also **send someone about his business.**
Send up 1. Write, usually requesting information. (Also **send off.**)
I'll send up for the firm's catalogue.
2. Satirize. Parody. (Also noun **send-up.**)
The play sends up the advertising industry.
Send word Dispatch a message.
I'll send word that we'll be arriving late.

Sensation **Create a sensation** Produce a startling effect.
Sense **Sense of humour,** *etc*. Ability to appreciate what is humorous, etc.

S

Come to one's senses 1. Recover consciousness.
2. Recover one's sense of proportion and of what is
intelligent and just.
Sixth sense Intuition.
Take leave of one's senses Appear to have lost one's
normal balance or sane state of mind.

Sensible **Sensible of** Aware; conscious of.

Separate **Separate the sheep from the goats** Separate
worthy people, or (more loosely) those suited to a
particular purpose, from those who are the reverse.
Separate the wheat from the chaff Separate what
is worth keeping from what is rubbish.

Sepulchre **Whited** *or* **painted sepulchre** One whose virtuous
appearance and manner conceals inward vice; a
hypocrite. [Or. Biblical.]

Serve **If my memory serves me right** If I remember
correctly.
Serve someone right Punish justly and appropriately.
Serve its turn Prove useful for a limited time.
Serve its purpose Be suitable for what it is required
to do. Opposite: **serve no purpose.**
The greenhouse is dilapidated, but it serves its purpose.
Serve two masters Observe two conflicting principles.
Serves him right He has received what he deserves.

Service **Render** *or* **do** *or* **perform a service** Be useful to;
assist.
Service flat One in which domestic help, meals, etc.,
are provided by the management.

Set **Set about** 1. Begin; commence.
I'll set about preparing supper.
2. Attack violently. Also **set on.**
The three thugs set about the barman.
Set one's affections on Concentrate one's liking
upon; desire intensely.
Set against 1. Opposed to.
His parents are very much set against the marriage.
2. Balanced against.
*The £5 you've paid now will be set against the £20 you
borrowed last year.*
Set apart Put on one side. Separate.
Set aside Disregard; place on one side.
Set-back A reversal or arrest of progress. A relapse.
*The injury to the full-back was a great set-back to the team's
chances.*

187

Set back Impede or reverse the progress of.
The drought will set the country's progress back several years.
Set down 1. Write; place on record.
2. Deposit passengers.
Set by Put on one side for future use.
Set by the ears Exasperate; cause to quarrel.
Set eyes on Emphatic form of 'see'.
I haven't set eyes on him for many years.
Set an example Exhibit oneself as an example or model to be followed.
Set fair Likely to be satisfactory.
Set a fashion Establish or begin a custom.
Set foot in Enter.
Set in Become established.
Set on foot Start; initiate.
Set forth, off, out Start; depart.
Set free, at liberty Release.
Set one's face against Oppose with determination.
Set one's hand to Undertake.
Set one's heart on Strongly desire to obtain.
Set one's house in order Arrange one's own affairs properly; correct one's own faults.
Set in Begin (applied to something which will continue for some time).
Winter has set in early this year.
Set off 1. Start on a journey.
He set off to Sheffield early next day.
2. Make more effective; embellish.
The roses set off the dark beauty of her hair.
Set on See **set about** (2).
Set out 1. State.
2. Begin journey.
3. Aim.
4. Show.
Set over Place (person) in authority over.
Set phrase Formal phrase.
Set piece Prepared performance.
Set purpose Determined purpose; one already decided.
It was his set purpose to discover his father's old home.
Set at rest Cause to subside; eliminate.
Set right Make correct.
Set sail See under *Sail*.
Set the seal on Complete; make final. (A legal document is not completed until the principals have signed their names against a seal.)

Set store by See under *Store*.

Set *or* **lay the table** Prepare it for a meal.

Set one's teeth on edge See under *Teeth.*

Set the Thames on fire Achieve sensational success.

Set-to Contest; fight.

There was a set-to when the police asked the demonstrators to disperse.

Set to Become active; busy.

If we set to, we shall soon have the room tidy.

Set up 1. Formally establish; cause to exist.

The Minister will set up a committee to investigate the matter.

2. Assume the right. Aslo **set up as.**

I don't set myself up as an authority on rare books.

Set upon Attack.

Settle **Settle down** Become established; adopt regular habits; live a settled and normal life.

Settle up Agree and pay (account etc.).

Seven **In one's** *or* **the seventh heaven** In a state of intense delight or ecstasy. [Or. The outmost of the Seven Heavens or 'layers' with which it used to be believed that the earth was surrounded.]

Severe **Leave severely alone** Avoid.

Sex **Weaker sex** Women. (Jocular.)

Shade **Put in the shade** Appear more prominent than. Outshine. Overshadow.

Their record of slum-clearance puts other towns in the shade.

Shadow **Cast a long shadow** Exercise influence.

Cast a shadow over Reduce success (fun etc.) of.

May your shadow never grow less May you always prosper.

Shadow of one's former self Reduced in vigour or health.

Shaggy **Shaggy-dog story** Long pointless joke.

Shake **Shake the dust from one's feet** Depart from, usually in contempt or anger.

Shake in one's shoes Tremble with fear and apprehension.

Shake off Get rid of.

I wish I could shake off this cold.

Shake one's head Express refusal, disagreement or concern.

Shake out Remove dust, etc., from garment, etc., by shaking.

Shake up 1. Mix by agitating.

2. Rouse.

Two shakes of a lamb's tale Very quickly.

Shame **A burning** *or* **crying shame** A great and terrible shame; one to make the cheeks burn with anger.

Put to shame Cause to feel ashamed, or inferior.

The boy's playing would have put many a professional to shame.

What a shame! How unfortunate!

Shank **Shanks' pony** One's own legs.

We missed the last train and used shanks' pony.

Shape **In good** *or* **poor** *or* **bad shape** In good (poor, bad) condition.

Share **Share and share alike** Divide everything equally.

The three partners in the business agreed to share and share alike.

Sharp **As sharp as a needle** Very sharp. Very intelligent.

Sharp practice Behaviour which, while still technically legal, practically amounts to swindling.

Sharp's the word; look sharp; be sharp Hurry up.

Sheep **Black sheep** A person with a bad record or reputation. [Or. A theory that, as among every flock of sheep there is always one which is black, so in every respectable family there is always one discreditable member.]

As well be hanged for a sheep as a lamb If one is in mild trouble, one might as well **go the whole hog** and incur serious trouble.

Cast sheep's eyes Gaze in a foolish and amorous way at a person.

See also under *Separate, Wolf.*

Sheer **Sheer off** Break off (usually applied to metal bolts, etc., coming apart under strain).

Sheet **Between the sheets** In bed.

Sheet anchor Chief support. [Or. Nautical. The sheet anchor is the largest and strongest of a ship's anchors.]

Shelf **On the shelf** No longer required to do active work; replaced by someone more effective. No longer capable of work. Also applied to a woman who is thought to be too old or unattractive to marry.

Shell **Come out of one's shell** Throw off one's reserve and become communicative.

Shift **Make shift** Contrive to carry on. See also *Makeshift.*

Shift for oneself Take care of oneself.

Thanks for your help; I can shift for myself now.

Shift one's ground Adopt a new point of view or position in an argument, discussion, etc.

Shilly-shally

Waste time trying to reach a decision. [Or. Probably a

corruption of 'Will I, shall I?']

Shine **Take the shine out of** Make appear inferior and
unimportant.

Ship **Shipshape (and Bristol fashion)** Tidy and in good
order. [Or. The reputation of Bristol as a port.]
When one's ship comes home *or* **in** When one
becomes rich.

Shoe **In a person's shoes** In a similar position to him.
Where the shoe pinches The real trouble or worry;
the chief cause of financial anxiety. [Or. The saying
'Only he who wears the shoe knows where it pinches'.]
See also under **Shake, Dead.**

Shoot **Shoot ahead** Make extremely rapid progress.
*The magazine was started only six months ago, but it has shot
ahead rapidly.*
Shoot one's bolt Make a final effort, having nothing
left in reserve.
[Or. Bolt = short, heavy arrow of crossbow.]
The team shot their bolt too early and were easily defeated.
Shoot up Rise or grow suddenly and rapidly.

Shop **Closed shop** Factory, or part of one, in which
employees have to be members of a trade union.
Talk shop Discuss one's profession, business, etc.
(usually on informal or social occasions).
Shut up shop Stop work.

Shorn **Shorn of** Stripped of.

Short **Bring** *or* **pull up short** Check.
Cut short Abbreviate. Interrupt.
Fall short of Fail to reach.
For short As a shorter form.
Make short work of Dispose of quickly.
Nothing short of Absolute.
Run short Have only small quantities remaining.
Sell short Disparage.
Short of Without sufficient.
I can't offer you tea, as we're short of milk.
Short change Give too little change from payment.
Short-circuit Deal informally and quickly with (an
official document, etc.), omitting the usual procedure.
Is there no way of short-circuiting these formalities?
Short cut A short way from one point to another, as
distinct from the usual one.
*The distance by the road is three miles, but there is a short cut
through the park.*

Short-handed *or* **short-staffed** With an insufficient
number of helpers; short of staff.
*I'm sorry to keep you waiting, but we are short-handed this week
through illness.*
In short Summarized; stated briefly.
The rumour, in short, is not to be trusted.
In the long run *or* **term** Over a long period of time.
In the short run *or* **term** Over a short period of time.
Short-lived Not of long duration.
Short of breath Panting (as result of illness, exertion,
etc.)
Short shrift Very little time for explanation before
inflicting punishment, or administering reproof,
correction etc. [Or. Shrift = confession to priest, prior to
doing penance and receiving absolution.]
He tried to explain the mistake, but got very short shrift.
In short supply Available in insufficient quantities to
meet the demand.
Short weight Less than was ordered or paid for.
(Make) short work of Dispose of quickly.
The children made short work of the chocolates.
Stop short Refrain.

Shot **A good shot** An accurate or near accurate attempt.
Opposite: **a bad shot.**
He made a good shot at repairing the toy.
Like a shot With extreme speed. Without hesitation.
A long *or* **random shot** A casual suggestion; a mere
guess.
A shot in the dark A guess.
A shot in the arm Encouragement. Stimulus.

Shoulder **Give the cold shoulder to** Treat coldly and formally;
snub.
Have broad shoulders Be able to bear much
responsibility.
Have on one's shoulders Support; bear.
It is a terrible responsibility to have on one's shoulders.
Head and shoulders See under *Head.*
Old head on young shoulders See under *Head.*
Put one's shoulders to the wheel Work hard and
steadily. [Or. The fable of the lazy man who had his
cart stuck in the mud. He appealed to Jove for help;
Jove retorted that the man should himself put his
shoulder to the wheel and try to move it before
appealing to the gods.]

Rub shoulders with Come into intimate contact with; become acquainted.

Shoulder to shoulder United in effort.

Straight from the shoulder Directly and forcibly. [Or. Boxing.]

Shout **All over bar the shouting** Virtually finished.

Shout at Speak loudly in rebuke.

Shout down Silence (person) by shouting.

Shout for Call for in loud voice.

Show **Give the show away** Betray one's secrets.

Nothing to show for Nothing produced by.

Show cause Give good reason.

Show-down A frank exposure; an open challenge.

Show off Display one's cleverness with the intention of attracting attention and obtaining praise.

Show of force Display of one's power.

Show of hands Raising of hands to vote.

Show of reason Apparent justice and logic.

The chef said, with a show of reason, that it was impossible to make an omelette without eggs.

Show one's hand Reveal one's strength or tactics.

Show up 1. Expose (usually to disadvantage).

The behaviour of those children shows up their parents.

2. Escort someone upstairs.

The visitors have arrived; show them up.

3. Be conspicuous, clearly visible (often to advantage).

The painting shows up well against that wall.

Shuffle **Shuffle off** Avoid. Abdicate. Hand over to someone else.

Shut **Shut down** Close. (Usually applied to business.)

Shut one's eyes to Pretend not to notice.

Shut out Exclude.

Shut the door on *or* **to** Make impossible.

Shut up shop Give up business; end one's occupation, either for the day, or permanently.

Side **Let the side down** Fail to conform with colleagues' standards, efforts, etc.

On every side; on all sides From every direction, every source.

On the safe side See under *Safe.*

On the side; as a side line In addition to one's normal work.

The garage mechanic earns quite a lot on the side.

Side by side Standing close together.

S

Side with Ally oneself with; openly sympathize with.
Split one's sides Laugh very heartily.
Take sides Make onself an ally.

Sight **At first sight** At the first (superficial) glance; immediately.
Catch sight of Begin to see.
In sight of Near enough to see.
We shall soon be in sight of Southampton.
In the sight of In the view of; as seen by.
In the sight of the world, they were a happily married couple.
Know by sight Be familiar with the appearance only.
I've never met him, but I know him by sight.
Lose sight of [LIT] Fail to see. Opposite: **catch sight of.**
At this distance you lose sight of the village.
[MET] Fail to realize, or to remember.
You've lost sight of the fact that you are no longer young.
Lose one's sight Become blind.
Out of sight Beyond one's vision.
Set one's sights on Aim at.
Sight for sore eyes A very welcome, cheering thing to see.
Out of sight, out of mind One forgets that which is not present.

Sign **Sign of the times** Indication of present-day thought and feeling.

Signal **Give the signal** *or* **sign** Indicate by sign or speech when some event should happen.
The captain gave the signal for the men to attack.

Silence **Keep silent; keep** *or* **maintain silence** Continue to remain silent.
Pass over in silence Ignore.
Silence is golden, but speech is silver To remain silent is better than to talk.

Silent **Silent majority** Majority of people (usually of moderate views) who do not draw attention to themselves or make themselves heard (e.g. by militant action).

Silk **Make a silk purse out of a sow's ear** Change the real character of a person; make a gentleman or lady of one who is not one; create something good out of poor materials.
Take silk See under *Take.*

Sing **Sing-song** 1. (Noun) An impromptu concert, usually held by a community—soldiers, campers, etc.

2. (Adjective) Monotonous; flat and lifeless.

The sentry repeated his instructions in a sing-song voice.

Sing the praises of Praise highly and in general terms.

Single **Single-handed,** Unaided.

Singleness of aim, purpose, heart Concentration; a single object in view.

Sink **Sink or swim** Rely on one's own efforts; succeed or fail.

Sit **Sit back** Relax.

Sit on one's hands Fail to act.

Sit tight Remain firmly in one's place.

Sit up Be startled.

That dress of yours will make the neighbours sit up.

Sit up for Wait after the usual bedtime for somebody's return.

We shall probably be late coming home, so don't sit up for us.

Six **At sixes and sevens** Muddled; in a state of confusion.

We have only just moved into the house, and everything is at sixes and sevens.

Six of one and half-a-dozen of the other An affair in which both sides deserve equal blame or merit.

The magistrates listened to the story of the quarrel between the two people, and decided that it was six of one and half-a-dozen of the other.

Skate **Skate on thin ice** Encroach on matter needing care.

Skeleton **Skeleton at the feast** Cause of worry or upset at enjoyable time.

Skeleton in the cupboard A disgrace which the family, community, etc., does its best to conceal.

Skeleton staff Small number of staff, just enough to keep things going.

Skin **By the skin of one's teeth** Very narrowly. Only just.

We caught the bus by the skin of our teeth.

Get under one's skin Annoy one.

Skin and bone Very thin.

Skin-deep Superficial; not lasting.

Beauty is only skin-deep.

Thick-skinned Insensitive (to criticism, other poeple, etc.).

Slap **Slap in the face** A rebuff; an insult.

Slap on the back Expression of congratulation.

Slate **Clean slate** No record of misdemeanours.

Wipe the slate clean Forget previous misdemeanours.

Sleep **Let sleeping dogs lie** Refrain from stirring up trouble.

Sleep on a matter Allow a time to pass before finally deciding.

I'll sleep on the matter, and write to you tomorrow.

Sleep like a top Sleep peacefully and deeply. [Or. When a top is spinning at its greatest speed, it appears motionless and is almost soundless.] Also **sleep like a log.**

Sleeping partner One who is a partner (e.g. in a business) but plays no active part.

Sleight **Sleight-of-hand** Extreme manual dexterity and quickness. (The phrase is generally used in connection with conjuring and in performing an illusion.)

Slide **Let things slide** *or* **drift** Do nothing; take no active steps; be negligent.

Slightest **Not in the slightest** Not at all.

Slink **Slink away** Retreat silently, secretly, guiltily, unobtrusively.

Slip **Give the slip** Escape, and remain uncaptured.

Let slip Remark without thinking.

Make a slip *or* **slip up** Make a slight (but frequently vital) error.

You've made a slip somewhere in these accounts.

Many a slip Many things may happen to prevent a desired or expected result. [Or. Proverb: 'There's many a slip 'twixt cup and lip'.]

Slip away, out, off, across, *etc.* Move unobserved or quietly or quickly.

Slip through one's fingers Escape; be lost.

Slip of a girl Slim, young girl.

Slip of the pen An error in writing.

Slip of the tongue A verbal error.

Slot **Slot in** Fit in (between two others). Accommodate.

The dentist slotted me in at short notice.

Slow **Slow(ly) but sure(ly)** Not quickly, but making progress.

Slow down Reduce speed.

Slow up Same as **Slow down.**

Sly **On the sly** Secretly and artfully.

Small **Feel (look) small** Be humiliated.

No small Considerable.

Small beer Trivial; unimportant.
The news is all very small beer.
Small talk See under ***Talk***.

Smoke **End** *or* **go up in smoke** Have no result; end in nothing.
No smoke without fire All rumour has some truth in it, or some justification.

Snake **Snake in one's bosom** Person ungrateful for kindness shown.
Snake in the grass A hidden or hypocritical enemy.

Snap **Snap at** 1. Try to bite (usually applied to animals).
2. Speak irritably to.
3. Accept eagerly.
Snap one's fingers at Disregard; treat with contempt.
Snap up Seize hastily.
It's a bargain I snapped up in the market.

Sneak **Sneak off** *or* **away** Depart furtively.

Sneeze **Not to be sneezed at** Not to be treated as unimportant or insignificant. (Always used in the negative.)
The firm is offering a salary which isn't to be sneezed at.

Sniff **Not to be sniffed at** Not to be treated with contempt.

So **Just so; quite so** I agree; it is as you have stated.
And so forth Similar objects; in a similar way, etc.
He dealt in chairs, tables, and so forth.
Similar to **and so on; et cetera.**
So far so good Good progress has been made up to now.
So-long Good-bye.
So long as Provided that.
So much for that That is the end of that.
So much so that To such an extent that.
So-so In inferior health; not too badly; moderately well.
His results in the exam were only so-so.
So-and-so 1. Such and such a person A general substitute for the specific name of a person or thing.
2. A mild term of abuse.
So to speak; in a manner of speaking Speaking generally, without being literally exact; speaking with a certain amount of metaphorical exaggeration.

Sober **Sober as a judge** Not at all drunk.
Sober down *or* **up** 1. Become more serious-minded and reliable.

The boy will sober down as he grows older.
2. Recover from a temporary attack of hysteria or drunkenness.
We put him on the bed to sober up.
Sober-sides Person of sedate temperament and habits.

Soft **A soft answer** A well-mannered answer.
Soft in the head Foolish.
Soft-hearted Sympathetic and understanding (sometimes too much so).
Soft job Very easy job (in view of the salary).
Soft option [LIT] An easy choice. [MET] Same as **soft job.**
Soft soap 1. Flattery; ingratiating behaviour.
2. (Verb) Behave ingratiatingly.
Soft-spoken Gently and politely speaking.

Sold **Sold a pup** Swindled; cheated.

Soldier **Come the old soldier (over)** Claim greater experience (than), and consequently superior wisdom.
Old soldier [LIT] A former soldier. [MET] Person of experience.
Soldier on Continue, despite the difficulties.
Soldier of fortune Originally a professional soldier who hired himself as such to any country. A wanderer who lives by his wits.

Some **Somebody (someone, some person, somehow, for some reason, something) or other** 'Other' is here used as a vague alternative to an unspecified individual or thing, i.e. somebody or other = 'any person'.
Somebody or other has left the gate open.

Something **See something of** Meet occasionally.
Something like 1. Approximately.
2. (A thing) rather like.
Something of To a certain extent.
He's something of a singer.

Song **For a song; a mere song** Extremely cheap; at a merely nominal price. Similar to **cheap as dirt.**
The painting was going for a song, so I bought it.
Make a song about Create a fuss, disturbance, quarrel about (usually for trivial reasons).
The repair-bill is not worth making a song about.

Soon **Sooner or later** Eventually; in the end.
Similar to **before long.**

Sore **Like a bear with a sore head** Grumpy.

Sight for sore eyes Welcome sight.

Stick out like a sore thumb Be prominent in an unpleasant or inappropriate way.

Sort **A good sort** A good fellow; a helpful person.

A sort of Something like.

Of a sort; of sorts Not fully deserving the name.
He's a billiards-player of sorts.

Out of sorts Not in good health; depressed and irritable. Similar to **off colour.**

Soul **Be unable to call one's soul one's own** Be dominated by a person.

Not a soul Absolutely no one.
When I reached the station, there was not a soul on the platform.

Soul-destroying Extremely dispiriting.

Soul of discretion The essence of prudence.

Sour **Sour grapes** Something referred to disparagingly, but only because it is out of reach. [Or. Æsop's fable of the fox who, after vainly trying to reach some grapes he wanted, consoled himself by saying that they were sour.]

Sow **Reap what one sows** Be faced with the results of one's own actions.

Sow the seeds of Originate; begin.

Sow the wind and reap the whirlwind Perform ill-advised action and produce even worse consequences.

Spade **Call a spade a spade** Speak quite plainly or bluntly.

Spanner **Throw a spanner in the works** Interfere with, and check another person's plans. [Or. A spanner is a small tool used for turning metal nuts.] Similar to **put a spoke in one's wheel.**

Spare **Not spare oneself** Use all one's efforts.

Spark **Spark off** Begin under stimulus.

Speak **In a manner of speaking** See **so to speak,** under **So.**

Nothing to speak of Not worth comments.

On speaking terms Just acquainted. Opposite: **not on speaking terms,** which also means 'having quarrelled'.

Plain speaking Uttering one's real and unflattering opinion. Also **speak one's mind.**
There was a good deal of plain speaking, and they parted in anger.

Speaks for itself Demonstrates without words; requires no explanation.

His record speaks for itself.
Speaking likeness A vivid and realistic likeness.
Speak out Express (opinion) freely.
Speak up 1. Speak more loudly.
2. Speak one's opinion (e.g. **for** or **against** something).
Also **Speak out.**
Speak volumes Convey much, while actually saying little or nothing.
Speak well of Praise. Be to the credit of.
Strictly speaking Speaking exactly, or according to a rule or promise.
Strictly speaking, I ought not to tell you this.

Spell **Spell out** Explain very clearly.
The solicitor spelled out the consequences of taking legal action in the matter.
Under the spell of Fascinated by (person) or with (thing).

Spick **Spick and span** Extremely neat and tidy. [Or. Nautical. A 'spick' is a spike or nail, a 'span' a chip of wood; a spick-and-span ship is one in which all wood and metal is new.]

Spike **Spike a person's guns** Take some (sudden) action which ends opposition. [Or. Military. Old-fashioned cannon were fired by applying a light to the 'touch-hole', one bored into the near end of the barrel. The object of an attacking enemy was always to hammer a spike or iron into this hole, making the cannon useless.]

Spin **Spin out** Draw out; prolong. Endure.
I don't think this gin will spin out for much longer.
Spin a yarn Tell a story. [Or. Nautical.]

Spirit **In high spirits** Cheerful. Opposite: **in low spirits.**
The spirit of the law The real meaning or intention of the law, as opposed to **the letter of the law**, the strict interpretation of its words.

Spit **Spit and polish** Cleaning (of room, etc.).

Spite **Cut off one's nose to spite one's face** Hurt oneself by hurting others.
In spite of Despite; notwithstanding.
In spite of oneself Though one would rather not have done it.
Out of *or* **from** *or* **in spite** With malicious intention.

Splash **Make a splash** Cause a sensation, excitement.
Spleen **Vent one's spleen** Show ill temper.

Splice **Splice the mainbrace** Take a stimulating drink to keep one's spirits up. [Or. Nautical. The 'mainbrace' is the rope which fixes the main (or chief) mast in position.]

Split **Split hairs** Quibble about trivial matters.

Splitting headache Very severe one.

Split second Very short moment of time.

Spoil **Spoiling for a fight** Anxious and eager to quarrel or fight.

Spoil-sport One who impedes (by his words or behaviour) the enjoyment of others.

Spoke **Put spoke in one's wheel** Frustrate one's purposes.

Sponge **Sponge on** Systematically and constantly obtain money from one's friends.

Throw up the sponge Submit. Admit defeat. [Or. Boxing, where sponge was formerly thrown into ring by a man's seconds to signify his withdrawal from the contest.]

Spoon **Born with a silver spoon in one's mouth** Born of rich parents; born lucky.

Wooden spoon Prize awarded to person coming last in race, competition, etc.

Spot **Have a soft spot for** Have room in one's affection for.

Spot Discover.

Spot cash Immediate payment in cash.

Spot check Random examination.

Spot the winner Bet successfully.

I was lucky enough to spot the winner in the two o'clock race.

On the spot 1. At that particular place; there.

The police were on the spot within ten minutes.

2. Immediately; without delay.

I'll attend to it on the spot.

Similar to **there and then.**

Put on the spot Place in a difficult position.

If it gets into the newspapers he'll be on the spot.

Sprat **Throw** *or* **set a sprat to catch a mackerel** Risk a little to gain much. Make a small gift or concession in the hope of obtaining a large one.

Spread **Spread-eagled** Having fallen to the ground with limbs spread out. [Or. Lashing of sailors in rigging with arms and legs extended, in manner reminiscent of common emblem of eagle with wings and legs spread out.]

Spread oneself Be lavish.

Spring   **Spring a leak** Begin to let in water.
Where did you spring from? Where have you suddenly come from?

Spur   **On the spur of the moment** Suddenly, without previous consideration.

Square   **All square** Level; equal.
If I buy the next round, we shall be all square.
Back to square one Back to the beginning.
Square a man Bribe him.
Square peg in a round hole Person not fitted for his position.
Square up to Confront.

Stab   **Stab in the back** Cowardly attack. Betrayal.

Stable   **Lock the stable door** Take precautions when the accident they are to prevent has already happened. [Or. Proverb: 'It is useless to lock the stable door when the steed is stolen.']

Staff   **Over-staffed** With more employees than are needed.
Under-staffed The reverse. Similar to **short-handed.**

Stake   **At stake** Dependent upon what is about to happen.
Have a stake in Be involved in (the welfare of).
All ratepayers have a stake in the matter.

Stand   **As matters** *or* **things stand** In their present condition.
Leave person standing Make much more rapid progress than person.
Long-standing Not recent.
Make a stand Refuse to budge.
Stand aghast Be shocked, appalled.
Stand alone Be without equal.
Stand aloof Remain detached; refuse to share or co-operate with.
Stand aside 1. [LIT] Stand where the progress of others will not be impeded. Also **stand back.**
2. [MET] Give someone else an opportunity.
Stand by 1. Wait in a state of readiness.
The troops have been ordered to stand by.
2. Support by word or deed.
He stood by his friend through all his troubles.
3. Be an observer.
I will not stand by and do nothing.
Stand on ceremony Behave stiffly and ceremoniously. (Usually used in the negative.)
Don't stand on ceremony—make yourself at home.
Stand a chance Have any possibility.

I don't think your horse stands a chance of winning.
Stand corrected Admit to being wrong.
I am sorry for the mistake—I stand corrected.
Stand down Retire.
Stand on one's dignity Show—often absurdly—a sense of one's importance.
Stand fast *or* **firm** Remain immovable.
Stand for Represent.
Stand one's ground Refuse to change one's statements or opinions.
Similar to **stand** *or* **stick to one's guns.**
Stand in for Act as replacement for.
Stand on one's own (two) feet *or* **legs** Accept full responsibility for one's own actions; accept no assistance.
Stand in the way of Obstruct.
Stand in a person's light Prevent his advancement; spoil his career. (Usually used in the negative.)
Stand-offish Haughty; consciously superior; curt.
Stand on Insist on.
Stand out 1. Remain in opposition; refuse to co-operate.
The conspirators did their best to persuade all the men to join them, but three stood out.
2. Be conspicuous.
The statue stands out against the trees.
Stand out for Insist upon.
The workers are standing out for higher wages.
Stand over 1. Stand near, usually to enforce an order.
She stood over the boy while he washed his face.
2. Put aside for a time.
The accounts can stand over till next week.
Stand on one's rights Insist upon one's legal entitlements.
Stand in good stead Prove useful to.
Stand still Remain motionless.
Standstill Stoppage. Usually **At a standstill** Not working. Not moving.
Stand to Similar to **Stand by** (1).
Stand to win *or* **lose** Be in a position where one is capable of winning (or losing).
Stand up 1. Stand on one's feet.
2. Be valid.
Stand up for Support openly, by speech or action.
Stand up to 1. Confront boldly; oppose.

2. Be capable of. Bear. Tolerate. Carry the weight of. Endure.

Standard **Standard of living** Degree of material comfort achieved by a person, society, etc.

Star **Star-studded** Having many 'stars' (famous people).
Star turn A 'turn' or act by a famous performer. Frequently applied to any conspicuous or successful incident.

Stare **Stare one in the face** Confront; be evident and obvious.
The troops saw defeat staring them in the face.

Stark **Stark staring mad** Extremely mad.

Start **A fresh start** A new beginning.
For a start In the first place.
Start life Begin one's career.
Start off Begin to move.
Start out Proceed (with an intention).
Start up 1. Begin (business).
2. Make (engine) work.
3. Move suddenly (from seat, in surprise, etc.).
To start with In the first place.

Stave **Stave in** Smash inwards. Crush out of shape.
If the fire takes hold the walls will stave in.
Stave off Avert. Ward off.
A late goal staved off defeat.

Steal **Steal a march on** Gain an advantage for which one's adversary was not prepared.
Steal the show Outshine others.
Steal one's thunder Forestall him. [Or. Playwright's remark when stage-effect of thunder he had intended for his own play was used first in another.]
Steal upon Creep softly upon.

Steam **Get up steam** Summon energy for a special effort.
Let off steam Get rid of surplus energy.
Run out of steam Lose impetus.

Steer **Steer clear of** Avoid; evade.
Steer a middle course Avoid extremes; act moderately; compromise.

Step **In one's (foot-)steps** Following one's example.
Out of step Not in comformity.
Retrace one's steps Return in the direction one had come.
He retraced his steps, looking for the purse.
Step by step Slowly and methodically.
Step down Give up position or post.

Step in Intervene.

Stepping-stone *or* **stones** [LIT] Stones in a stream used to enable one to cross with dry feet. [MET] Anything which may act as a means to an end (usually to an improvement).
He regards his present job purely as a stepping-stone.

Step up Increase.

Take steps Start a course of action.

Stew **Stew in one's own juice** Suffer the consequences of one's own (misguided) actions.

Stick **In a cleft stick** In such a position that it is very difficult to make a decision.

Stick-in-the-mud An unenterprising, unambitious person.

Stick at nothing Stop at nothing; be restrained by no scruple or impediment.

Stick out Same as **stand out** (2).

Stick in one's throat [LIT] Choke one. [MET]. Cause disgust or aversion.

Stick to Remain faithful to.

Stick to one's guns Not to be budged from one's position.

Stick up to Offer resistance to.

Stiff **Stiff as a poker** *or* **a ramrod** *or* **buckram** Rigid; very formal.

Stiff upper lip Firmness of character.

Still **Still life** A phrase applied by artists to compositions in which there are only inanimate objects—flowers, fruit, furniture, etc.

Still waters run deep Streams which flow silently are usually deep. Quiet, undemonstrative people are frequently those who have depths of emotion, etc., even though they are successfully concealed.

Sting **Sting in the tail** Unpleasantness or disadvantage mentioned last.

Stir **Cause a stir** Create commotion.

Stir the blood Inspire.

Stock **In stock** Readily available, not needing to be specially obtained.

Lay in a stock of Acquire supplies of.

On the stocks Being made, but not finished. [Or. Shipping.]
I have two novels on the stocks.

Stock rises Reputation increases.

Stock still Absolutely motionless.

Stock-in-trade [LIT] A tradesman's stock, or supply of goods for sale. [MET] Any possession, tangible or otherwise, which one employs in one's business or profession.

Her stock-in-trade consisted of plenty of confidence, a knowledge of French, and a charming smile.

Stockpile Store.

Take stock of Consider the value or possibilities of.

He took stock of his present position.

Stone **Heart of stone** Want of human feeling.

Leave no stone unturned Use every possible effort to find out; investigate thoroughly.

People who live in glass houses should not throw stones Those who are vulnerable should not provoke attack.

Stone blind *or* **deaf** Totally blind or deaf. Also, with the same effect, **stone cold** and **stone dead.** (But not, for some reason, stone dumb.)

Stone's-throw A short distance (theoretically, as far as one can throw a stone).

The house was within a stone's-throw of the sea.

Stone-walling Persistent refusal to discuss, act, etc. [Or. Cricket: not trying to score.]

Stony-broke Entirely without money.

Stool **Fall between two stools** Fail as a result of not selecting one of necessary alternative courses of action.

Stoop **Stoop to conquer** Humiliate onself to achieve success in the end.

[Or. Goldsmith's comedy, *She Stoops to Conquer.*]

Stop **Come to a full stop** Cease completely.

A dead stop A complete and sudden halt.

The car came to a dead stop in the middle of the road.

Stop-gap Temporary solution.

Stop-gap measures will not solve this crisis.

Stop at nothing Ignore all impediments.

Store **In store** About to come.

I think you've a surprise in store.

Set store by *or* **on** Value; attach importance to.

Storm **Bow before the storm** Yield to public indignation.

Storm in a teacup Much excitement and trouble over a trivial matter.

Take by storm Capture (hearts of people) by vigorous action.

Story **Cut a long story short** Omit details of narrative.
The old, old *or* **same old story** The familiar pattern of events.
The story goes It is said.
Stout **Stout-hearted** Brave.
Straight **Keep a straight face** See under *Face*.
Play a straight bat Behave or speak without equivocation.
Put things *or* **the record straight** Express matters as they are, to remove muddle.
Straight away; straight off Immediately. Without hesitation.
The doctor will see you straight away.
Straightforward 1. Without complications.
2. Honest.
Straight from the shoulder See under *Shoulder*.
Straight tip A definite hint; also private and accurate information. [Or. Betting.]
Strain **Strain at a gnat and swallow a camel** Object to some trivial matter while condoning or permitting a far greater offence. [Or. Bible.]
Strain every nerve Use all efforts.
Strain one's eyes 1. Make an extra effort to see.
If you strain your eyes, you can just see the church.
2. Tire one's eyes.
Don't strain your eyes by reading such small print.
Strained relations Tension as result of disagreement etc.
Stranger **Be a stranger here** Not live here.
Be no stranger to Be accustomed to.
Straw **Clutch** *or* **grasp at a straw** *or* **straws** Grasp at anything, however trivial, to escape disaster; gain hope from the slightest sign that may appear favourable. [Or. The saying that a drowning man will clutch at even a straw to save himself.]
The last straw Any final unendurable event; a culminating injury. [Or. Proverb: 'It is the last straw that breaks the camel's back.']
Make bricks without straw See under *Brick*.
A man of straw See under *Man*.
Not care a straw *or* **two straws** Care nothing at all.
A straw will show which way the wind blows A trivial thing will indicate what is likely to happen.

(Hence, **a straw** *or* **straws in the wind.** Hints which indicate **which way the wind is blowing,** i.e. what is likely to happen.)

Stream **Go** *or* **drift with the stream** Follow the example of the majority.

Strength **From strength to strength** From one success to greater ones.

In strength In large numbers.

On the strength of Relying on.

Stretch **At a stretch** 1. With an effort; only by straining one's resources.

We can manage to entertain ten people at dinner at a stretch.

2. Continuously.

Some lorry-drivers are working ten hours at a stretch.

By no stretch of the imagination In no way which it is possible for one to conceive.

Stretch one's legs Take exercise by walking.

Stretch a point Make an exception to a rule. Extend an arrangement, rule, law, etc., beyond its legitimate extent.

Strict **Strictly speaking** Using words with precise meaning.

Stride **Get into one's stride** Become accustomed to and settle into one's job, etc.

Make rapid strides Progress quickly.

Take in one's stride Cope with easily.

Strike **How does that strike you**? What do you think of that?

It strikes me It seems to me.

On strike Refusing to work until some grievance is corrected.

Strike a bargain Reach an agreement.

Strike a blow for Do something on behalf of.

Strike at Aim a blow at.

Strike at the root of Threaten destruction to.

Strike back return a blow.

Strike the happy medium Arrive at the best possible compromise.

Strike home Strike a vital blow; strike directly at the heart or emotions.

It was only a short speech, but it certainly struck home.

Strike while the iron is hot Take advantage of a suitable opportunity.

Strike off Remove from an official list or record.

His name was struck off the register of doctors.

Strike on Luckily encounter.

Strike out 1. Make violent movements with one's arms or legs.

2. Similar to **strike off.**

Strike terror, fear, *etc.* Create terror; terrify.

Strike up Begin.

Within striking distance (of) Near enough (to).

String **First** *or* **second string** Principal *or* alternative person or thing one relies on.

String together [LIT] Link, as by a string or cord. [MET] Arrange in sequence.

I've strung together a few ideas for discussion.

Stroke **A stroke (of work)** Any work. (Usually used in negative.)

I haven't done a stroke all weekend.

A stroke of genius Brilliant idea or act.

A stroke of luck Unexpected good fortune

At a stroke By one action.

On the stroke (of) Punctually (at).

Put one off one's stroke Cause one to falter in what one is doing.

Strong **Strong box** A metal box designed to protect valuable papers from fire or thieves.

Stuck **Stuck up** Vain; arrogant.

Study **In a brown study** See under *Brown.*

Make a study of Pursue knowledge in.

Stumble **Stumble upon** Discover by chance.

Stumbling-block Obstacle.

Stump **Stumped for** At a loss for.

Stung **Stung** *or* **wounded** *or* **cut to the quick** See under *Cut.*

Subject **Change the subject** Talk of something else.

On the subject of Concerning.

A sore subject A subject about which one is particularly sensitive.

A subject for A matter for. A cause of.

Success **Nothing succeeds like success** One success leads to another.

Such **Such-and-such a person** See **so-and-so.**

Such as it is If one can call it by that name.

Such being the case Considering the present state of affairs.

Suchlike Things, people, etc., of that kind.

I don't much care for night-clubs and suchlike.

Sudden **All of a sudden** Without warning.

Suit **Follow suit** Do the same. [Or. Card-playing: play card of same suit.]

Suit the action to the word Do what one has promised, threatened, etc.

Suit yourself Do as you wish.

Sum **Sum up** Give a final résumé and analysis of what has occurred.

Summer **Summer time** The official alteration of Greenwich time, in order to allow more hours of daylight in summer to be used.

Sun **A place in the sun** Favourable situation.

Catch the sun Be sunburnt.

Under the sun In the whole world.

There's nothing new under the sun.

Sunday **Month of Sundays** Long period.

Sunday best Best clothes one has.

Sure **Make sure; make certain** Render absolutely certain.

Sure enough In accordance with something anticipated.

I said you'd come, and sure enough here you are.

Sure as Fate Beyond a doubt, with absolute certainty.

Surprise **Taken by surprise** Suddenly surprised; astonished.

To my surprise Contrary to what I expected.

Suspense **In suspense** In a condition of uncertainty.

Swallow **One swallow does not make a summer** One piece of good fortune (news, luck, etc.) does not mean that others will follow.

Swallow an insult Submit to an insult without protest.

Swallow up Engulf; cause to disappear.

An earthquake can swallow up an entire town.

His wife's debts swallowed up all his savings.

Swan **Swan-song** Final performance of career.

Swear **Swear by** Have great belief in. Recommend. Resort to frequently.

My wife swears by these indigestion-tablets.

Swear like a trooper Use particularly bad language. [Or. A trooper is a soldier, a member of a troop of horse.]

Sweat **By the sweat of one's brow** By hard (physical) work.

In a (cold) sweat [LIT] Perspiring. [MET] 1. In a state of anxiety.

2. In a hurry.

Sweated labour People employed for long hours for low wages.

Sweep **Make a clean sweep (of)** Get rid or dispose (of).
Sweep the board Win everything that is to be won.

Swell **Swell the ranks of** Add to an already large number of people or things.

Swim **Go swimmingly** Proceed smoothly and well; become a complete success.
I am sure your party tomorrow will go swimmingly.
In the swim Fully involved in what is going on.
We're new to the district, and not yet in the swim.
Swim with the tide Go with the majority.

Swing **In full swing** Making full progress.
The fête was in full swing when the storm came.
Go with a swing Proceed in a lively and enjoyable manner.

Swoop **At one fell swoop** In one complete and sudden disaster.

Sword **Cross swords with** Quarrel with. Engage in rivalry or controversy with.
He's not a man I'd like to cross swords with.
Sword of Damocles A disaster liable to occur at any moment; a threat to one's peace and happiness. [Or. The story of Damocles who, being invited by Dionysius to a splendid feast, looked up from his seat to see a sword suspended above his head by a single hair.]
Put to the sword Executed.

Sworn **Sworn enemies** Irreconcilable ones.

Syllable **In words of one syllable** In the simplest and plainest words possible.

System **Get something out of one's system** Rid oneself of its influence on oneself.

T

T **Cross the T's** Be very accurate. Correct or finish something in detail.
To a T Exactly. [Or. The T-shaped piece of wood used by carpenters to make sure that joints are exactly at right angles.]
This measurement is correct to a T.

Table **Turn the tables on someone** Convert relatively weak position to strong one.

Tack Course of action. Thus **change tack, on the right, wrong, tack,** etc.

Tag See **rag tag and bobtail**

Tail **Tail between one's legs** Cowed and humiliated, like a frightened dog.

Tail off Become weaker.

Tail wind Following wind.

Turn tail Turn one's back and run away.

With one's tail up In good spirits.

Take **Taken aback** Disconcerted; surprised.

The man was utterly taken aback when they recognized him.

Take account of See **take into account.**

Take after Resemble, physically or otherwise.

Mary takes after her father, and is very musical.

Take against Begin to dislike.

Take back Withdraw.

I take back everything I said.

Take the bit between one's teeth See under *Bit.*

Take the bull by the horns Confront a difficulty boldly and without any evasion.

Taken by Attracted by.

Take care Be careful.

Take care that you don't slip on the frosty road.

Take a cue Understand a hint. Follow someone's example. [Or. The 'cue' is the word which indicates when an actor is to appear.]

Take down 1. [LIT]

Take down that book (or *take that book down*) *from the shelf.*

2. [MET] Record; write.

Take down this letter, please.

Take down a peg See under *Peg.*

Take effect Come into operation. Make an impact.

The new regulations will take effect from next year.

Take one's fancy Charm; attract; interest.

I saw nothing in the shop to take my fancy.

Take flight; take to flight Depart quickly.

The thieves, hearing footsteps, took to flight.

Taken for a ride Deceived.

Take for granted Assume as a fact.

Take in good *or* **bad part** Accept good-naturedly or angrily.

I hope you'll take my advice in good part.

Take in hand Undertake. Control.

The workers will take the repairs in hand next week.

Take into one's head Decide (to do).
Take to heart Be seriously affected.
He has taken your words to heart, and will try to be more careful in future.
Take heed of *or* **to** Attend; be warned by.
Take heed of what I've told you.
Take a hint Pay attention to, and act on, a gentle suggestion, without needing explicit guidance.
Take hold of Seize; grasp.
The boy took hold of the ladder, and began to climb.
Take in 1. Mislead; deceive.
We were completely taken in by his story.
2. Receive, as a means of livelihood.
Miss Brown takes in lodgers.
3. Escort to a dining-room, etc. [Old f.]
Our host took in the principal guest.
Take in hand Accept responsibility for.
Take ill Become unwell.
Take it or leave it Do what you wish.
Take into account Include in one's calculations, plans, ideas, etc.
I didn't take into account the possibility of such a long delay.
Take it badly Respond (to news) with distress.
Take it from me Accept what I say as true. Also **take my word for it.**
Take leave of Say farewell.
Take leave of one's senses Cease to behave wisely. Do something rash.
Take a liking, dislike, fancy, *etc.*, **to** The same as 'like', etc., except that the effect is rather more emphatic and spontaneous.
Take off 1. Mimic.
He took off the headmaster perfectly.
2. Rise from the ground.
The aeroplane will take off at three o'clock.
Take-off Piece of mimicry or caricature.
Take one's leave Say farewell and depart.
Take a lot of doing Be difficult to do.
Take one's time Refrain from hurry.
Take oneself off Depart, generally abruptly or indignantly.
They took themselves off without saying good-bye.
Take offence *or* **umbrage** Be annoyed; angry.
He always takes offence at any kind of criticism.

Take on Accept responsibility for.
I've taken on the organization of our Hospital Fête.
See **take upon oneself.**
Take out 1. Obtain the issue of (in a legal sense).
I am taking out a patent for the invention.
2. Extract.
The dentist took out five of Mary's teeth.
3. Accompany (for a walk, etc.); in charge of.
Father isn't at home; he's taken out the dog.
Take it out of one 1. Exhaust; weaken.
So much hill-climbing takes it out of me.
2. Have revenge. (More usually, **take it out on.**)
Just because you're in a bad temper, don't take it out on the dog.
Take over Take the place of someone else.
You stay with the children until ten o'clock, and then I'll take over.
Take-over bid Attempt by a company to purchase another.
Take pains *or* **trouble** Make a considerable effort.
I took pains to explain the facts clearly.
Take part in Share; co-operate; act with others.
Her sister takes part in all local events.
Take a person's part Support; identify oneself with.
The boy's mother will naturally take his part.
Take place Happen; occur.
The race will take place tomorrow.
Take the rough with the smooth Accept philosophically both pleasant and unpleasant things.
If one becomes a teacher, one must be ready to take the rough with the smooth.
Take sides Support one adversary against another.
A judge should remain impartial, and not take sides.
Take silk Become a Queen's Counsel, an honour which entitles a barrister to wear a silk gown in Court, instead of the cloth one previously worn.
Take one's stand Decide upon a mental attitude; base one's argument.
Take stock of Examine thoroughly and in detail.
He decided to take stock of the present condition of affairs.
Take by storm Capture by a violent attack. [Or. Military.] Captivate sensationally.
The film has taken everywhere by storm.
Take to Form a liking for.

The baby took to the kitten at once.
Similar to **take a liking to.**
Take to one's bed Go to bed, usually for some time, as the result of illness, etc.
My husband feels so ill that he has taken to his bed.
Take to task Blame; reprove.
His wife took him to task for his forgetfulness.
Take too much Become intoxicated.
Though Bill enjoys a drink he never takes too much.
Take in tow [LIT] Attach a cable, etc., to a vehicle, ship, etc., to pull it along. [Or. Nautical.] [MET] Take charge of; be responsible for.
Take on trust Believe without evidence or proof.
We are prepared to take on trust the facts you have told us.
Take up 1. Absorb; occupy.
Most of their time is taken up in decorating the house.
2. Lift.
We will take up the carpet and send it to be cleaned tomorrow.
Take up the threads Resume after an interruption.
Take up with Become friendly or intimate with.
Take upon oneself Assume or accept responsibility without being asked.
Take the will for the deed Accept the desire to be kind and helpful, even if nothing practical results.
Taken with Captivated by.

Tale **Live to tell the tale** Come through ordeal.
Old wives' tale Superstitious tradition, often foolish but believed to be true by some people at the moment and many in the past. Also, an unconvicing story.
Tale-bearer One who spreads rumours, and who tells malicious stories of other people.
Tell its own tale Need no explanation.
Tell tales out of school Reveal another person's private affairs; discuss them with inappropriate people, or at inappropriate times.
Thereby hangs a tale There is an interesting story or explanation concerned with that event. [Or. Quotation from Shakespeare's *The Taming of the Shrew*.]

Talk **Do the talking** Act as spokesman.
Idle talk Foolish, useless talk; gossip.
Know what one is talking about 1. Understand what one says.
2. One is an expert.
Money talks Having money gives one power.

Small talk Talk concerning trivialities; formal and polite conversation.

Table-talk Conversation of the friendly and entertaining type which takes place among intimates at a meal. Applied especially to the talk of famous people.

Talk back Reply (defiantly).

Talk the back *or* **hind legs off a donkey** *or* **horse** Be very talkative.

Talk out Discuss until conclusion is reached.

Talk over 1. Discuss.

We talked over his plans for the future.

2. Convince; bring to one's own way of thinking. Similarly, **talk round.**

He wouldn't come at first, but we talked him round.

Talking of As we are discussing.

Talking of money, have you paid the gas bill yet?

Talk through one's hat Talk nonsense.

Tangent **Go off at a tangent** Diverge from main topic of conversation.

Tar **Tarred with the same brush** Having the same defects as someone else.

She is rather conceited, and her son is tarred with the same brush.

Task **Take person to task** Upbraid him.

Hard task-master Person (or thing) imposing heavy burden.

Taste **Leave a nasty taste in the mouth** Cause unpleasant memories or feelings (at end of matter).

There's no accounting for taste Everyone has different tastes, some of them difficult to understand.

A taste for A natural appreciation of, or liking for.

I have no taste whatever for Japanese art.

Tear **Tear to tatters, ribbons,** *etc.* [LIT] Tear roughly into small pieces. [MET] Destroy (e.g. someone's argument).

Tear oneself away Make oneself leave (usually used in negative).

It was such a good exhibition that I could hardly tear myself away.

Tear one's hair Be angry, very anxious, perplexed.

I was tearing my hair with impatience at the delay.

Tears **Bathed, drowned** *or* **dissolved in tears** Weeping excessively.

Crocodile tears Hypocritical grief; tears shed by one who is not, in fact, grieving at all. [Or. The legend, based on the sucking and oozing sounds made by the movement of crocodiles in the swampy ground in which they live, that the animals deliberately weep noisily, so that travellers go to rescue what they imagine to be a lost child.]

Reduce to tears Compel to weep by pity or distress (or, occasionally, by excessive laughter).

Tease **Tease out** Separate (parts of problem, discussion, etc.) into components.

Teens **In one's teens; teenage** At any age from thirteen to nineteen inclusive.

Teeth **Armed to the teeth** Having many weapons.

Get one's teeth into Start work seriously on.

In the teeth of In spite of; without regard to.

They married in the teeth of her parents' opposition.

Lie in one's teeth Tell serious and blatant untruths. (Emphatic form of 'lie'.)

Make someone's teeth chatter Cause one to tremble or shiver so much that the upper and lower teeth click together.

Put teeth into Give effectiveness (to law, rules, etc.)

Set one's teeth on edge [LIT] Cause a grating or tingling sensation around one's teeth, through their contact with acid, etc. [MET] Cause a general discomfort at some particularly harsh sound, or by embarrassing action or speech.

For heaven's sake oil that wheel—it sets my teeth on edge.

Show one's teeth Threaten.

Skin of one's teeth See under *Skin.*

Tell **As far as one can tell** As far as one knows.

Tell one's beads Say a series of prayers as one passes one's fingers over the beads of a rosary; say the Rosary. ('Tell' in this sense means 'count'.)

Tell off 1. Select a number of persons by name for a special purpose.

The captain told off six men to act as escort to the prisoners. 2. Reprove. Express one's views frankly and unfavourably.

I told him off for keeping me waiting.

Tell that to the Marines (or, more correctly, **the Horse Marines**, such a corps being non-existent, as Marines are a sea-going force) Tell that story to someone who doesn't exist, since no one who does exist is likely to believe it.

You never can tell Appearances are misleading.

Temper **Lose one's temper; be out of temper** Exchange
one's good temper for a bad temper; be angry, irritable,
annoyed, in an unpleasant mood. Opposite: **keep
one's temper.**
Temper the wind to the shorn lamb Arrange
matters to suit the weakest element.

Ten **Ten to one** It is ten chances to one that it will happen;
very probably. (Similary other numbers.)
Tell him you've broken the vase; ten to one he won't be angry.

Tenterhooks

On tenterhooks In a state of acute anxiety or
suspense. [Or. Tenterhooks are hooks on which cloth is
stretched after being woven.]

Terms **Come to terms** Reach a formal and businesslike
arrangement.
If you're willing to sell your house, we can soon come to terms.
Couched in terms Expressed in words.
In terms of In the language of.
On good *or* **bad terms with** Having a friendly *or*
unfriendly relationship with (normally applied to
relationships between people). Similarly **on speaking
terms** = in a relationship which is such that both
parties speak to one another.
*We have always been on bad terms (we are not on speaking
terms) with our neighbours.*
On one's terms With the conditions (e.g. price, rules)
laid down by one.

Test **Put to the test** Make (person or thing) undergo
examination or trial.
Stand the test of time Continue to be effective
despite normal effects of passage of time.

Thank **Thank goodness, heaven, etc.** A general ejaculation
of gratitude.
Thank one's (lucky) stars Be grateful. [Or. The stars
are supposed to protect a person and bring good
fortune—and the reverse.]
*You may thank your lucky stars that you weren't in the house
when the party was on.*
Thanks to Owing to; because of.
No thanks to No credit or gratitude is due to.

That **At that** Thereupon. Then.
At that, the meeting broke up.
In that Since. In so far as.

I could understand his point of view, in that I'd been in a similar position myself.

That will do No more, or nothing else is required. That is sufficient.

That's more like it You (or thing, progress etc.) are becoming more satisfactory.

That's that A concluding emphasis to a statement. *I refuse, and that's that.*

That is to say To express differently, or more fully. *He's a cutler—that is to say, he sells knives and sharp tools.*

Then   **Then and there** Immediately. On the spot. Also **there and then.**

There   **There you are** This is what you need.

Thick   **In the thick of** In the densest, most congested part [LIT and MET]. *We were in the thick of the crowd. Don't disturb me—I'm in the thick of a job.*

Thick and fast In large numbers very quickly.

Thick end of the stick Worst aspect of the bargain.

Thick-skinned Not sensitive to reproach, criticism, etc. *He's too thick-skinned to see the impression he makes.*

Through thick and thin Through every trouble or difficulty, good fortune or bad fortune.

Thin   **Into thin air** So as to be invisible.

Thin end of the wedge Small but dangerous precedent.

Thin on top Balding.

Thing   **And another thing** Moreover.

Just one of those things Something unavoidable.

Make a thing of Create fuss over.

Just the thing; the very thing Exactly what is needed or appropriate. *This carpet is just the thing for the bedroom.*

Know a thing or two Be experienced, shrewd.

Of all things From among all the things which might have happened. *And now—of all things!—we shall have to move house.*

On to a good thing Engaged in a profitable or beneficial activity. *As the only vet in the town, he's on to a good thing.*

Taking one thing with another Weighing the advantages against the disadvantages; considering all the circumstances.

The thing (to do) *or* **the done thing** The correct procedure. The custom. The fashion.

Think **Think a lot of** Esteem highly.

Think back to Recall to mind.

Think better of it Abandon an unwise decision.
He was going to argue with the shop-assistant, but thought better of it.

Think big Have ambitious thoughts, plans, etc.

Think fit *or* **proper** Decide; consider suitable or appropriate.

Think for oneself Be capable of independent thought.

Think highly *or* **much of** Admire.

Think little *or* **nothing of** Treat casually; regard as normal.

Think no end of Have a very high opinion of.

Think no more of Forget.

Think out Meditate upon; consider.
We must think out some other way of repairing it.

Think over Consider at some length.
I'll need a few days to think it over.

Think through Consider until problem is solved or conclusion reached.

Think twice Consider very carefully.

Way of thinking Point of view; personal aspect.

This **This, that and the other** Various unspecified things.

Thorn **A thorn in the flesh** *or* **in one's side** An infliction; an annoyance which one has to endure. [Or. The custom of the ancient Pharisees of putting thorns in their garments to prick their legs when walking.]

Thought **A penny for your thoughts** What are you thinking about?

Quick as thought Instantly.

Second thoughts Further consideration.
On second thoughts, I'll go by train.

Take no thought for Do not worry or concern yourself about.

Take thought Consider thoroughly.

Train of thought Direction in which one's thinking is moving.

Thread **Hang by a thread** Be in precarious position or state.

Lose the thread (of an argument, etc.) Stop understanding.

Pick up the thread(s) Resume after an interruption.

It's difficult to pick up the thread of this book after a week.
Thread *or* **edge one's way** Move to one's
destination through narrow or crowded streets.
We threaded our way through the crowds at the station.

Threshold **On the threshold** [LIT] The 'sill' (horizontal piece of
wood or stone) that forms the bottom of the door-frame
at the entrance of a building. [MET] The beginning of
anything.
*The scientist felt he was on the threshold of solving a tremendous
mystery.*

Throat **Cut one's own throat** Damage oneself.
Cut one another's throats Damage one another (in
competition, etc.).
Ram down one's throat Bring forcibly to one's
attention.

Through By means of.
He obtained the information through his own efforts.
Through and through Thoroughly.

Throw **Throw away** Lose by neglect or recklessness.
He threw away his chances of winning.
Throw dust in the eyes of Obscure the facts;
mislead.
*The Prime Minister was accused of throwing dust in the
public's eye.*
Throw good money after bad Risk further loss in
attempt to make good a previous one.
Throw in Give in addition.
*The herrings were ten for £1 and the fishmonger threw in an
extra one.*
Throw in the towel Surrender.
Throw light upon Make plainer.
This information may throw light upon the mystery.
Throw off Discard. Get rid of.
He appears to have thrown off his cold.
Throw off the scent Distract from what is of true
importance, from the true facts. [Or. Hunting.]
*The police were completely thrown off the scent, and arrested the
wrong man.*
Throw oneself into Engage energetically in.
Throw one's hand in Abandon (project, etc.).
Throw one's lot in with Join.
Throw open Make accessible.
They intend to throw open the house to the public.

Throw out Reject. Distract.

Throw out a suggestion Make a suggestion, usually tentatively.

Throw over Abandon; discard; have no further association with.

Throw up the sponge Surrender; abandon abruptly; admit complete defeat. [Or. Boxing. The sponge used to bathe the boxers' faces was thrown into the air when the loser admits his defeat.]

Thumb **Thumb-nail sketch** 1. Small, quickly done picture. 2. Brief description in words.

Under one's thumb Under one's control or influence.

Thunder **Like a thunderclap** *or* **thunderbolt** Causing great astonishment.

The news of his resignation was like a thunderclap.

Thunders of applause Applause so noisy and continuous that it suggests thunder.

Thunderstruck Overcome with astonishment.

Tick **Tick off** Check (by placing a small mark, e.g. against items in a list).

Tide **Tide over** Continue until changed and usually improved conditions take place.

I need £1 to tide me over till I can get to the bank.

Tie **Black tie** A black tie worn with a dinner-jacket. (The idiom is used as indicating the whole outfit.)

White tie Similarly, a white tie worn with white waistcoat, coat with 'tails', and black trousers—the more formal evening dress.

Tiger **Paper tiger** Fierce-looking but ineffectual person.

Tight **On a tight-rope** Precariously balanced.

Tight-fisted Mean.

Tight-lipped Uncommunicative.

Time **Against time** with all speed.

Ahead of time Before the expected time.

All the time Continuosly.

At one time Formerly.

At times At intervals; occasionally.

He seems at times to know more than he says.

Similar to **now and then; now and again.**

Beat time The action of a conductor indicating the 'beats' in the music with his baton.

Before one's time Before one was born.

Compare **born before one's time.**

Bide one's time Wait patiently. [Or. 'Bide' is an

abbrev. of 'abide' = stay, remain.]
If we bide our time it will all come right.
For the time being Temporarily; during the time that is immediately coming.
We are going to Rome as soon as we can, but are staying in London for the time being.
From time to time Occasionally.
I only go to the cinema from time to time.
A good time 1. A highly pleasurable time.
Jane and Joan are at Brighton, having a thoroughly good time.
2. A considerable period.
I am going into the town, and shall not be back for a good time.
Hard times Times of poverty, suffering, or discomfort.
He went through hard times when he was young.
Have no time for Be unable or willing to spend time dealing with.
High time Fully time.
It is high time that we went home.
In (the) course of time Eventually; after some time had passed.
In time 1. Before it is too late.
The doctor came in time to save her life.
2. After some considerable time had passed.
In time he forgot all about her.
In good time Early; with time to spare.
Be at the station in good time.
In one's own good time At a time convenient to oneself.
In one's own time Outside working hours.
In the nick of time Just in time; almost, but not quite, too late.
The door of the tiger's cage was shut in the nick of time.
In no *or* **less than no time** Very soon; almost immediately.
We shall be ready in less than no time.
Similar to **in half a tick; two-twos; half a jiffy.**
Keep good (bad time) (of clock, etc.) Be accurate (inaccurate).
Lose no time Act at once.
Many a time Repeatedly; frequently.
Many a time we walk by the river.
Once upon a time Some time ago; in the past. (The traditional beginning to children's stories.)
Once upon a time there lived a king with three sons.

Overtime Extra time; additional hours of work for which payment is made.

Part-time Time which does not occupy all the usual working day.

Marjory has a part-time job taking care of young children.

Pass the time of day (with) Exchange greeting (with a person).

Play for time Delay so as to gain time.

Pressed for time Short of time; very busy.

I can't stay more than ten minutes, as I am pressed for time.

Stand the test of time Remain valid, unaltered, strong, etc., despite the passage or effect of time.

Unlike some laws, this one has stood the test of time very well.

Stated time A time already fixed.

Take time by the forelock Act promptly and without delay. [Or. Time is always represented as an old man, bald except for a 'forelock' or tuft of hair over his forehead.] Similar to **strike while the iron is hot.**

Time after time Repeatedly.

The fence has had to be rebuilt time after time.

Time and again Frequently.

The children have been warned about the danger time and again.

Time immemorial see **Time out of mind.**

Time's up The stated time has come to an end, is finished.

Time's up—you must say good-bye.

Time of day The time, the hour.

What's the time of day?

Time of life Age.

At my time of life I can't be expected to dance.

Time of one's life A most enjoyable period.

I had the time of my life at the party.

Time off Time spent away from work.

Time on one's hands Time to waste, to spare; superfluous time.

As I had a good deal of time on my hands, I decided to explore the City.

Time out of mind; from time immemorial
Longer than can be remembered. [Old f.]

Time was There was a time.

Time will tell All will become known with the passage of time.

Times out of *or* **without number** Many times; times beyond counting.

Times, days, years, *etc.,* **to come** In the future.
In times to come none of us will have to work.

Work against time Use special efforts to finish a piece of work within a stated time.
We are working against time to complete the house by Christmas.

Tip **On the tip of one's tongue** (Word) known to speaker but forgotten. On the verge of being spoken.

Tip the balance Exert influence in favour of one of two sides.

Tiptoe **On tiptoe** [LIT] Standing on the tips of one's toes. [MET] a state of excitement and tension.
The children were on tiptoe when the day of the party arrived.

Tip-top Excellent; the best of its kind.
We had a tip-top breakfast at the hotel.

Tit for tat An equivalent; something, frequently unpleasant, given in return for something else.

Tittle-tattle Idle, chattering gossip.

To **To and fro** (= To and from.) From one spot to another and back again.
The sentry paced to and fro.

Toe **Toe the line** Conform, usually under pressure, to rules, etc.
The Party expects M.P.s to toe the line.

Tread on one's toes Offend one's feelings, prejudices, etc.

Together **Together with** With; also.
I am selling the house, together with the furniture.

Token **By the same token** Further; moreover. Similarly.

Tom **(Any) Tom, Dick or (and) Harry** Persons taken at random. Any unspecified people.
It's not the sort of club that admits any Tom, Dick or Harry.

Ton **Like a ton of bricks** Very heavily or severely.
Weigh half a ton Be very heavy.

Tone **Tone down** Reduce severity (of remarks, statement, etc.).

Tongue **Give tongue** Repeat. [Or. Hunting. Hounds are said to give tongue, or utter their peculiar cry, when the fox is seen.]

Hold one's tongue Become silent; cease to speak.

Keep a civil tongue in one's head Avoid impoliteness.

Lose one's tongue Be too bashful to speak. Opposite: **find one's tongue.**

On the tip of one's tongue On the verge of being spoken; almost but not quite uttered. (Word) known to speaker, but forgotten.

Tongue-tied Silent through embarrassment or fear.

Wag one's tongue Talk indiscreetly, or too much.

Too many tongues have been wagging for the matter to remain confidential any longer.

With one's tongue hanging out Very thirsty.

With one's tongue in one's cheek Without meaning what one says; insincerely.

Too **None too** Less than.

Tooth **A sweet tooth** A liking for sweet things—jam etc.

Long in the tooth Old. [Or. Horses, where age can be estimated from length of teeth because the gums recede.]

Tooth and nail With extreme fierceness.

Top **From top to toe** [LIT] From one's head to one's feet. [MET] From beginning to end.

She was impeccably dressed from top to toe.

On top of 1. In addition to.

2. In control of.

On top of the world In excellent spirits.

Top gear The highest gear of a car engine.

Top speed; full speed As fast as possible.

Top of the tree *or* **ladder** The highest point in one's business or profession.

He has reached the top of the tree as a surgeon.

Top up Fill up something partly empty. Finish; conclude.

Please top up the oil and water.

See under ***Sleep.***

Topsy-turvy

In a state of confusion or disarray. Inverted, the normal position reversed.

After the party, the whole room was topsy-turvy.

Similar to **upside down.**

Toss **Toss up** Decide by spinning a coin. See **heads or tails.**

Hence **win the toss, lose the toss.**

A toss-up A complete uncertainty; as likely as unlikely.

It's a toss-up whether I will be able to come.

Touch **Finishing touches** Final details.

In touch with In communication, or contact, with.

I haven't been in touch with him for some years.

Lose touch Cease to have any communication with.

Opposite: **Keep in touch (with).**
I used to see him a lot, but I've lost touch with him lately.
Out of touch 1. Not in communication.
2. Lacking up-to-date knowledge.
Personal touch Detail(s) showing individual influence or concern.
Touch and go Extremely doubtful or precarious.
It was touch and go whether we should arrive in time.
Touch on Same as **Touch upon.**
Touch up Restore or improve by a number of small details (especially with a brush or pen).
Touch upon Refer to briefly.
Touch wood Expression meaning 'I hope my luck continues'.

Tower **Ivory tower** Pleasant shelter from harsh reality.
We are living in an ivory tower if we think we can ignore the growth of world population.
Tower of strength A great support and help.
In a towering passion *or* **rage** Dominated by tremendous danger.

Town **Man about town** Socialite.
On the town Enjoying oneself in places of entertainment.
Talk of the town Subject of general conversation or gossip in a town.
Up to town Into London.

Track **Beaten track** [LIT] A pathway which has been beaten or flattened by many feet. [MET] A regular routine; customary procedure.
They live on Dartmoor, well off the beaten track.
Cover one's tracks Conceal what one has done.
Keep track of Follow course or progress of. Opposite: **lose track of.**
On the wrong track Follow wrong course in argument, investigation, etc. See also *Tack.*
Track down Find.
See under *Keep.*

Trade **Of a trade** Following the same occupation.
Trade on Take advantage of.
Trick of the trade Device known only to those in particular profession, job, etc.

Trail **Trail one's coat** Attempt to start a quarrel or argument. [Or. To trail or drag one's coat behind one was an accepted method of issuing a general challenge; any person stepping on the coat was considered to have insulted its owner.]

Trail off Become weaker and feebler.
He began by shouting, but his voice trailed off into a mere whisper.

Tread **Tread on the heels of** Follow immediately after.
Tread under foot Treat with contempt. Usually **trodden under foot.**

Treasure **Treasure (up)** Retain, as something precious and valuable.
We should treasure every moment of such a day as this.

Tree **Grow on trees** Be plentiful.

Trial **Give a trial** Test. Similar to **try out.**
Trial and error Repeated attempts, expecting failure, until success is achieved.
Trial of strength Contest to discover who is stronger or strongest.

Tribute **Pay tribute** [LIT] To pay a fixed amount to a ruler or other governor. [MET] Admit one's indebtedness to some helper or benefactor.
Tribute to Sign of merit in.

Trice **In a trice** [Old f.] [LIT] A period of time equal to one-third of a second. [MET] Very quickly.

Trick **Up to one's tricks** Aware of one's characteristic behaviour, devices, etc.
Up to one's (old) tricks (again) Behaving in characteristic manner (deviously, mischievously, etc.).

Trivet **Right as a trivet** In sound health or condition. [Or. Trivet = tripod for holding cooking pots. Right = steady, therefore good.]

Trivial **The trivial round** The routine of everyday life; the succession of small regular duties. [Or. Abbrev. of lines from Keble's hymn, 'The trivial round, the common task, will furnish all we need to ask'.]

Trot **Trot out** Quote, often glibly or predictably; exhibit; produce in support.
He trotted out the old proverb that there's no time like the present.

Trouble **Go to the trouble of doing** Concern oneself to do. Also **take the trouble to.**
Look for trouble 1. Wish to cause dissension, conflict, etc.
2. Take risks.

No trouble No inconvenience.

Trouble brewing Trouble is likely to occur.

Trouble in store Trouble likely to occur at some later time.

Trousers **Wear the trousers** Be dominant. (Usually of women).

Truck **Have no truck with** Refuse to deal with.

True **(Run) true to form** (Happen) predictably, in accordance with expectation or past experience.

Trump **Trump-card** Piece of valuable information, knowledge, etc., or an unexpected idea, produced surprisingly to outwit or defeat an opponent. [Or. Card-playing. 'Trump' is an abbrev. for French *triomphe*, a game of cards = triumph, and a trump-card is a 'triumph' or winning card.]
The Prime Minister played his trump-card by saying that negotiations had in fact already begun.

Trump up Falsely state; tell maliciously and untruthfully.

Trumpet **Blow one's own trumpet** Boast of one's own work or actions.

Trumpet-call [LIT] Tune played by a trumpet or trumpets alone, usually in manner of a summons. [MET] An urgent summons to action.
His speech was a trumpet-call for public protest.

Trust **Take on trust** Accept without proof.

Trust with Consign to without serious misgivings.

Truth **Home truths** Unpalatable facts about oneself.

The naked (plain, simple, sober, *or* stark) truth The truth, and nothing but the truth.

Arrive at the truth Discover what really occurred.

Truth is stranger than fiction Things which actually happen are sometimes more unexpected than the things which are invented in literature.

Try **Try conclusions** Start a struggle that must have a definite ending.

Try one's hand at Attempt.
I'm going to try my hand at cooking while Jane is away.

Try on Put on a garment to see if it fits.

Try out Put to the test.

Tub **Tub-thumper** Ranting orator.

Tuck **Tuck up** Wrap closely in bedclothes, etc.

Tug **Tug-of-war** Conflict in which each side seeks to retain own position rather than occupy other's. [Or. Game between two teams pulling opposite ends of rope.]

Tune **Call the tune** Control events.

Change one's tune Assume a different style of manner or language. Similar to **sing a different tune.**

In tune In agreement. In harmony. Opposite: **out of tune.**

To the tune of At a cost of.

The town is building a new hall to the tune of three million pounds.

Tunnel **Tunnel vision** Inability to understand more than one view.

Turn **As it turned out** As it resulted; happened; as the sequel.

Everyone thought farmers would be ruined, but as it turned out they were more prosperous than before.

At every turn Continually.

By turns In rotation. Alternatively.

Do a good _or_ **bad turn** Help (or the reverse).

Done to a turn Cooked perfectly.

In turn In succession.

Not know which way to turn Not know what course of action to follow or where to find help.

Not turn a hair Remain calm, in control, unperturbed.

On the turn Changing.

Out of turn Before or after the proper time.

Take a turn Pass from one state of health to another.

Take turns; take it in turns Act in rotation or regular order.

We took turns in mowing the lawn.

To a turn Exactly.

Turn about Face in opposite direction.

Turn to (good) account Use; make use of successfully.

Turn adrift Cast out to wander. [Or. Nautical. A vessel is adrift if it is floating without control wherever the winds and current may take it.]

Turn against Change from like to dislike; regard with aversion.

Turn around Same as **turn round.**

Turn-about Change (of opinion, policy, etc.).

Turn aside Alter the direction in which one is going. Temporarily leave one occupation for another.

Turn away Refuse to meet.

Turn one's back on Deliberately ignore.

Turn the corner Pass a crisis successfully.

The patient has turned the corner, and will recover.
Turn a deaf ear to Refuse to listen to.
Turn down 1. [LIT] Fold over and flatten down.
He turned down the collar of his coat.
2. [MET] Refuse or decline definitely.
He turned down every offer of help.
Turn of events Change in the course of events, or
happenings.
*A year later, owing to a strange turn of events, I found myself
in Paris again.*
Turn of phrase Manner of speech.
Turn one's hand to Undertake a variety of work, or
work that is not one's normal occupation.
*I'm a carpenter by trade, but I can turn my hand to bricklaying
or painting.*
See under **Head.**
Turn an honest penny See under **Penny.**
Turn in Deliver.
Turn inside out [LIT] Turn so that the inner is
outside, and vice versa. [MET] Examine or explore with
extreme thoroughness.
I've turned my desk inside out, but cannot find the missing paper.
Turn off *or* **on** 1. Stop (or start) something by turning
(a tap, knob, switch, etc.).
2. Turn (car, oneself) in different direction.
Turn on Become aggressive towards.
Turn out 1. Manufacture.
We can turn out three thousand cups a week.
2. Compel to leave; evict.
*The family were turned out of their cottage because they could
not pay their rent.*
3. Empty (usually to tidy).
He turned out his desk.
4. Transpire. Be the final outcome.
It turned out that he was George's father.
5. Similar to **turn off.**
Turn-out 1. Display.
The Lord Mayor's show was a magnificent turn-out.
2. Number of people coming (to attend, vote, etc.).
Turn over 1. Cause to fall over.
2. Hand over.
Turn-over The money taken in a business, shop, etc.
Turn over a new leaf Change for the better.
Turn out well Suceed in life.

He's a sensible and clever boy, and ought to turn out well.
Turn round Face in opposite direction.
Turn *or* **tilt the scales** [LIT] Make the scale fall, and so register something slightly heavier than the weight on the opposite side.
He turned the scale at eleven stone.
[MET] Finally decide some matter which is in doubt.
Turn of speed Capacity for speed.
This car has a fine turn of speed.
Turn the tables Reverse the position.
Turn tail Turn and run away.
Turn the tide Reverse the course of events.
Turn of the tide [LIT] The point at which the sea ceases to flow out and begins to flow back, or vice versa. [MET] The point at which success is followed by failure, or vice versa.
Turn to Begin work.
Turn and turn about First one, then the other, for equal periods.
Turn turtle Turn upside down in the sea.
Turn up 1. Arrive; appear.
Our guests did not turn up until nearly midnight.
2. Find.
Turn up one's nose Sneer.
Now she has become well known she turns up her nose at plain food.
Turn upon Blame or attack.

Tweedle **Tweedledum and Tweedledee** People whose opinions (or appearance) are alike [Or. Poem of John Byrom satirizing rival musicians whose music was in fact similar.]

Twiddle **Twiddle one's thumbs** Waste one's time. Be forced to be kept idle. Similar to **kick one's heels.**

Twinkle **Twinkling of an eye** Very quickly. [Or. 'Twinkling' means a rapid twist or turn, and is of the same origin as 'wriggle'.] Also **in a twinkle.**

Twist **Twist one's arm** [LIT] Hurt one's arm by twisting it. [MET] Bring pressure to bear to persuade someone. [Or. Method of torture.]
I think he'll come if you twist his arm.

Twister One who 'twists', or systematically cheats.

Two **In two-twos** In a moment; almost instantly.
Put two and two together Draw conclusion from given facts.

Two-faced Hypocritical.
Two penny-halfpenny Cheap. Insignificant.

U

Under **Come under** Be classified with.
Cups and saucers come under crockery.
Fall under [MET] Similar to **come under.**
Under a cloud In disgrace.
Underdog Person in an inferior position.
The English are reputed to have a special sympathy for the underdog.
Under one's wing Under one's protection, guidance.
Under the sun Anywhere in the world.
Under way See under *Way.*

Understanding
Come to an understanding Agree and co-operate, after discussions and explanations.
On *or* **with the understanding** According to an agreement, instruction, etc.
You may go to the disco, on the distinct (clear) (precise) understanding that you are back before midnight.

Up **All up** Hopeless.
On the up and up Improving.
Something is up Something is wrong. Something unusual is happening.
Up against Close to.
Up and about Well enough to leave one's bed after an illness.
Up and down 1. [LIT].
2. To and fro.
Ups and downs Good times and bad times.
Up in arms Indignant; resentful.
Up to date See under *Date.*
Up and doing Active; busy.
We must be up and doing if we are going to catch the train.
Up-end Place so that the small or narrow end is uppermost.
We shall have to up-end it to get it out of the room.
Up to the eyes Immersed; completely occupied with.
I am up to the eyes in work.
Up to the hilt To the limit, the greatest possible extent. [Or. The hilt is the handle of a sword, at which the blade ends.]

The property is mortgaged up to the bilt.

Up to the mark In one's normal state of health; capable of doing something.

Up to now Until the present time.

Come up to the scratch See under *Scratch.*

Up to a thing or two Alert; shrewd.

Up to something Privately planning; plotting some scheme.

I guess by the look on her face that she is up to something.

Up stage [LIT] The front of the stage, the position of most prominence. [Or. Theatre.] [MET] Haughty, conceited behaviour.

Up to it Capable of doing anything.

The hill is steep: are you up to it?

(Not) up to much (Not) good.

I didn't think the party was up to much.

Up to you The responsibility is yours.

Up a tree In a state of desperation.

What's up? What is hapenning?

Upon **Upon which** When this occurred.

The boy admitted that he stole, upon which his father thrashed him.

Uppers **On one's uppers** Very poor; completely destitute. [Or. When the sole of a shoe is completely worn out, the wearer is walking on the 'uppers' or upper layers of leather.]

Upper crust Aristocracy.

Upper hand Mastery.

Upside **Upside-down** Inverted.

Upward **Upward of** More than.

Use **Make use of** Utilize, employ.

Used to Accustomed to.

Use up Finish. Consume the remainder of.

Useful **Make oneself useful** Give assistance.

V

V **V-sign** Gesture of hand with first and second finger extended, the others clenched, as sign of contempt (when back of hand faces outward) or victory (when palm faces outward).

Vain **In vain** Ineffectively; without any result.

Take in vain Treat lightly.

Vale **Vale of years** Old age.

Valour **The better part of valour** Discretion. Carefulness. Wise action. [Or. Proverb: 'Discretion is the better part of valour.']
The general decided on the better part of valour, and surrendered.

Value **Set a value on** Estimate the value of.

Van **In the van** In the front. [Or. Nautical, from the French *avant*. Abbrev. for 'vanguard'; the foremost or leading position.]

Variance **At variance** In a state of quarrelling or disagreement.

Veer **Veer round** Change one's opinions, language, behaviour, mood, etc.
At first Simon agreed with me; then he veered round and agreed with Brian.

Veil **Draw a veil over** Remain silent about; conceal.
Take the veil Become a fully initiated nun.

Velvet **Velvet glove** Gentleness. See under *Fist.*

Vengeance **With a vengeance** To an excessive degree.
There will be trouble with a vengeance when the boss hears what happened.

Vent **Give vent to** Give expression to; allow (one's emotions) to escape.
See *Spleen.*

Ventilate **Ventilate a grievance** Same as **air a grievance.**

Venture **Nothing venture (nothing win** *or* **gain)** One must be bold (if one wishes to win something).
Venture on Take the risk of making.

Verdict **Bring in** *or* **return a verdict** The legal phrase for a jury recording a decision.

Verge **Verge on** Come close to.

Very **The very thing** See **just the thing,** under *Thing.*
Very well See under *Well.*

Vested **Vested interest** [LIT] Permanent rights. [MET] Personal involvement; keen commitment.

Vet Abbrev. for 'veterinary surgeon', one who examines and cures sick animals. Now frequently used as a verb in the sense of examining and, where necessary, correcting any form of work.
I shall be glad if you'll vet what I've written.

Vex **Vexed question** Difficult, often-debated problem.

View **Bird's-eye view** A comprehensive view from above, such as a bird would obtain.
You get a bird's-eye view of Paris from the Eiffel Tower.

Bring into view Reveal to one's sight.

Extreme views Opinions which do not find favour with the majority.

In full view (of) Plainly visible (to).

To have in view To be contemplating, planning.

In view of After consideration of.

In view of what you tell me, I shall not go.

In my view In my opinion.

One-sided view A prejudiced and limited outlook.

On view Available for inspection.

Point of view Position from which opinion is expressed.

Taking a long view Planning over a long period.

With a view to With the purpose of. In the hope of.

Violet **Shrinking violet** Shy person.

Viper **Viper in one's bosom** Person who betrays one who has befriended him or her.

Virtue **By** *or* **in virtue of** As a result or consequence of.

By virtue of his position, the Lord Mayor is the chief magistrate of the city.

Make a virtue of necessity Gain an advantage, or pretend to be acting virtuously (e.g. out of a sense of duty or goodwill, etc.), when one is in fact under compulsion.

Have the virtue of Have the good quality of.

This sofa has the virtue of being convertible into a bed.

Visit **Visit the sins on** Punish a person for the sins someone else has committed. [Or. Bible: 'I will visit the sins of the fathers upon the children.']

Voice **Give voice to** Express; state publicly.

In good voice Having voice in good condition (for singing, etc.).

Raise the voice Speak more loudly. Opposite: **lower the voice**. Speak more softly.

At the top of one's voice As loudly as possible.

A voice in the matter A share in the control; a right to express one's views.

With one voice Unanimously.

Vote **Vote down** Reject by voting.

Vote in Elect by voting.

Vote on Judge by voting.

W

Wag **Tongues are wagging** There is gossip.

Wagon **Hitch one's wagon to a star** 1. Entrust oneself to luck or belief in good fortune.
2. Support person in hope of sharing their success.

Wait **Wait and see** Await outcome of events.
Wait (up)on 1. Pay a formal visit. (Now almost obsolete.)
2. Attend to the wants (of).
The dinner was good, but there weren't enough people waiting on the guests.
Wait up Not go to bed (expecting someone's arrival).
You wait Abbreviation for 'You wait and find out what will happen'.

Waiting **Play a waiting game** Delay so as to gain later advantage.

Wake **In the wake** In the footsteps or path of. [Or. Nautical. The 'wake' is the track left by a vessel as it passes through the water.]
Refugees follow in the wake of war.

Walk **Walk into** Encounter through unwariness.
Walk of life Occupation; profession.
Walk off one's feet Exhaust one by walking.
Walk-out Departure, usually as mark of protest.
The orchestra staged a walk-out when the conductor prolonged the rehearsal.
Walk out on Leave, unexpectedly and usually in pique (so that difficulties are caused).
You can't really blame his wife for walking out on him.
Walk over 1. Treat with contempt.
2. Win because of lack of competition.
A walk-over An extremely easy victory.
Walk the streets 1. [LIT] E.g. because of loneliness.
2. Be a prostitute.

Wall **Go to the wall** Fail as result of competition.
Walls have ears Beware of eavesdroppers.
Weakest to the wall Whoever is least able to compete will fail. See under **Weak.**
With one's back to the wall Desperately, as a final defence.

Wane **On the wane** Diminishing; decreasing in power. [Or. Astronomy. A star 'wanes' when its light decreases.]

Want **For want of** Because of lack of.
It is rotting for want of paint.

Found wanting Discovered to be unsatisfactory.

In want of In need of.

War **Be in the wars** Show signs of physical damage.

Cold war Unfriendly relations between nations shown by propaganda, lack of diplomatic or economic co-operation, etc., but not by fighting.

Wage war Conduct war.

War to the knife *or* **the death** A bitter and ruthless struggle.

War of nerves Unfriendly relationships between nations, with attempts to undermine confidence, morale, etc., or to make threats, but not to fight.

Warm **Make it (things) warm for someone** Create difficulties for person.

Wart **Warts and all** Including blemishes.

Wash **Come out in the wash** Reach satisfactory conclusion.

Wash one's dirty linen in public Discuss or reveal one's own shortcomings, scandals, etc., publicly.

Wash one's hands of Refuse any responsibility for.

Do as you like; I wash my hands of the whole business.

Wash out [LIT] Remove by washing.

I've washed out the stain on your coat.

[MET] Obliterate.

He tried to wash out the memories of the past.

Washed-out Tired, incapable of effort, as result of energetic activity (or over-indulgence).

Waste **Go** *or* **run to waste** Be wasted.

Waste one's breath Talk in vain.

You'll simply be wasting your breath if you talk to him.

Watch **On the watch** In a state of watchfulness. Similar to **on the alert.**

Set a watch Arrange for systematic watching.

A watched pot never boils Time seems long when one is waiting for something to happen. [Or. Proverb.]

Watch it *or* **yourself** *or* **your step** Take care.

Water **Hold water** 1. [LIT] Contain without leaking.

That bucket won't hold enough water.

2. [MET] Be true, and capable of being tested.

His account of the robbery won't hold water.

In deep water(s) In great difficulties.

In hot water In trouble.

Of the first water Of the finest possible quality; to the greatest degree.

Make one's mouth water Be intensely attractive,

delightful to eat or see.

Pour cold water on Prevent. Discourage.

Still waters run deep A reserved disposition or manner may conceal strong emotions or unexpected characteristics.

Throw cold water on Depreciate; discourage.

Water down Weaken.

Water under the bridge What has happened and cannot be changed.

Wave **Wave aside** Dismiss as irrelevant.

Wave down Halt by signalling with wave of hand.

Wax **Be wax in one's hands** Be subservient to one.

Wax and wane Increase and decrease.

Way **Across the way** *or* **street** *or* **road,** *etc*. On the opposite side.

All manner *or* **sorts** *or* **kinds of ways** A large variety of ways.

All the way The whole distance.

By the way Incidentally. (The phrase is used when a speaker wishes to pass abruptly from one subject to another which has little or no connection with it.)

By way of 1. By passing through.
We came by way of Banbury.
2. As substitute for. With the intention of making.
He sent her flowers by way of an apology.

Clear the way Remove obstacles.

Come one's way Become available.

Find a way Discover a method.

Find its way Reach destination.

Get in *or* **out of the way** Obstruct (or the reverse).
Please get out of my way.
Is this ladder getting in the way?

Get into the way of Acquire the habit of doing.

Get one's own way Get what one wants.

Give way 1. [LIT] Break.
The railings gave way, and three people fell in the river.
2. [MET] Yield.

Go one's way 1. Depart.
2. Be favourable to one.

Go one's own way Follow one's personal desires, without accepting guidance or advice.
Similar to **have one's own way; follow one's own devices.**

Go out of one's way Make special effort.

Go the way of all flesh. Die.
Have a way with Be skilful in dealing with
Have one's own way Do as one wishes.
In a bad way In an unsatisfactory condition.
In a fair way Likely to.
In a small way In modest circumstances.
He's a builder, but only in a small way.
In a way In certain respects; to a certain extent.
In many ways In many respects. Also **in more ways than one.**
In no way Not at all.
In the way Obstructing; forming an obstruction.
I can't empty the bottle—there's a piece of cork in the way.
In the way of In a position to obtain.
She put me in the way of several good bargains.
Lead the way 1. Act as leader.
2. Show by example what ought to be done.
A long way off Very distant.
Look the other way Pretend not to notice.
Lose one's way Go astray.
Make one's way 1. Progress; travel on one's journey.
2. Succeed in one's profession.
Make way [LIT] Step aside. [MET] Retire from office.
Nothing out of the way Nothing unusual.
On the way Coming.
Once in a way Occasionally.
One way and another Taking everything together.
One way or another By some means.
Out of the way Difficult to find.
2. Completed.
3. In less inconvenient place.
Out of one's way Not as one has planned.
Over the way Same as **across the way.**
Parting of the ways Time for important decision.
Pave the way for Take steps to prepare for some change or future development.
The withdrawal of the troops paves the way for the granting of independence to the country.
Pay one's way Not be in debt.
Under way Beginning; moving. [Or. Nautical.]
Way of life Style in which one leads life.
Way of thinking Opinion.
Way of the world What normally happens in life.
Ways and means Methods of overcoming difficulties.

Wing one's way Travel swiftly, as a bird flies.

Weak **In a moment of weakness** At a time when one was not fully in control of oneself.

The weakest goes *or* **go to the wall** Those least able to help themselves are pushed aside or ignored. [Or. Said to be the benches lining the wall of the Chapel of the House of Commons, specially put there for the old or sick, at time when no other seating existed. Originally, therefore, the expression was one of concern.]

Weak in the head Idiotic.

Weak-kneed Easily intimidated.

Wear **Fair wear and tear** The normal lessening in value due to constant use.

Wear away Cause to disappear by friction.

Wear down Exhaust. Tire.

Wear one's heart on one's sleeve See under *Heart*.

Wear one's years well Not show signs of age.

Wear off Diminish and finally disappear.
The effects of the shock will soon wear off.

Wear on Pass or diminish slowly.
The hours wore on; night came.

Wear out 1. [LIT] Render useless by wear.
My boots are worn out.
2. [MET] Exhaust.
She had not slept all night and was completely worn out.

Wear thin Approach its end.

Wear well *or* **badly** Last a long (or short) time. Remain in working order, or presentable, for a long (short) time. (Also, jocularly, of people: retain (or lose) one's strength of youthfulness.)

Worse for wear Damaged.

Weather **Make heavy weather of** Treat as though it were a very serious matter. Find difficult.

Weather the storm Survive. ('Storm' is frequently used for financial and other troubles.)

Wedge **The thin end of the wedge** A small or trivial beginning which is likely to develop into something of much greater importance.

Weigh **Weigh down** Overburden.

Weigh heavy on Depress.

Weigh in 1. Enter a race or contest, having been weighed.
2. Enter forcefully.

Weigh one's words Choose what one says very carefully.

Weigh up Estimate. Come to a judgment about.

Welcome **Outstay one's welcome** Outstay as visitor for longer than is expected or convenient.

Well **As well** Also.

Come early, and bring your sister as well.

As well as In addition to.

Let well alone Do not interfere.

Very well A general expression of agreement and assent.

(All) well and good Unemotional or neutral acceptance of decision, etc.

If you decide not to believe me, well and good.

Well and truly Thoroughly.

Well built *or* **well set-up** Physically well constructed; fit.

Come off well Have good success or luck.

Well disposed (to) Inclined to favour.

The Council is well disposed to the idea.

Do oneself well Live in comfort. Enjoy oneself.

Do well out of Profit from.

Well done! Exclamation of approval.

Well founded Justifiable.

Well, I never! Abbrev. of 'Well, I never heard anything so extraordinary!' A common expression of astonishment.

Just as well Fortunate.

Leave well alone Refrain from having any dealings.

Well-lined purse Plenty of money.

Well off See under *Off.*

Well out of something Fortunate not to be involved in something any longer.

I never enjoyed the job and am well out of it.

Well-rounded *or* **-turned phrases, sentences,** *etc.* Elegant and graceful speech.

Well-to-do Fairly rich.

Wish person well Hope person prospers.

What **I tell you what** I make this suggestion.

I tell you what—let's go to a cinema.

Know what's what Be able to discriminate between what is of value and use, and what is not.

What for? Why?

What have you Anything else similar.

What's-his-name; what do you call him? A substitution for a name one has forgotten.
This morning I met that tall man with red hair—old what's-his-name.
Similar to **so-and-so.**

Wheat **Sort (separate) the wheat from the chaff** Distinguish between the useful and the useless.

Wheel **Put a spoke in one's wheel** Interfere with one's plans.
Similar to **throw a spanner in the works.**
Wheel and deal Scheme (usually in politics).
Wheels within wheels Small, often unknown motives and influences, which contribute to the general result. Secret procedures.

Wherewithal **The wherewithal** That which is necessary to accomplish something. Money.

Whether **Whether or no** Whether or not.

While **A good while** A long time.
A little while A short time. Opposite: **a long while.**
I'll telephone you in a little while.
For a while For some time.
Once in a while At long intervals. Occasionally.
Similar to **from time to time.**
See under *Worth.*

Whip **Have the whip hand** Be in a position to control.
Whipping-boy Scapegoat.

Whistle **Clean as a whistle** Very clean(ly).

Whit **Not a whit** Not at all. [Or. Whit = a speck, the smallest visible particle of matter.]
Bleed white Extract (from person or business, etc.) all possible wealth.
White *or* pure as driven snow Absolutely white. [Or. Driven snow is snow that has been 'driven', or blown, by the wind.]
White as a sheet Extremely pale; colourless.
White at the lips Extremely angry. Very afraid.
White hope Person expected to succeed.
See also under *Feather, Lie, Tie.*

Whole **On the whole** Having considered all sides of the matter.
I think, on the whole, we had better stay at home.
Whole-hearted Enthusiastic. Without doubts.

Why **The why and wherefore** The reasons for any action

or the existence of any condition. The explanation.

Wide **Wide awake** 1. [LIT] Entirely awake.

2. [MET] Alert, aware.

Give a wide berth to Avoid.

It is advisable to give a wide berth to that particular shop.

Wide of the mark Inaccurate. [Or. Shooting.]

You're very wide of the mark if you think I want to work here all my life.

Widespread Found in many places.

Wild **Wild and woolly** Incoherent. Idiotic.

Wild goose chase A practically hopeless search or other enterprise.

Wild guess Utterly haphazard guess.

Out in the wilds Far from civilisation. Not in a town. (Usually jocular.)

Wildfire **Like wildfire** With extreme rapidity. [Or. An inflammable mixture very difficult to extinguish. It was used in fighting at sea.]

Wile **Wile away (the time,** *etc.*) Pass, occupy (the time).

Will **Against my will** Contrary to my wishes.

At (one's own sweet) will Exactly as one pleases.

Free will Right, or power, to decide one's own course of action.

Hence **of my own free will**: without any compulsion being exercised on me.

Where there's a will there's a way If there is determination to do something, a means of doing it will be found.

A will of one's own Spirit, determination, of one's own.

Our baby is only a month old, but he's already shown that he has a will of his own.

Willy-nilly Just as one pleases. Whether one likes it or not. [Or. Abbrev. of the old 'will-he, nil-he'.]

With a will Energetically.

With the best will in the world However well disposed one may be.

Win **Win hands down** Succeed very easily.

Win over Convert to one's own point of view; persuade to become one's ally.

Win the day Be victorious.

Wind **Close to the wind** See under **Sail**.

Get wind of Obtain early information about something that is likely to happen.

It's an ill wind that blows nobody good It is a
very unfortunate event which is of no benefit: someone is
almost sure to profit from a loss. [Or. Proverb.]
In the wind Likely to happen.
Like the wind Extremely quickly.
Sail near (close to) the wind See under *Sail*.
Sound in wind and limb Healthy.
See how the wind blows Test opinion.
Straw in the wind See under *Straw*.
Take the wind out of one's sails Disconcert, usually
by gaining an advantage over one, e.g. by anticipating
one's arguments or suddenly revealing a secret.
Which way the wind blows What developments
are likely to happen. What opinions are being held.
What the position is, or is likely to become.
Windbag Person who talks too much.
Wind of change Tendency to reform.
Wind up Conclude; bring to an end.
See under *Second*.

Wing **Clip the wings** See under *Clip*.
Stretch (spread) one's wings Exert one's (new-found)
power, influence, etc.
Take under one's wing Protect (as a hen takes her
chickens under her wing).
Please take the new typist under your wing until she settles in.
Take wing Start flying.
Waiting in the wings Ready to become prominent [Or.
Theatre, where 'wings' adjoin stage.].

Wink **As easy as winking** Very easy.
Forty winks A short sleep.
Not a wink No sleep at all.
Wink at Tactfully ignore.

Wire **Get one's wires crossed** Be or talk at cross purposes.
Be confused.

Wise **None the wiser** No more informed than previously.
Wise after the event Knowledgeable when it is too
late. Failing to foresee.

Wish **Wish to goodness** Wish intensely, emphatically.
(Polite version of 'Wish to God'. 'Goodness' is similarly
used in 'Hope to goodness' and 'Trust to goodness'.)
Wish a person joy Wish him, or her, luck;
congratulate.
Wish a person joy of Hope he may find some
pleasure or satisfaction in.

Wishful thinking Thinking, or belief, based on wishes rather than facts.

Wishy-washy

Feeble. Unsystematic.

Wit **Addle one's wits** Make one's mind hopelessly confused. [Or. 'Addled' is applied to an egg upon which the bird has been sitting for some time, and then has deserted.]

At one's wits' end See under *End.*

Have *or* **keep one's wits about one** Be alert, observant and intelligent.

Live by one's wits Make one's living by ingenuity.

Withers **Wring one's withers** [Old f.] Cause acute distress. [Or. The 'withers' of a horse are the muscles joining the back and shoulders, and these are often made painful by a badly fitting saddle. Hamlet's 'Our withers are unwrung' means 'We are not in pain'.]

Within **Within an ace of** Close to.

Within call *or* **hail** Near enough to hear the sound of a voice.

Within (easy) reach Accessible; capable of being reached, physically or by communication.

Within oneself Not using one's whole energies.

Wives **Old wives' tale** Superstition.

Wolf **Cry wolf** See under *Cry.*

Keep the wolf from the door Live without suffering acute poverty.

Lone wolf Person who prefers to act alone.

Throw to the wolves Sacrifice.

Wolf in sheep's clothing A plausible deceiver; one whose apparent harmlessness conceals his true character. [Or. Biblical: also Æsop's fable, in which a wolf covered himself with the sheep's skin and succeeded in deceiving a herd of sheep—but not the shepherd.]

Wonder **Do wonders** Have remarkable success.

Nine days' wonder An event which causes great excitement for a short time and is then forgotten.

No wonder Not surprising. (The phrase is often used on its own, meaning 'I am not in the least surprised'.) *It is no wonder that she is always tired.*

Small wonder Same as **no wonder.**

The wonder is What is surprising is.

Wonders never cease How surprising! (Ironical or jocular.)

Work wonders Have excellent results.

Wood **Cannot see the wood for the trees** Is prevented from seeing the main issue because of details.

Out of the wood Free from difficulties.

Wool **Be wool-gathering** Allow one's thoughts to wander. Similar to **day-dreaming.**

Pull the wool over one's eyes Deceive one.

Word **As good as one's word** Faithful in keeping a promise.

Break one's word Fail to keep one's promise.

Fine words butter no parsnips Words are less adequate than deeds.

Give one's word Make a promise.

Hard words Harsh and unpleasant statements, not necessarily true.

Have the last word Make the final (and supposedly decisive) contribution in a discussion, quarrel, etc.

Have a word with Talk briefly to.

Have words Quarrel.

In a word In brief. To sum up.

In other words Expressed in different words.

In so many words Verbally and explicitly.

Keep one's word Do as one promised.

The last word The latest, or best, of its type.
The train is the last word in speed and comfort.
See also **have the last word.**

Leave word Leave a message.

Lost for words Too surprised to speak.

Man of few words Reticent one.

A man of his word One who can be trusted to keep a promise.

Put into words Express in words that which one thinks.

Say the word Give permission or instruction.

Say a good word for; put in a good word for Speak in favour of.

Say a few words Make a brief speech.

Send word Transmit a message.

Take at one's word Accept a statement literally, and as the truth.
Also **take one's word for it.**

Upon my word! Exclamation, expressing astonishment. [Old f.]

Waste words Talk in vain. Talk with no result.

Word for word Exactly as spoken or written; verbatim.

This is, word for word, the message he gave me.
Word of honour Solemn promise.
A word in the ear A private statement, or hint.
Word in edgeways Any entry into a conversation.
She talks so much that one can't get a word in edgeways.
(By) word of mouth Verbally; spoken, as contrasted with written, speech.
Word in season Well-timed advice.
Word-perfect Exact, absolutely accurate.
Words fail me I am too surprised (shocked, etc.) to speak.

Work **At work on** Engaged or employed on.
Donkey-work Rough or hard work, necessary for the completion of a task. [Or. A 'donkey-engine' is a small engine which supplies power for minor work on board ship.]
Have one's work cut out Have a difficult task.
Make short work of Finish quickly.
The new machine makes short work of the washing.
Set to work Begin work.
Work off Get rid of by working.
Work one's passage Earn a privilege or advantage by doing work in return. [Or. Nautical. A passenger who has no money to pay his fare and works as a seaman instead, is said to work his passage.]
Work out 1. Solve.
Have you worked out the sum yet?
2. Be calculated.
The cost works out at £4 a square metre.
3. Plan.
I'll work out the details of our holiday over the weekend.
Work up 1. Create by degrees.
From one small shop, he worked up to a very fine business.
2. Rouse or excite.
It was a thrilling game, and the spectators became very worked up.
Work upon Exert influence upon.

World **All the world and his wife** Everyone; all the people there are.
For all the world 1. Precisely.
She looks for all the world like her sister.
2. Under any circumstances.
I wouldn't like his job for all the world.

Make the best of both worlds Satisfy two opposing demands; compromise.

A man *or* **woman of the world** An experienced person; one familiar with the customs and habits of society.

The best of both worlds Benefit from two quarters.

The way of the world The customary behaviour of mankind, especially civilized, sophisticated mankind. (The phrase is generally used ironically.)

The (whole) world over Everywhere.

What in the world Whatever. (Used for special emphasis.)

I can't understand what in the world she's bought it for.

Worm **Even a worm will turn** Even the weakest person may be goaded into defiance or rebellion. [Or. Proverb.]

Worm (one's way) in Insinuate.

Worm out Discover by persistent questioning.

Worn **Worn out,** *etc.* See under *Wear*.

Change for the worse Deterioration.

The worse for wear [LIT] Damaged by use. [MET] Not at one's best; tired out; unwell.

Worst **At the worst** In the worst possible circumstances; even if the worst happens.

If the worst comes to the worst If matters become as bad as they can possibly be.

Worth **For all one's worth** With all one's efforts.

For what it is worth If it has any value.

Worth one's salt; worth one's keep See under *Salt*.

Worth its *or* **one's weight in gold** Very valuable or useful.

Worth while; worth one's while; worth it Worth spending time or trouble over.

I would try to sell the business, but it isn't worth while.

Wrap **Take the wraps off** Reveal.

Under wraps Secret.

Wrapped up in Entirely devoted to; absorbed in.

He is wrapped up in his family.

Write **Write off** Treat as no longer of any value.

Writing **The writing on the wall** Clear warning of disaster. [Or. Biblical. The writing on the wall was the warning given to Belshazzar as a plain indication that unless he altered his conduct, the end would be disaster.]

Wrong **Get person wrong** Misunderstand him.

Go wrong Make an error.

In the wrong Having made error.
The wrong way round Opposite to what it should be.
Wrong-headed Perverse and obstinate.
Wrought **Wrought up** Worked up. Tense and excited.

Y

Year **All the year round** Throughout the year.
Getting on in years Becoming old.
Year in, year out Continuously.
Years of discretion An age at which one is supposed to have acquired a certain amount of wisdom and discretion.
Yellow **Yellow-livered** Cowardly. [Or. A tradition that the liver of a coward has a streak of yellow in it.]
Yellow press Sensational newspapers, usually with chauvinistic tendencies.
Yellow streak Capacity for cowardice.
Yeoman **Yeoman service** Sound and excellent work.
Yet **As yet** Until now.
As yet, I have seen no signs of deterioration.
Yours **You and yours** You and your family.
Yourself **Pull yourself together** Take control of your feelings.